SEE NO EVIL
The JFK Assassination and the U.S. Media

KENNEDY EXTRA
PRESIDENT DEAD
Shot by Assassin

New York World-Telegram
PRESIDENT SHOT DEAD

Highlights of Kennedy's Career

Jim DeBrosse

SEE NO EVIL: THE JFK ASSASSINATION AND THE U.S. MEDIA
COPYRIGHT © 2018 JIM DEBROSSE

Published by:
Trine Day LLC
PO Box 577
Walterville, OR 97489
1-800-556-2012
www.TrineDay.com
TrineDay@icloud.com

Library of Congress Control Number: 2018932325

DeBrosse, Jim.
–1st ed.
p. cm.

Epub (ISBN-13) 978-1-63424-163-2
Mobi (ISBN-13) 978-1-63424-164-9
Print (ISBN-13) 978-1-63424-162-5
1. Kennedy, John F. -- (John Fitzgerald), -- 1917-1963 -- Assassination. 2. Mass
media -- Social aspects -- United States -- History -- 20th century . 3. United
States -- History -- 1961-1974. 4. Kennedy, John F. -- (John Fitzgerald), -- 1917-
1963 -- Public opinion. 5. Mass media and culture. 6. Mass media criticism. I.
DeBrosse, Jim. II. Title

FIRST EDITION
10 9 8 7 6 5 4 3 2 1

Printed in the USA
Distribution to the Trade by:
Independent Publishers Group (IPG)
814 North Franklin Street
Chicago, Illinois 60610
312.337.0747
www.ipgbook.com

For those who seek the truth, no matter where it leads.

Acknowledgements

Based on my dissertation for the E.W. Scripps School of Journalism at Ohio University, this book would have never happened without the help of three people to whom I am in debt.

My friend and former newspaper colleague Mary McCarty, who gave me the germ of the idea by insisting that someone look into the media bias against Oliver Stone's film *JFK*.

My friend and academic advisor Mike Sweeney, who was open-minded and courageous enough to see my dissertation through to its successful conclusion.

My editor and publisher Kris Milligan, whose fearless defense of the First Amendment elevates him to a position in the publishing industry that few, if any, can match.

Table of Contents

Introduction

"Something Stinks about the Whole Affair"

Millions of baby boomers like myself have seared into their collective memory the black-and-white TV images they saw flash before their eyes in the early afternoon of November 24, 1963. In those few seconds, Lee Harvey Oswald, accused killer of President John F. Kennedy, was being escorted in handcuffs through the basement of Dallas police headquarters when a large man in a dark suit and hat stepped from the small crowd in front of Oswald and jabbed something toward Oswald's mid-section – a motion followed instantly by the sound of a gunshot and the sight of Oswald crumpling. Then sheer chaos erupted – men shouting, forms grappling, the camera view jiggling – until the man who was later convicted as Oswald's killer, Jack Ruby, was pinned to the floor.

Even at so young an age (I was eleven at the time), I realized I had witnessed a terrible moment in the nation's history and that, at some primal level, this was unlike the countless staged shootings I had watched on TV and in the movies. I wondered, too, with an aching wince what it must feel like to be shot in the gut at such close range.

Eleven-year-olds typically do not think in terms of conspiracies, but my father – an intelligent, working-class man with a deep cynicism born of life's disappointments – certainly did. Like many Americans, he saw in the execution-style murder all the signs of a cover-up, and would continue to insist it was so, long after the Warren Commission issued its report nine months later that both Oswald and Ruby had acted as lone deranged killers. Did my father's views influence my own? Certainly, they must have at some level. But within weeks after the televised murder – and the far more traumatic shock of the assassination and burial of a president our Catholic community had nearly canonized – my adolescent life returned to the normalcy of school, sports, television, and comic books. I had no inkling until decades later that Ruby had been convicted and sentenced to death for Oswald's murder and that the decision had been reversed on appeal. Ruby died of cancer before going to trial a second time.

Likewise, for the country as a whole, it did not take long for the memory of JFK's assassination to be lost in the maelstrom of racial strife, a deeply divisive war in Vietnam, and the murder of two more of the nation's heroes – Robert F. Kennedy and Martin Luther King Jr. Two years after the assassination of RFK, I entered college at Harvard University in 1970, soon to be caught up in the ongoing sexual revolution, the trappings of the counterculture, and the growing anti-war movement. With each passing month, the loss of all three charismatic leaders seemed to recede into the irrelevant past as we, members of the "now" generation, sped forward into the promise of a just and harmonious future that we felt certain we could achieve if only the older generations would step aside and let us take control.

Then came the end of the war, and Watergate, and the demise of the Nixon presidency just as I was launching my career in journalism. I was determined to make a difference, as Bob Woodward and Carl Bernstein had, in helping shape the discourse and polity of American life, one story at a time. Like most Americans during the three decades that followed, I never gave much thought to JFK's assassination – or to Oswald and Ruby – until the release, in 1992, of Oliver Stone's *JFK*.

The film struck me, as it did many of its critics, as too broad and unfocused in its finger pointing. It seemed that nearly everyone, with the exception of embattled New Orleans District Attorney Jim Garrison and his dwindling allies, were somehow involved in the assassination and its cover-up. Even so, I thought the film was courageous and thought-provoking, having brought into public view many of the flaws, inconsistencies, and outright deceptions of the Warren Report that JFK researchers had been writing about for decades.

I started reading up on the topic and I noticed something else – none of the dozens of researchers in the field were working reporters for news organizations. How had my profession failed to investigate what many have called the "Crime of the Century"? Adding hypocrisy to the industry's shame, journalists of every mainstream medium – TV, newspapers, and magazines – had ripped into Stone and his film for daring to question the very assumptions that the news industry had left unexamined for thirty years.

An important distinction must be made here between journalists employed by the mainstream media and those who work for themselves or alternative media outlets. Several well-known researchers critical of the Warren Report are former employees of mainstream news organizations who later chose to conduct their investigations free of corporate media constraints. Jefferson Morley left the *Washington Post* and became editor of the JFKFacts.org, a website dedicated to finding concrete answers to JFK assassination mysteries. Jim Marrs, an investigative reporter for the *Fort Worth Star-Telegram*, turned freelance writer in 1980 and nine years later published *Crossfire: The Plot That Killed Kennedy*, the principal basis for Stone's *JFK*. Carl Bernstein, who won a Pulitzer Prize for exposing the Watergate scandal in 1974, left the *Washington Post* in 1976 before investigating the close ties between the CIA and the elite media for *Rolling Stone*. Other notable Warren Report critics came up through the ranks of non-mainstream media, including David Talbot, a former senior editor of *Mother Jones*; Robert Hennelly, an investigative reporter for public radio; Jerry Policoff, a senior editor at the non-profit OpEdNews.com; and Anthony Summers, an Irishman who had been a producer for British public TV before publishing *Conspiracy* in 1980.

Nearly two decades after the release of Stone's film and more than three decades after launching my career as a journalist, I retired as an enterprise reporter from the *Dayton Daily News* to pursue a doctoral degree in journalism. As I started my third year of graduate school, I still had not arrived at a dissertation topic that excited me – something I confessed to Mary McCarty, my longtime friend and colleague at the *Dayton Daily News*. In her gentle style of scolding, Mary told me that someone – me! – should look into why the media had been so unmerciful in its criticism of Stone. Several days later, she emailed me an article by investigative reporters Robert Hennelly and Jerry Policoff, "JFK: How the Media Assassinated the Real Story," that had appeared originally in the *Village Voice*.

The 2002 article disclosed in detail how the industry had failed not only to investigate the JFK assassination but also that many of its most respected news organizations had been complicit from the beginning in advancing the Warren Commission's lone gunman theory.[1] After reviewing hundreds of documents related to coverage of the assassination, Hennelly and Policoff found an undeniable pattern of media collusion in a cover-up, including these details:

- Only four hours after the assassination, *Time-Life* purchased exclusive rights to a key piece of evidence, the 8-millimeter home movie of the JFK assassination sequence shot by Dallas clothing manufacturer Abraham Zapruder. *Life* withheld the film from public view for twelve years while reproducing only selected frames in its magazine to eliminate any conflict with the Warren Report's finding that the shots fired at the president came from the rear. Shots from the front would have indicated a second shooter other than Oswald.[2] *Time-Life* executives maintained that they withheld the complete film, and in particular infamous frame 313 showing the president's head exploding and jerking backwards, because of its graphic and disturbing content.[3]

- Within days of the assassination, the Department of Justice used its influence at the paper's highest levels to kill a *Washington Post* editorial calling for an independent investigation free of FBI, CIA, and other governmental influence.[4]

- The *New York Times* edited a book based on the Warren Commission hearings, *The Witnesses*, that omitted any testimony deviating from the official account of a lone assassin, including a witness who told the commission he had seen two men on the sixth floor of Texas Book Depository where Oswald allegedly shot at JFK and had heard shots coming from the railroad yard in front of the president. Missing, too, were statements from three Secret Service agents present at the autopsy who contradicted the official finding of a rear-only entrance wound to the head and from numerous witnesses, including Zapruder, that the shots had come from in front of the president.[5]

- *Life's* October 2, 1964, cover story on the Warren Report was written by former commission member Gerald Ford and, even after the magazine hit the newsstands, underwent two revisions and expensive replating to remove evidence that appeared to contradict the report. The first revision eliminated a photo of the stricken president slumping back against the seat and leaning to the left, an indication of someone shooting from the front of the motorcade. The second changed the caption on a photo to support the Warren Commission's findings of rear shots only.[6]

- In 1964, *Time* blamed the wave of conspiracy rumors in Europe on "leftist" writers and publications trying to blame the assassination on a "rightist conspiracy." Later that year, the magazine dismissed the first book criticizing the Warren Report, *Who Killed Kennedy*, because its author, Thomas Buchanan, had allegedly been "fired by the *Washington Star* in 1948 after he admitted membership in the Communist Party."[7]

- In 1966, under pressure from critics of the Warren Report, the *New York Times* and *Life* launched their own investigations. The *Times* probe lasted only a month even though its team of reporters and editors found "a lot of unanswered questions" that were never pursued, according to team member Martin O. Waldron. *Life*'s November 25, 1966 cover story, "Did Oswald Act Alone? A Matter of Reasonable Doubt," was accompanied by an editorial calling for a new investigation, both of which were then attacked by its sister publication, *Time*, as pursuing a "phantasmagoria." The investigative team's first article was its last. *Life* later sued its former investigative consultant, Josiah Thompson, for using sketches of the Zapruder film in his book *Six Seconds in Dallas* that challenged the Warren Commission findings. The magazine lost the copyright suit because it failed to prove damages. Thompson had offered all the book's proceeds to *Life*.[8]

- In 1967, a CBS documentary series on the assassination was secretly reviewed and perhaps altered by former Warren Commission member John Jay McCloy, whose daughter, Ellen McCloy, was then administrative assistant to CBS News President Richard Salant. The documentary included eleven CBS marksmen who tried to re-create Oswald's alleged feat of firing three shots with two hits on a moving target in 5.6 seconds. Incredibly, seventeen of the thirty-seven test runs were disqualified "because of trouble with the rifle." By eliminating those "malfunctions," the marksmen, on average, were able to match Oswald's three shots in 5.6 seconds. What CBS did not tell its viewers, however, was that the marksmen were using a rifle that could fire faster than the one used by Oswald, who was reportedly a poor shot, and that their average number of hits was only 1.2 compared with Oswald's two. Cronkite summed up for audiences: "It seems equally reasonable to say that Oswald, under normal circumstances, would take longer. But these were not normal circumstances. Oswald was shooting at a president. So our answer is: [he was] probably fast enough." In other words, shooting at a president, by some contorted logic, gives an assassin hyper-natural powers. One of the eyewitnesses interviewed for the CBS documentary, Orville Nix, later told his granddaughter that his interview was repeatedly cut short until he eliminated any reference, as instructed by the producers, to having heard shots from the infamous grassy knoll in front of the president's motorcade.[9]

- In 1970, someone at the *New York Times* who has never been identified changed the headline to, and deleted two paragraphs from, John Leonard's combined book review of Jim Garrison's *A Heritage of Stone* and James Kirkwood's *American Grotesque*. The headline in the first edition, "Who Killed John F. Kennedy?

Mysteries Persist," was changed to "The Shaw-Garrison Affair" in subsequent editions. The deleted paragraphs from the first edition included these words: "But until someone explains why two autopsies came to two different conclusions about the President's wounds, why the limousine was washed out and rebuilt without investigation, why certain witnesses near the 'grassy knoll' were never asked to testify before the Commission, why we were all so eager to buy Oswald's brilliant marksmanship in split seconds, why no one inquired into Jack Ruby's relations with a staggering variety of strange people, why a 'loner' like Oswald always had friends and could always get a passport – who can blame the Garrison guerrillas for fantasizing? Something stinks about the whole affair."[10]

Policoff has documented other instances where the mainstream media were more government propagandists than government watchdogs in supporting the Warren Report. In 1967, a CBS inquiry theorized that the three jiggles in the Zapruder film – the only known footage of JFK's assassination– corresponded to the three shots fired by Oswald from the Texas Book Depository. The jiggles were explained as Zapruder's involuntary response to the sound of shots fired. What CBS didn't tell viewers is that there were five jiggles in all during the sequence in question.[11]

JFK researcher Edward J. Epstein used the CBS inquiry to back the Warren Report in a bitter attack on its critics in an April 20, 1969 *New York Times Magazine* article, "The Final Chapter in the Assassination Controversy?" Epstein had been aware of the CBS deception and had said so in a letter to another JFK researcher, Sylvia Meagher, more than a year before: "I am shocked that five not three frames were blurred. If this is so, CBS was egregiously dishonest and the tests are meaningless." Meagher wrote a letter to the editor of the *Times* documenting the contradiction between Epstein's letter and his article, but received no reply. Meagher's letter never ran.[12]

At least two mainstream journalists helped sabotage New Orleans District Attorney Jim Garrison's investigation into businessman and CIA informant Clay Shaw and his ties to Lee Harvey Oswald and CIA-backed anti-Castro groups. *Life* staff member Tom Bethal was assigned to work with Garrison in what Garrison believed would be a friendly story about his prosecution of Shaw. But Bethal handed over Garrison's trial strategy, his list of witnesses, and their expected testimony to Shaw's defense team.[13] *Newsweek* reporter Hugh Aynesworth fed the same inside information to the intelligence unit of the Dallas Police Department.[14]

Not to be outdone for skullduggery, *Washington Post* editor Ben Bradlee helped CIA counterintelligence chief James J. Angleton confiscate the personal diary and papers of JFK's closest mistress, Mary Pinchot Meyer, on the night after her death in 1964.[15] Meyer, who was Bradlee's sister-in-law and the former wife of CIA operative Cord Meyer, was murdered under mysterious circumstances while walking home from her art studio along a deserted stretch of the C&O Canal Towpath in Georgetown. In his book *The Georgetown Ladies' Social Club*, biographer C. David Heymann claims that, shortly before Cord Meyer's death, he sneaked into his nursing home room and asked him who he thought had killed Mary. According to Heymann, Cord "hissed ... the same sons of bitches who killed John F. Kennedy."[16]

At least one prominent Washington journalist used his influence to sway the direction of the JFK investigation. LBJ took a call the day after Oswald's murder from Joseph Alsop, one of the top syndicated columnists of the Cold War era, who offered the new president some "public relations" advice. Alsop urged Johnson, who was leaning toward a joint FBI-Dallas police probe of the JFK murder, to put a blue ribbon commission in charge to assure Americans of the investigation's thoroughness and independence and to spare Attorney General Robert F. Kennedy the emotional burden of handling the FBI case. Interestingly, for guidance on creating that commission, Alsop suggested that LBJ call Dean Acheson, the respected elder statesman who had resigned as Kennedy's advisor during the Cuban missile crisis because JFK had refused to take his advice and bomb the Cuban missile sites; Assistant Attorney General Nicholas Katzenbach, who on the same day as Alsop's phone call had sent a memo to LBJ aide Bill Moyers stressing that "all measures" be taken to assure the public that Oswald was the lone shooter; and top network news executive Fred Friendly of CBS, which would produce three of the staunchest defenses of the Warren Report over the next 12 years.[17]

Even journalists in the leading leftist media, whom one would expect to question a government report that many critics say had been rushed to its conclusions, fell into line behind the Warren Report, as E. Martin Schotz details in his book, *History Will Not Absolve Us*. Notable Warren supporters among the left include columnist Alexander Cockburn and the editors of *The Nation,* and even the skeptic's skeptic, I.F. Stone.[18] Before the release of the report, *The Nation* had raised the possibility of Oswald's ties to the CIA and FBI and also doubted whether he had possessed the financial means and marksmanship to have assassinated JFK on his own.

But with the release of the commission's report in September 1964, the editors did a complete turnabout, enthusiastically endorsing the commission's findings and calling it "conclusive."[19] Under growing pressure from critics, however, *The Nation* ran an article in June of 1965 in two installments by investigative journalist Fred J. Cooke that questioned many of the conclusions of the report, but with a disclaimer from the editors that the article represented only the views of Cooke. A month later, *The Nation* ran a follow-up piece ridiculing critics of the Warren Report, including Cooke. When Cooke complained vehemently to then-editor Carey McWilliams and asked *The Nation* to print his rebuttal, he was refused.[20]

Some might dismiss this shameless journalistic behavior as the workings of a post-World War II and pre-Watergate media that were far more subservient than the media today to the wishes of government leaders and far more intent on maintaining public confidence in the stability and incorruptibility of the nation's leadership.[21] As *New York Times* columnist C.L. Sulzberger wrote soon after the report's release: "It was essential in these restless days to remove unfounded suspicions that could excite latent jingo spirit. And it was necessary to reassure our allies that ours is a stable reliable democracy."[22]

The problem, though, as this book will show, is that the mainstream media – in particular the top newspapers, book publishers, and traditional TV networks – have continued well beyond the Watergate era and into the present day to promote the findings of the Warren Commission and to marginalize those who question it. Perhaps most disappointing is that Bradlee, who was a close friend of JFK and the editor whose paper fearlessly exposed the Watergate conspiracy, never used the resources of either *Newsweek*, where he was Washington bureau chief during the Kennedy years, or the *Washington Post*, where he took over as managing editor in 1965, to look beyond the Warren Commission's findings. In 1975, when *Rolling Stone* reporter Robert B. Kaiser asked Bradlee why he had never pursued the case, Bradlee fired back, "I've been up to my ass in lunatics," and then added, "Unless you can find someone who is willing to devote his life to [the case], forget it."[23] Bradlee died in 2014.

TV networks have used the power of their medium primarily to conduct simulations – both computerized and "real-life" – straining to prove various technical aspects of the Warren Report while ignoring the broader body of evidence that points to a conspiracy, including the testimony of scores of credible eyewitnesses and the often intertwining relations that Oswald and Ruby had to both organized crime and covert government operations.[24] But that didn't stop CBS correspondent Tracy Smith from touting the efforts of CBS and other mainstream media to get at the truth during a fiftieth anniversary broadcast: "An unending parade of investigators and news outlets, not the least of which was CBS News, spent years and whatever money it took to find evidence – any evidence – that the official story wasn't the whole story."[25]

TV news anchors have been especially shameless in expressing their bias toward the Warren Report. "Twenty-First Century technology concludes Oswald was the only shooter," Bob Schieffer says near the end of a *48 Hours* special in 2013 on the JFK assassination. "And despite all the theories and all the investigations over the last fifty years, no one has yet produced credible evidence of a conspiracy behind Oswald."[26]

At the end of a *Today* show marking the fiftieth anniversary of the assassination, TV news heavyweights Dan Rather and Tom Brokaw both tell viewers where they stand on the Warren Report, despite their "open-mindedness" as veteran journalists. "I love to doubt as well as to know," Rather says, "but I do believe one gun, one shooter. I think it was Lee Harvey Oswald, the shooter. I don't believe that he was part of a conspiracy, but I'm open if somebody comes forward with convincing evidence or testimony…" To which Brokaw adds his amen: "That's where I am as well."[27]

The deeper question, of course, is why do JFK conspiracy theories still threaten the powers-that-be more than a half-century after the assassination? Nearly everyone who might have been involved in a conspiracy is dead and gone. Who, or what, is being protected?

As a longtime journalist and now journalism assistant professor, I understand the importance of fairness, thoroughness of research, and keeping an open mind to differing points of view. But as a confessed conspiracy theorist, I make no apologies. To make clear what I mean by a "conspiracy theorist," I rely on a definition from Washington-D.C.-based journalist and blogger Sheila Casey: "Someone who has a theory about a very specific kind of conspiracy: one operating at the highest levels of our government, or above or outside our government."[28]

As Casey argues, there is nothing unreasonable about having theories or being a theorist. "It doesn't mean [theorists] are flying blind, untethered by facts. They use the facts they already know to create theories about things that are still unknown."[29] Certainly, in the case of JFK's assassination, much is still unknown despite "six official inquiries over the past fifty years, hundreds of books and dozens of documentaries [as well as] the release of four million pages of long-secret documents" shaken loose by Stone's *JFK* in 1992, says former *Washington Post* reporter and JFK researcher Jefferson Morley.[30] Morley lists among the chief unknowns hundreds of records related to the assassination still sealed by the CIA, many of them linked to legendary spymaster and CIA chief of counterintelligence James J. Angleton or operatives who reported to him.[31] It was Angleton's counterintelligence staff that first drew government attention to Oswald's alleged contacts in Mexico City with KGB station chief and suspected assassination specialist Valery Kostikov.[32]

Perhaps most tantalizing of all are the suspected documents related to George Joannides, the CIA's chief of psychological warfare operations in Miami in 1963. Joannides supervised a group of Cuban exiles in New Orleans who publicized Oswald's pro-Castro activities before and after the assassination. In 1978, he deceived congressional investigators about his role with the exile group and, two years later, received a CIA medal for his service.[33]

The JFK Records Act of 1992 mandated the release of all documents related to the assassination within 25 years, but gave the president the authority to withhold any documents that would harm an active agent or an ongoing operation, whether in defense, intelligence or law enforcement, or harm the conduct of foreign relations. In addition, the President must certify that "the identifiable harm is of such gravity that it outweighs the public interest in disclosure."(fn 44 U.S.C. §2107 note § 5(g)(2)(D).) The deadline was October 26, 2017. From July 24 through Nov. 17, 2017, a total of 1,211 formerly withheld documents were declassified and another 30,123 redacted documents were released in full to the National Archives, according to the Mary Ferrell Foundation website.[34] But President Donald Trump is still holding back an unspecified number of documents, hundreds of which are of keen interest to researchers, at the request primarily of the CIA and FBI.

It's hard to believe that there are agents still breathing and operations still ongoing that would be jeopardized by the release of information gathered 54 years ago. And it's even harder to imagine that the exposure of any agent or operation now in place could outweigh the benefit of Americans finally gaining some deeper insight into how and why a president of the United States was murdered and who might have been responsible. Harm to the conduct of our foreign relations, however, is another matter to be discussed later in this book.

Soon after the release on Nov. 4, 2017, Trump directed federal agencies to review again the remaining classified material, including any unreleased files and those with redacted information, over a 180-day peri-od to end April 26 of this year. The White House cited national security concerns for the delay, but CIA officials issued a more specific statement that they were concerned about "the names of CIA assets and current and former CIA officers, as well as specific intelligence methods and partner-ships that remain viable to protecting the nation today."[35] The notion that there are ongoing partnerships that need to be protected leads to an obvi-ous question: partnerships with whom or what country? And how could such a partnership merit more consideration than shedding light for the American people on a pivotal event in their nation's history?

But even if the files are released in full, they're not likely to solve the essential mysteries in the JFK case, say nearly all assassination researchers – even those who support the Warren Report. They argue that too much of what the government knew about people with knowledge of the assas-sination, or those with reason to take part in a conspiracy or cover-up, has been hidden from the public record, destroyed, or deemed not relevant.[36]

The Secret Service has admitted destroying some of its records about what happened in Dallas on Nov. 22, 1963, and Army and Navy intelli-gence officials have acknowledged destroying files on Oswald and with-holding information on other key actors, even from government investi-gators who probed Kennedy's killing in the two decades that followed. Missing, too, is part of a CIA report on Oswald about his defection to the Soviet Union and his activities there before returning to the U.S. The deepest mysteries of all, though, remain hidden in the files maintained by Angleton, the paranoid and troubled head of CIA counterintelligence who often kept many of his own secrets, and those of his division, from the rest of the CIA operation.[37]

After the release of the latest files last fall, John Turnheim, the federal judge who chaired the Assassinations Records Review Board from 1992 to 1996, told *Politico* that documents his board did not think relevant to the assassination could be now, in light of new details that have surfaced.[38] Those include the suspected files of Joannides.

JFK researchers say the limited files available on Oswald – a Marine who defected to the Soviet Union with valuable information about the CIA's super-secret U2 surveillance of that country – is in itself a smoking gun. A whole volume of information on Oswald compiled by the agen-cy's Office of Security has simply vanished. The CIA's trail of paper and inter-office coding related to Oswald indicates that the agency – more specifically, Angleton's counterintelligence division – had a keen and continuing interest in his activities from the time he defected to the Soviet Union to the time he took up residence in Dallas. In fact, one of the few revelations in the latest release of documents – a discovery made by researcher and author Jefferson Morley – shows that Angleton knew that Oswald had made contact with KGB officials during a trip to Mexico City but that Angleton never relayed that information to the FBI once Oswald returned to Dallas. A week later, Kennedy was dead.[39]

Agency mismanagement may explain some of the gaps in the official record, but certainly not all, especially when so much of the missing information are pieces to the puzzle that remain unsolved, says John Newman, a political science professor at James Madison University and 20-year veteran of Army intelligence. "There was a consistency to the type of information that went missing," Newman told Politico. "We should have screw-ups on things that don't matter."[40] Even former government investigators say they are frustrated with the latest release of documents. G. Robert Blakey, chief counsel for the House Select Committee on Assassinations probe from 1977 to 1979, told Politico the record is still far from complete. He blames the CIA for stymying the record.[41]

Besides the sealed CIA files, only eighty-eight minutes of taped communications to and from Air Force One during the four-hour flight that transported JFK's body from Dallas to Washington, D.C., have been released to the public, and the location of the original White House Communications Agency tapes remains unknown.[42]

Ignoring the oft-cited rule of investigative reporting – "follow the money" – not a single U.S. news organization has ever looked into the operations and funding sources of Permindex and its parent company Centro Mondiale Commerciale (CMC), a phony world trade promotion group and an elaborate ruse for laundering money. The Rome-based company was exiled to South Africa for its covert efforts to undermine leftist political groups in Europe and publicly accused by French President Charles de Gaulle of financing assassination attempts on his life.[43] Clay Shaw, the target of Garrison's investigation, was a board member of Permindex with documented ties to the CIA. The company's chief shareholder for unnamed parties was Louis Mortimer Bloomfield, a Montreal lawyer who represented the wealthy Bronfman family, raised money for Israeli causes, and also worked for U.S. intelligence.[44]

Casey uses a layman's logic to arrive at the gist of a more conceptual argument that historian John Lewis Gaddis developed in *The Landscape of History: How Historians Map the Past*. Gaddis tells us that historians (and

I would argue the same for journalists) move naturally between evidence and theory in reconstructing, or what he calls "retrocasting," history.

> We have no way of knowing, until we begin looking for evidence with the purposes of our narrative in mind, how much of it is going to be relevant: that's a deductive calculation. Composing the narrative will then produce places where more research is needed, and we're back to induction again. But that new evidence will still have to fit within the modified narrative, so we're back to deduction. And so on.... That's why the distinction between induction and deduction is largely meaningless for the historian seeking to establish causation.[45]

Some respected JFK researchers, including Morley, have fallen into the trap of thinking that "facts" and "evidence" alone can somehow lead us to the truth in the JFK mystery without plausible theories and causes to guide us. Morley, who claims he is neither for nor against the Warren Report, or any theory in the case, argues that conspiracy theories are "a no-win game" and "a dead-end for everyone."[46]

"I don't even want to go there," he said in an interview for this book. "You spend all your time arguing about this theory or that theory. But to me, what happened in 1963 is much more interesting, and there is only so much time [left] to focus on that" before all the evidence and witnesses disappear.[47]

But, as Gaddis would counter, what focus are we talking about? On whom or what or where or even when? How do we know that 1963 is the only "interesting" year leading up to the Kennedy assassination? Again, it takes theories and well-founded speculation about causes and linkages not only to help investigators know where best to look for evidence but also to make sense of what they find. Induction without deduction, and vice versa, is a non-starter for JFK research.

As for the disappearing evidence in the Kennedy assassination, Gaddis writes that historians "can never expect to get the full story of what happened."[48] He backs his argument with a quote from another noted historian, David Hackett Fischer: "The historian's evidence is always incomplete, his perspective is always limited, and the thing itself is a vast expanding universe of particular events, about which an infinite number of facts or true statements can be discovered."[49] To fill in the inevitable gaps, historians must rely on a combination of imagination, theory, carefully researched historical context, and "a preference for parsimony in consequences, but not causes" in order to understand how past processes have produced present structures.[50] "Causes always have antecedents," Gaddis writes. "We may rank their relative significance, but we'd think it irresponsible to seek to isolate – or 'tease out' – single causes for complex events. We see history as proceeding instead from multiple causes and their intersections."[51]

Gaddis's approach is instructive to both journalists and historians grappling with the seemingly endless complexities and mysteries of the JFK assassination. Indeed, some JFK researchers, including author and historian Michael L. Kurtz, have already run up the white flag.[52] In the space of fifty years, they argue, too many witnesses have died and too much evidence has been lost, distorted, and destroyed to ever solve the riddle. For some journalists, that means accepting the Warren Commission as the final word. "Our best guess: Official history (Lee Harvey Oswald acted alone) is based on what we do know, while unofficial history (Kennedy was killed in a conspiracy) is based on what we don't know – on contradictions, ambiguities, mysteries," *Washington Post* staff writer Joel Aschenbach wrote in a scathing review of Stone's *JFK*.[53]

But what we do not know about the Kennedy assassination – "its contradictions, ambiguities and mysteries" – is the continuing challenge for responsible historians and journalists. That challenge should not be an excuse to accept a narrowly focused narrative that fails to capture both key evidence and compelling context for one of the pivotal events of the twentieth century.

Among its many findings that require a leap of faith, the Warren Report expects Americans to believe that Jack Ruby, a strip-joint owner and former gun-runner to Cuba with deep ties to organized crime, murdered Oswald to spare the wife of his beloved president the ordeal of having to testify at trial. Really? The same Jack Ruby who, in the three months leading up to the assassination, made more than seventy long-distance calls to organized crime figures?[54] Who never bothered to watch the motorcade of his beloved president on that fateful day and instead was hanging out in the advertising department of the *Dallas Morning News* just five blocks away?[55] The same man who stalked Oswald for nearly two days before finding the right opportunity to kill him? Who begged the Warren Commission members to remove him from Dallas to the safe haven of Washington, D.C., so he could tell them the truth?[56]

The majority of Americans still do not buy the Warren Commission's narrative – 61 percent, according to a Gallup poll taken less than a week before the fiftieth anniversary of the assassination.[57] Pro-Warren researchers such as historian Max Holland and Wall Street lawyer-turned-author Gerald Posner dismiss the public's skepticism as either part of the nation's cultural vein of paranoia or its emotional inability to accept that a lone loser with a twelve-dollar, mail-order rifle could have so easily brought down what Americans remember as their brief and shining Camelot.[58] Perhaps, but a more plausible explanation might be found in the words mysteriously deleted from John Leonard's *New York Times* book review: "Something stinks about the whole affair."

There are journalists and academics who say it is time to put the assassination behind us. Fifty years of digging and debate, they say, have produced no clear answers, just more bitterness and divisiveness. Among them, surprisingly, is America's leading dissident intellectual, Noam Chomsky, who told a gathering of his faithful in Hungary in 2004 that 9/11 conspiracy theories are akin to "the huge energy that's put out on trying to figure out who killed John F. Kennedy. Who knows? And who cares? ... It's just taking energy away from serious issues onto ones that don't matter."[59]

Chomsky believes strongly that Kennedy would have continued the same policies as his successor, Lyndon Baines Johnson.[60] In a July 15, 2014 email to the author, he wrote:

> There is a significant question about the JFK assassination: was it a high-level plot with policy implications? That's quite important, and very much worth investigating. I've written about it extensively, reviewing all of the relevant documentation. The conclusion is clear, unusually clear for a historical event: no.
>
> That leaves the question open as to [who] killed him: Oswald, Mafia, Cubans, jealous husbands, ...? Personally, that question doesn't interest me any more than the latest killing in the black ghetto in Boston. But if others are interested, that's not my business.

But it should be. On the most obvious level, accepting the assassination of a U.S. president without trying to clarify who was culpable and for what reasons may encourage further assassinations by those who feel they have a right to subvert our nation's democratic processes. On a psychological level, acceptance without persistence or resolution denies Americans the right to understand fully their history, their heritage, and their national identity. "Who we are is where we have been," Gaddis writes,

15

and "past processes are responsible for present structures."[61] As this book will explore in a later chapter, there was at least one clear policy change in the transition from the Kennedy to the Johnson administrations: U.S. willingness to supply offensive weapons to Israel and to look the other way as Israel secretly developed a nuclear arsenal in the tinder box of the Middle East. And the man at the center of nearly every JFK conspiracy theory, James J. Angleton, was the CIA liaison to Israel's Mossad and had been known to use CIA and Mossad agents almost interchangeably for counterintelligence work he wanted done – top-secret work that was often known only to him.[62]

Since the murder of JFK, our history has repeatedly taken us to places involving deception and crime at the highest levels of government – The Gulf of Tonkin, Vietnam, Watergate, Iran-Contra, Iraq, Guantanamo Bay and, most recently, the National Security Agency's massive surveillance of U.S. citizens. Americans' trust in government has continued to tumble with each new disturbing revelation. As a first step to restoring that trust, the media – the guardians of the public trust – must search widely and delve deeply into the events surrounding November 22, 1963, for that is when the honesty and transparency of the nation's leadership seemed to jump the tracks.

This book will examine the last thirty years of new books, new theories, and newly released information about the assassination of JFK, as well as the reactions to those developments in the nation's TV networks, news magazines, and top newspapers – specifically, the *New York Times* and the *Washington Post*. The examination will encompass more than just media "coverage" of JFK assassination theories – a word that implies that the media have been mere passive observers to the debate. Instead, the focus here will be on media "treatment" of those theories, a word that recognizes the media have been an active force in shaping the controversy from its very beginnings. In that broader sense, this book will show how America's mainstream media have choked the parameters of the debate and stifled the search for answers to the Crime of the Century.

Endnotes

1. Robert Hennelly and Jerry Policoff, "JFK: How the Media Assassinated the Real Story," *Village Voice* 37, no. 13 (1992): 33. Academic Search Complete.

2. Hennelly and Policoff, "How the Media Assassinated," *Village Voice*.

3. Michael Benson, *Who's Who in the JFK Assassination: An A-to-Z Encyclopedia* (New York: Citadel Press, 1993), 432.

4. Hennelly and Policoff, "How the Media Assassinated," *Village Voice*.

5. bid.

6. Ibid.

7. Ibid.

8. Ibid.

9. Ibid.

10. Ibid.

11. "CBS News Inquiry – The Warren Report," *CBS News*, June 25-28, 1967, Part II, p. 15 of transcript; and Jerry Policoff, "How All the News About Political Assassinations in the United States Has Not Been Fit to Print in the *New York Times*," Ratville times, accessed August 12, 2015, http://www.ratical.org/ratville/JFK/PA-NYT.html

12. Policoff, "How All the News," s times.

13. John Simkin, "Richard (Dick) Billings," Spartacus Educational, last modified August 2014, http://spartacus-educational.com/JFKbillings.htm

14. Ray and Mary La Fontaine, *Oswald Talked: The New Evidence in the JFK Assassination* (Gretna, Louisiana: Pelican Publishing, 1996), 342.

15. Peter Janney, *Mary's Mosaic* (New York: Skyhorse Publishing, 2102), 114.

16. C. David Heymann, *The Georgetown Ladies' Social Club* (New York: Atria Books, 2003), 168.

17 Gary King, "Journalists and JFK: How to Succeed in the News Media," Citizens for the Truth about the Kennedy Assassination, May 2011, http://www.ctka.net/2011/journalist_&_JFK_King.html, accessed September 2, 2016; "LBJ Phone Calls," Mary Ferrell Foundation, https://www.maryferrell.org/pages/LBJ_Phone_Calls.html, accessed September 2, 2016.

18. E. Martin Schotz, *History Will Not Absolve Us* (Brookline, MA: Kurtz, Ulmer & DeLucia Book Publishers, 1996), 15.

19. Ibid., 230.

20. Ibid., 228.

21. Larry J. Sabato, *Feeding Frenzy: How Attack Journalism Has Transformed American Politics* (New York: Free Press), 1991.

22. C.L. Sulzberger, *New York Times*, September 24, 1964, p. 28.

23. David Talbot, Brothers: *The Hidden History of the Kennedy Years* (New York: Free Press, 2007), 391.

24. See "Re-Enactment of Shooting of President Kennedy," *NBC Nightly News*, November 13, 2008, LexisNexis Academic; "Kennedy Assassination: New Techniques for Analyzing Evidence," *Good Morning America,* ABC, November 20, 2003, LexisNexis Academic; "The Kennedy Assassination – Thirty Years Later," *Larry King Live,* CNN, November 22, 1994, LexisNexis Academic; and "For November 11, 2013," *CBS This Morning*, November 11, 2013, LexisNexis Academic.

25. "For November 17, 2013," CBS, *Sunday Evening News*, November 17, 2013, LexisNexis Academic.

26. "Examining the Assassination of President Kennedy, 50 Years Later," *48 Hours*, CBS, November 16, 2013, LexisNexis Academic.

27. "Remembering the Kennedy Assassination," *Today*, NBC, November 22, 2013, Lexis-Nexis Academic.

28. Sheila Casey, "Confessions of a Conspiracy Theorist," *Dissident Voice*, October 24, 2008, http://dissidentvoice.org/2008/10/confessions-of-a-conspiracy-theorist.

29. Ibid.

30. Jefferson Morley, "Jefferson Morley: What We Still Don't Know about JFK's Assassination," *Dallas Morning News*, October, 25, 2013, LexisNexis Academic.

31. Jefferson Morley, "1,100 JFK Documents Ignored in Obama's Push to Open Records," JFKFacts.org, May 14, 2013, http://jfkfacts.org/assassination/news/key-jfk-files-ignored-in-obama-declassification-drive/.

32. Edward Jay Epstein, *Legend: The Secret World of Lee Harvey Oswald* (New York: Reader's Digest Press, 1978), 253.

33. Ibid.

34. "2017 Document Releases," Mary Ferrell Foundation, https://www.maryferrell.org/pages/2017_Document_Releases.html.

35. KelseyTamborrino, Bryan Bender, Cristiano Lima and Louis Nelson, "Trump blocks release of some JFK assassination records," Politico.com, https://www.politico.com/story/2017/10/26/trump-blocks-release-of-some-jfk-assassinationrecords-244223.

36. Bryan Bender, "What you won't find in the final JFK records release,"Politico.com, https://www.politico.com/story/2017/10/26/jfk-assassination-files-release-244227.

37. Ibid.

38. Ibid.

39. Ibid.

40. Ibid.

41. Ibid.

42. Morley, "What We Still Don't Know," *Dallas Morning News*, and "Audio – Other," Mary Ferrell Foundation, https://www.archives.gov/research/jfk/select-committee-report/part-1d.html.

43. Joan Mellen, *A Farewell to Justice: Jim Garrison, JFK's Assassination, and the Case That Should Have Changed History* (New York: Skyhorse Publishing, 2013), Kindle edition, location 2797.

44. Marrs, *Crossfire*, 498-99.

45. John Lewis Gaddis, *The Landscape of History: How Historians Map the Past* (New York: Oxford University Press, 2002), 107.

46. Jefferson Morley, interview by author, April 1, 2014.

47. Ibid.

48. Gaddis, *Landscape of History*, 107.

49. Isaiah Berlin, "The Concept of Scientific History," in *The Proper Study of Mankind: An Anthology of Essays*, eds. Henry Hardy and Roger Hausheer (New York: Farrar, Straus & Giroux, 1998), 34-35.

50. Gaddis, *Landscape of History*, 62, 65, 105.

51. Ibid., 65

52. Michael L. Kurtz, *The JFK Assassination Debates: Lone Gunman versus Conspiracy* (Lawrence: University Press of Kansas, 2006), 222-25.

53. Joel Aschenbach, "JFK Conspiracy: Myth vs. the Facts," *Washington Post*, February 28, 1992, LexisNexis Academic.

54. Kurtz, *JFK Assassination Debates*, 199.

55. Seth Kantor, *Who Was Jack Ruby?* (New York: Everest House, 1978), 38-9. Kantor writes that Ruby was at the desk of ad salesman Jack Newnam, where Ruby had gone to deliver weekend copy for his nightclubs and to make good on an overdue bill for a previous ad. Ruby was complaining to Newman about the "lousy taste" of the full-page ad in that day's paper criticizing Kennedy for being soft on communism when news of the gunshots reached the newspaper. Ruby had been especially troubled that the ad had been signed by someone with a Jewish name, Bernard Weissman.

56. See Peter Dale Scott, *Deep Politics and the Death of JFK,* (Berkeley: University of California Press, 1993), 184; and G. Robert Blakey and Richard N. Billings, *Fatal Hour: The Assassination of President Kennedy by Organized Crime* (New York: Berkley Books, 1992), 361, 365.

57. David Jackson, "Most Still Believe in JFK Assassination Conspiracy," *USA Today*, November 20, 2013, http://www.usatoday.com/story/theoval/2013/11/17/john-kennedy-assassination-conspiracy-theories-gallup/3618431/.

58. Gerald Posner, *Case Closed: Lee Harvey Oswald and the Assassination of JFK* (New York: Random House, 1993), x; and Max Holland, "Paranoia Unbound," Wilson Quarterly 18, no. 1 (Winter 1994): 88.

59. Douglas Herman, "Does Noam Chomsky Matter Any More?" Rense.com, May 28, 2008, http://www.rense.com/general82/chom.htm.

60. "What Does Noam Chomsky Say About the JFK Assassination?" 22November1963.org.uk, http://22november1963.org.uk/noam-chomsky-jfk-assassination.

61. Gaddis, *Landscape of History*, 35-52, 62.

62. Michael Holzman, *James Jesus Angleton, the CIA, and the Craft of Counterintelligence* (Amherst: University of Massachusetts Press, 2008), 151.

★ ★ ★ ★ ★
TOMORROW'S
WEATHER
SHOWERS
Low 57, High 70

CHATTANOOGA NEWS-FREE PRESS

★ ★
NIG
FI
30 P

Full Associated Press and United Press International Wirephoto and News Service

VOL. XXXI, NO. 72   CHATTANOOGA, TENN. 37401, FRIDAY, NOVEMBER 22, 1963   Second-class mail privileges authorized at Chattanooga, Tennessee   SEVEN

KENNEDY MURDERE
BY GUNMAN IN TEXA

JFK Lashes Critics In 'Campaign' Style

(Editor's Note: This is the speech President Kennedy was scheduled to make in Dallas.)

DALLAS (UPI)—President Kennedy, campaigning as though it was election time, came to the Goldwater stronghold of Texas today and denounced the "nonsense" of opponents who demand violent action against national enemies and cuts in federal spending.

Midway through his two-day swing through five cities of the Lone Star State, the President lashed at "dissident voices ... finding fault but never favor."

Despite drizzle and lowering skies, the President brought out throngs of people, not all of them friendly.

The President was making a three-pronged drive through Texas, which he carried by only 43,000 votes in 1960. He was seeking to charm the people, heal a rift in the state Democratic party and defend his programs in an area where criticism has been loud.

HITS CONSERVATIVES

Speaking at a lunch in the Trade Mart at Dallas, the President criticized the ultra-conservatives as people "perceiving gloom on every side and seeking influence without responsibility."

"Other voices are heard in the land," he said, "voices preaching doctrines wholly unrelated to reality, wholly unsuited to the '60s, doctrines which apparently assume that words will suffice without weapons, that vituperation is as good as victory and that peace is a sign of weakness.

"We cannot expect that ev—

(Continued on Page 2, Column 3)

NEWS STUNS OFFICIALS

Mayor, Others Hit With Deep Shock

Chattanooga reacted with stunned disbelief today to the news that President Kennedy has been shot to death in Dallas.

Local officials and business and civic leaders reached shortly after the tragic news issued the following comments:

Congressman Bill Brock said upon hearing of President Kennedy's death:

"There is no way I can express my real sense of shock and very deep regret over this tragic and tragic news. At this moment I know that his wife and family have the sympathy of every American. We are assured that the American tradition and ideals, furthered by his bound-

(Continued on Page 2, Column 6)

Bulletins

DALLAS, Tex. (AP)—The Dallas police department today arrested a 24-year-old man, Lee H. Oswald, in connection with the slaying of a Dallas policeman shortly after President Kennedy was assassinated. He was also being interrogated to see if he had any connection with the slaying of the President. Oswald was pulled screaming and yelling from the Texas Theater in the Oak Cliff section of Dallas.

He brandished a pistol which officers took away from him after a scuffle. Police Officer M. N. McDonald, who was cut across the face in the scuffle, quoted Oswald as saying after he was subdued, "Well, it's all over now."

A large crowd had congregated around the theater and witnessed the arrest. Police had to hold the crowds back because many apparently connected the arrested man with the slaying of the President.

The officer who was slain, J. D. Tippett, had been killed by a man answering the description of Oswald in the neighborhood a short time before. Tippett had been slain with a pistol.

DALLAS, Tex. (AP)—A Secret Service agent and a Dallas policeman were shot and killed today some distance from the area where President Kennedy was assassinated.

No other information

(Continued on Page 2, Column 7)

PRESIDENT SHOT—Mrs. John F. Kennedy (arrow) bends over her husband, slumped down out of sight, seconds after a bullet struck him in a Dallas motorcade. An unidentified man stands on the car bumper. The President was rushed directly to a hospital in this car.—(AP Wirephoto.)

BEFORE TRAGEDY—President Kennedy is shown in the motorcade as it moved toward the downtown area of Dallas shortly before his party was fired upon. In the center of the photograph is Gov. John Connally.—(UPI Telephoto.)

Bullet Hi
Connally

PRESIDENT KENNEDY

By MERRIMAN SMITH

DALLAS (UPI) — President was assassinated today in a burst of downtown Dallas. Texas Gov. John was shot down with him.

The President, cradled in his w had been rushed in his blood-spatte sine to Parkland Hospital and ta emergency room. An urgent call we neurosurgeons and blood.

The President, 46 years old, once in the head. Connally was hit i and wrist.

Vice President Lyndon Johns the same motorcade and was immed rounded by Secret Service men unt take the oath of office as President.

Police found a foreign-make r iff's officers were questioning a ye picked up at the scene.

The President was conscious rived at the hospital. Father Huber Trinity Roman Catholic Church v and administered the last rites of th

Johnson, who now becomes Pr the United States, was in a car behin nedys and Connallys. He rushed to tal and was whisked away by Secre men. His whereabouts were kept se

Throughout the trip, when Ke Johnson had been in the same moto have ridden in separate cars as an s curity measure. The Kennedys had p spend the night at Johnson's home

The top of the famous bubblet down. Neither of the women appear been hurt, at least not seriously.

Three gunbursts of fire, appare automatic weapons, were heard.

The Secret Service men, who stantly at the President's side, loose matic weapons and drew pistols but late.

The shooting occurred just eas

(Continued on Page 2, Column 2)

AT HALF-MAST — Chattanooga's Federal Building flag was lowered to half-mast as soon as the President's death was ... —(Staff Photo by

AT AIRPORT—President Kennedy greets a well wisher at Dallas Airport shortly after his arrival today. In the center is Gov. John Connally of Texas. Mrs. Kennedy is at right—

LYNDON JOHNSON
New President of the United States

Chapter 1

A Nation Still Divided

More than fifty years after President John F. Kennedy was slain in broad daylight among hundreds of witnesses, the nation's mainstream media still insist on dividing JFK researchers into two camps – those who rely on conspiracy "theories" and "circumstantial evidence" to answer their own persistent questions and those who rely on "facts" and "hard evidence" to arrive at the highly circumscribed conclusions of the Warren Commission. But is a bullet found on an empty stretcher in the basement of Parkland Hospital – its origins and handling unknown – harder evidence than a respected reporter having seen and talked with Jack Ruby at Parkland in the hours after the assassination? Is a rigged simulation by CBS illustrating that Lee Harvey Oswald may have been able to fire three shots in the requisite 5.6 seconds with his Mannlicher-Carcano rifle harder evidence than Oswald associate and New Orleans businessman Clay Shaw's position on the board of directors of a shell corporation publicly accused of financing political assassinations? Is the testimony of witnesses who say they saw Oswald murder Dallas Police Officer J.D. Tippit harder evidence than those who say they encountered phony Secret Service agents in Dealey Plaza who blocked them from pursuing the source of shots they had just heard from the grassy knoll?

Anyone who has delved deeply and with an open mind into the assassination is forced to acknowledge that the line between theory and evidence grows increasingly blurred the closer one looks at both the surrounding circumstances and the publicized facts of JFK's death. Writing in *Time* magazine for the fiftieth anniversary of the assassination, reporter David Von Drehle concludes that "the search for meaning in the hideous brutality of Dealey Plaza long ago became as much about faith as forensics. Not religious faith, necessarily, but that set of beliefs that frames our approach to data and mystery. Each of us must have some sort of faith because we can never have perfect knowledge, no matter how much information we accumulate. Faith fills in the gaps."[1]

Von Drehle's finely spun prose, however, blurs another distinction – between what he calls "faith" and what I will call an "investigative lens." A lens, unlike faith, does not demand that we leave logic behind when trying to determine which set of "facts" best explains a mystery. A lens can be focused more tightly or more widely to discover and analyze an array of evidence. It can also be filtered or unfiltered to ignore or trace the connections among the evidence in its view. An investigative lens is therefore highly subjective; its view is focused and/or filtered according to one's theories, prejudices, and even intuitions, often without the investigator's awareness. Regardless of their subjectivity, some investigative lenses are clearly superior to others in making sense of past events for which there is imperfect knowledge – an argument that has perhaps been advanced best by historian John Lewis Gaddis. But before we can begin comparing the effectiveness of different lenses in probing the JFK assassination, we must look at the major assassination theories that have shaped those lenses and, in turn, been shaped by them.

In September of 1964, after deliberating nine months, the Warren Commission concluded that a lone marksman, Lee Harvey Oswald, armed with a bolt-action rifle on the sixth story of the Texas School Book Depository, shot the president as his limousine passed on the street below. The commission claimed to have found no evidence of a conspiracy, but sealed most of the documents related to the assassination until 2039. The commission's stated aim, General Counsel Lee Rankin told the *New York Times* in January 1964, was to "reassure this country and the world not only that we can protect our President but that accused criminals can be treated fairly."[2]

Twenty-five years later, in 1979, the House Select Committee on Assassinations (HSCA) released its own report criticizing the commission for a slap-dash investigation and determining that there probably was a conspiracy in the assassination. The panel found that 1) organized crime as a whole was not involved in the conspiracy but that individual members may have been, 2) that the Soviet Union and Cuba were not involved, 3) that the CIA and FBI were not involved, and 4) that a second gunman had fired from a position in front of the motorcade.[3] The committee's finding of a second gunman was based on a recording of police radio transmissions during the assassination that has since been discounted. Experts at the time concluded that the recording contained evidence of four shots, including one from the front of the president. However, more recent research has shown that the police radio that picked up the alleged shots was two miles from Dealey Plaza where the assassination occurred.[4] The committee declined to speculate on exactly who might have been involved in the conspiracy or why, citing a lack of funds to continue the probe.[5]

Defenders of the Warren Report have argued that the elimination of the acoustical evidence of a second gunman in the House committee investigation nullifies the HSCA report and reinstates the Warren Report to its primacy as the government's official version of the assassination. But Rep. Louis Stokes, the Ohio congressman who chaired the House committee probe, has said that is far from the case, noting that the Warren Commission began with the conclusion that Oswald had acted alone. "Our committee did pursue a theory that there may have been a conspiracy," Stokes said on ABC's *Nightline* in 1992, soon after the release of Stone's *JFK*. "We also found that some of the information that was not given to the Warren Commission was part of what did lead us to our conclusion (of a conspiracy.) That is, the CIA … withheld certain information from them, and so they could not have pursued a conspiracy investigation."[6]

Rather than following up on HSCA leads pointing to a conspiracy of organized crime figures and anti-Castro activists in the JFK assassination, the *Washington Post* and especially the *New York Times* did their best to pooh-pooh the two-and-a-half year congressional investigation. The *Times* previewed the release of the committee report quoting unnamed officials that there was little chance of identifying and prosecuting the conspirators given that so many suspects in the case were now dead or missing.[7] The *Times* then followed the release of the HSCA findings with a long magazine piece defending the Warren Commission Report, written by the commission's former counsel, David Belin.[8] The *Washington Post* chose to summarize the progress of the committee in a skeptical piece written by George Lardner Jr., beginning with this dismissive lede: "Having satisfied itself that Lee Harvey Oswald killed John F. Kennedy and Jack Ruby killed Lee Harvey Oswald, the House Assassinations Committee yesterday began concentrating on more difficult questions. Now in the final week of its public inquiry into the president's assassination, the committee served up a potpourri of tantalizing but inconclusive leads…"[9]

In the last half century, the Warren Report, named after commission chair Chief Justice Earl Warren, has been discredited by both independent and government researchers for having distorted, overlooked, and suppressed evidence in the case.[10] Even researchers who support the essential conclusions of the commission – that Lee Harvey Oswald assassinated the president entirely on his own – concede that its work was a rush job aimed at quelling rumors of a Castro- and/or Soviet-backed conspiracy and heading off a possible nuclear war.[11] President Lyndon Johnson himself feared that America's Cold War enemies were behind the assassination. He later revealed to his former press secretary and distinguished journalist Bill Moyers his thoughts soon after that horrific day in Dallas: "What raced through my mind was that, if they had shot our president driving down there, who would they shoot next and what would they – what was going on in Washington and when would the missiles be coming?"[12]

A memo by Walter Jenkins, an aide to Johnson, quoted FBI Director J. Edgar Hoover as telling the new president just hours after Ruby had killed Oswald, "The thing I am most concerned about, and [Deputy Attorney General] Mr. [Nicholas] Katzenbach, is having something issued so that they can convince the public that Oswald is the real assassin."[13] The next day, just three days after the president's assassination, Katzenbach issued a memo on behalf of Johnson and Hoover to Moyers:

> It is important that all of the facts surrounding President Kennedy's assassination be made public in a way which will satisfy people in the United States and abroad that all the facts have been told and that a statement to this effect be made now. The public must be satisfied that Oswald was the assassin; that he did not have confederates who are still at large; and the evidence was such that he would have been convicted at trial. Speculation about Oswald's motivation ought to be cut off, and we should have some basis for rebutting thought that this was a Communist conspiracy or (as the Iron Curtain press is saying) a right-wing conspiracy to blame it on the Communists.[14]

"Unfortunately," Katzenbach added, "the facts on Oswald seem too pat – too obvious (Marxist, Cuba, Russian wife, etc.)."[15]

The very makeup of the Warren Commission fails to inspire confidence in its conclusions. Among LBJ's seven appointees was Allen Dulles, the former CIA chief fired by JFK for the Bay of Pigs fiasco. The CIA's liaison to the commission was the longtime head of the agency's counterintelligence division, James J. Angleton, whom many JFK researchers believe was at the center of the conspiracy and its cover-up.[16] Another appointee, Republican Congressman and later President Gerald R. Ford, was so close to the FBI that he secretly, and illegally, fed the FBI classified information while he served on the committee.[17]

The work of the commission has been criticized by both lone gunman and conspiracy theorists over the years for a wide range of issues: 1) deferring to the investigations of the FBI and CIA rather than launching its own, 2) failing to pursue Lee Harvey Oswald's and Jack Ruby's possible ties to organized crime, the anti-Castro community, the FBI, and the CIA, 3) discounting the testimony of scores of credible witnesses, and, 4) being deceived by the CIA on at least one subject known to be relevant to the probe – U.S. attempts to assassinate Cuban leader Fidel Castro.[18]

The litany of doubts raised by critics of the report has become part of the nation's cultural iconography. Among them are the oft-ridiculed Single Bullet Theory that accounts for seven wounds in two men while remaining essentially intact, the backward snap of Kennedy's exploding head during the fatal shot captured in the Zapruder film, and the numerous eyewitness accounts of shots from the grassy knoll in front of the advancing motorcade. Further muddying the commission's findings were Oswald's insistence that he was a "patsy" – an innocent man set up to take the blame for others – and, of course, his subsequent execution-style murder by Ruby. Top government officials, past and present, have privately and publicly expressed their doubts about the Warren Report. They include Texas Governor John Connally, who was wounded while riding in the limousine with the president; President Johnson, who organized the commission; and Attorney General Robert F. Kennedy, who secretly conducted his own investigation into his brother's murder until he, too, was assassinated in 1968.[19] More recently, Secretary of State John Kerry and Robert F. Kennedy Jr. have come forward publicly to add their voices to the chorus now questioning the lone gunman theory.[20] Robert Jr. told a Dallas audience in 2013 that his father thought the Warren Report "was a shoddy piece of craftsmanship," then added his own comment that "the evidence at this point, I think, is very, very convincing that it was not a lone gunman." When asked if the plot might have involved the mob or Cubans, Robert Jr. added, "Or rogue CIA agents."[21]

Many legal experts doubt that Oswald, if he had lived, could have been convicted at trial. JFK researchers point out that little of the crime scene evidence from the murders of both the president and Oswald would have been admissible in court. Secret Service agents cleaned the president's limousine before bullet fragments and tissue could be photographed and collected as evidence.[22] No photographs of Kennedy's clothing were taken in their original condition after the shooting, discounting them as evidence for entry and exit wounds.[23] An unfired bullet in the chamber of the rifle allegedly used by Oswald was never photographed or checked for fingerprints.[24] While Dallas police could find only smudges on the outside of the rifle, they did claim to find Oswald's palm print on the barrel inside the rifle's stock. The FBI later found no trace of the palm print or of it having been lifted from the rifle barrel.[25] Not a single witness can verify that Bullet 399, the so-called Magic Bullet entered into evidence as the one that wounded both Kennedy and Connally, was the same bullet found on a stretcher in the basement of Dallas's Parkland Hospital and assumed to have fallen from Connally's body.[26] It is little surprise then that both U.S. Supreme Court Justice Abe Fortas and former Watergate special prosecutor Leon Jaworski have said nearly all the evidence gathered in the assassination would have been disallowed in court because of its mishandling.[27]

The Warren Commission ignored or discounted scores of well-placed witnesses whose testimony did not fit its lone gunman thesis. Of the 126 witnesses questioned by the commission, fifty-one placed the shots as coming from the grassy knoll, thirty-two said they came from the Texas School Book Depository, and five cited more than one location. Thirty-eight witnesses had no opinion, but most were not asked.[28]

Discounted testimony included that of journalists and law enforcement officers.[29] Four employees of the *Dallas Morning News*, all of whom were standing north of Elm Street as the president's limousine approached them as it traveled west, told the press that they had heard shots behind them and to their right in the area of the grassy knoll. None was called as a witness by the commission.[30] Seth Kantor, a Scripps-Howard reporter who knew Ruby personally and later wrote a book profiling Ruby and his extensive links to organized crime, told the commission that he had seen and talked to him at Parkland Hospital just hours after the assassination. But when Ruby denied being there that day, the commission ruled that Kantor must have been mistaken.[31] However, after reading Kantor's 1978 book on Ruby, Warren Commission attorney Burt W. Griffin changed his mind. Now a retired Cuyahoga County, Ohio, judge, Griffin conceded that "the greater weight of the evidence" indicates that Kantor did see Ruby at Parkland.[32]

In 1975, while researching his book on Ruby, Kantor learned that the record of one of his phone calls from Parkland – to Scripps-Howard Florida correspondent Harold "Hal" Hendrix – was still classified for reasons of national security. Kantor had been told by his editor that day to call Hendrix for details on Oswald. Indeed, Hendrix had more information on Oswald, who had just been arrested in Dallas and named the chief suspect in the assassination, than anyone at the scene of the crime. Hendrix, who had earned the nickname "Spook" from his journalistic colleagues, had long been part of the CIA's network of journalists-propagandists known as Operation Mockingbird.[33]

Dallas County Deputy Sheriff Roger Craig claimed that when he arrived in Dealey Plaza after hearing shots, he saw a white male he later identified as Oswald run from the direction of the Texas School Depository and hop into a light green Rambler station wagon being driven by a dark, Latino-looking man. Craig said heavy traffic prevented him from stopping the vehicle before it sped away but that he related his story to a man at the scene who said he was with the Secret Service.[34] Craig and other reliable witnesses said they had talked to or encountered several Secret Service agents in Dealey Plaza immediately after the assassination. The Secret Service, however, denies that any of its agents had remained in the area after the shooting.[35]

To a lesser extent, the credibility of the HSCA report has also been questioned by JFK researchers, including most recently the committee's former chief investigator, G. Robert Blakey, an expert on organized crime who says he learned decades later that the CIA had withheld information from the committee. Documents released through the JFK Assassination Records Act of 1992 revealed that CIA officer George Joannides had been involved in a disinformation campaign to link Oswald to Castro – a CIA ruse that was withheld from both Warren Commission and HSCA investigators.[36]

The medical evidence in the JFK assassination is perhaps the least reliable of all. The findings of the HSCA in 1979, followed by the release of documents and witness interviews by the Assassination Records Review Board almost two decades later, "clearly demonstrate a systematic campaign of deceit, deception, and cover-up in the medical evidence," historian Michael Kurtz writes in The JFK Assassination Debate.[37] Doctors at Parkland who first saw Kennedy's body all agreed that there was an entrance wound in his throat and a large exit wound in the back of his head, indicating passage of a bullet from front to back.[38] However, navy physicians who later performed the official autopsy at Bethesda Naval Medical Center – none of whom had experience with gunshot wounds – found only rear-entry wounds, one whose location in the report was moved upward four inches from the shoulder to the base of the neck by Warren Commission member Gerald Ford so that it would conform with the trajectory of the Single Bullet Theory. Several photographers at the autopsy say the photos in the National Archives do not match those they took during the proceedings.[39] Nor has a single witness in the emergency room at Parkland Hospital or at the autopsy in Bethesda been able to authenticate all the photos in the National Archives "as consistent with what he or she observed."[40] Several critical items from the medical inventory have disappeared from the archives, including the president's brain, photos of the interior of his chest, and slides of the tissue around the margins of his wounds that would have indicated whether they were inflicted upon entry or exit.[41]

Missing, too, is a nearly triangular piece of JFK's skull, dubbed the Harper Fragment, found by Billy Harper in the infield of Dealey Plaza while snapping pictures twenty-eight hours after the assassination. Harper took the bloody piece of bone to his uncle, Dr. Jack C. Harper, who then turned it over to Methodist Hospital in Dallas, where three different pathologists identified it as occipital bone from the rear of the head, thus indicating a head shot from the front of the motorcade and a second gunman.

The FBI turned the fragment over to JFK's personal physician, Admiral George Burkley, who promptly lost it. Photographs of the fragment taken by one of the Dallas pathologists, A.B. Cairns, resurfaced in time for the HSCA investigation, whose panel of forensics experts determined that the fragment was from the parietal region of the skull at the top and right side of the head, supporting a rear head shot with forward spray as it appears in the Zapruder Film. Warren critics have their own pathologists who say the original identification was the correct one. They also point out that the original determination by the Dallas pathologists predated any evidence or theories about the direction of the headshot and that it agreed with the testimony of dozens of eyewitnesses who later said they saw a large blow-out at the back of Kennedy's skull.[42]

Adding to the debate are questions surrounding the location of the fragment in Dealey Plaza. In 1969 and again in 1996, Harper placed the position of the fragment on a map 117 feet forward of where the Zapruder film shows Kennedy receiving the fatal head shot. Warren supporters say this is further evidence of a rear head shot but Warren foes say the fragment couldn't have possibly traveled that far against a 14 mph head wind and that Harper's memory may be faulty or the fragment may have been moved during the twenty-eight hours following the assassination.[43]

Skeptics of JFK conspiracy theories often argue that "if there had been a conspiracy, someone would have talked." In *Brothers: The Hidden History of The Kennedy Years*, JFK researcher and *Salon.com* founder David

Talbot is the most recent to note that key suspects tied to the assassination have indeed talked, including Lee Harvey Oswald, who insisted he was "a patsy" up to the moment of his death. The list also includes CIA agents David Atlee Phillips and David Morales, both of whom were involved in covert anti-Castro operations in the early 1960s; organized crime lieutenant Johnny Roselli, who was murdered after talking to investigative journalist Jack Anderson for a column that relayed the claim that Robert Kennedy approved an assassination plot [against Castro] which then backfired against his brother[44]; and CIA master spy and Watergate conspirator E. Howard Hunt, who left behind an audiotape after his death in 2007 in which he confesses to being loosely involved in the assassination plot and names a host of familiar suspects in the "big event" in 1963, including CIA operatives Phillips and Morales, several Cuban exiles, a French assassin, and even LBJ.[45]

JFK researchers point out that many other key witnesses and suspects never had the chance to make their case. Deputy Sheriff Craig was among scores of witnesses and persons of interest in the assassination to die under what many researchers have called "suspicious" circumstances.[46] Craig, who testified for the prosecution in Jim Garrison's unsuccessful attempt to convict New Orleans businessman Clay Shaw of conspiracy in the JFK murder, was twice driven off the road, twice shot at by snipers, and was seriously injured in a car explosion shortly before his death. Craig was one of several eyewitnesses who said they encountered bogus Secret Service agents in Dealey Plaza immediately after the shooting. Craig also said he saw someone who looked like Oswald run from the Texas School Book Depository after the shooting and enter a light-colored Nash Rambler with an overhead luggage rack, driven by a Latino-looking man.

When Oswald was later asked by police about the vehicle, he said, "That station wagon belongs to Mrs. Paine. Don't try to tie her into this. She had nothing to do with it." Ruth Paine, indeed, owned a station wagon fitting that description. She and her friend, CIA informant George de Mohrenschildt, were perhaps Oswald's closest friends in Dallas. Paine and de Mohrenschildt found Oswald the job at the book depository that would be in a key location along the route selected for Kennedy's motorcade.[47] Craig died May 17, 1975 of what was ruled a self-inflicted gunshot wound after appearing in a series of radio talk shows in which he had discussed the assassination.[48]

Researchers, however, have long debated what constitutes "suspicion" in the deaths of individual witnesses as well as in the broader sense of statistical probabilities. Citing actuarial data compiled by the *London Times*, Jim Marrs noted in *Crossfire: The Plot that Killed Kennedy* that the eighteen material witnesses who died within three years of the assassination – all but four of them from murder, suicide, or car accidents – represent a 1 in 100,000 trillion chance even if they had all died of natural causes. This number was later revised by applied mathematician and software consultant Richard Charnin to reflect the smaller universe of JFK witnesses. Charnin calculated the chances that 33 of the 1,400 witnesses would die of unnatural causes within three years of the assassination at *one in 137 trillion*. Normally, one would expect only two or three such deaths during the same period.[49]

John McAdams, a political science professor and staunch lone gunman theorist, concedes in his book *Assassination Logic* that the five murders of organized crime witnesses are toughest to explain,[50] especially those of Sam Giancana, who was under a Senate Intelligence Committee's witness protection program at the time he was shot once in the back of the head and six times around his mouth, and of Roselli, who was garroted and dismembered after talking to Anderson and also agreeing to testify before the Senate.[51] Other notable persons who died suspicious deaths include de Mohrenschildt, Oswald's closest friend and some researchers say his CIA handler, who was found dead of a gunshot wound to the mouth on the day he agreed to talk to the HSCA, and New York newspaper columnist Dorothy Kilgallen, who died of a drug and alcohol overdose just days after interviewing Jack Ruby in prison and telling friends she was going to "break open the Kennedy case." Pathologists have disagreed on whether the overdose was accidental or intentional, or even if the amount of barbiturate taken was lethal.[52] A day later, the close friend and JFK mistress with whom Kilgallen had entrusted her notes, Florence Pritchett Smith, died of a cerebral hemorrhage most likely related to her leukemia. Even so, Kilgallen's notes were never found.[53]

Although Kilgallen later became a gossip columnist and TV personality on the quiz show *What's My Line*, she had first gained acclaim as an investigative crime reporter and took up the mantle again in the wake of the Kennedy assassination. She wrote a series of columns critical of the Warren Report and eventually teamed up with renowned JFK researcher Mark Lane, author of *Rush to Judgment*. Kilgallen's hairdresser, Marc Sinclaire, was the first to find her body, upright in her bed, and noted to close friends of Kilgallen a number of irregularities: 1) she was wearing clothing she would have never worn to bed, 2) she still had on her false

eyelashes even though she never slept with them on, and 3) she was reading a book that she had already finished and discussed with him several
weeks before.[54]

The death of possible conspiracy witness Melba Christine Marcades,
aka Rose Cheramie, was chronicled in the intense opening sequence of
JFK. The scene takes place two days before the Kennedy assassination
on a deserted Texas back road, where a woman is thrown from the back
door of a sedan and left on the road bloodied and cursing. Cross-cut with
actual footage of Kennedy's motorcade just moments before the assassination, the film shows the woman in a hospital bed screaming at doctors
that "they're going to kill Kennedy!" Cheramie was indeed dumped on a
Texas back road and run over by second car. She would die days later in
the hospital from her head injuries, but not before telling Louisiana State
Police Officer Francis Fruge and several nurses at the hospital her prediction that JFK would be assassinated in Dallas.[55] Cheramie had been a drug
runner associated with members of organized crime, including Ruby, and
had worked as a stripper at Ruby's nightclub. Soon after the assassination,
she told Fruge and several doctors at the hospital that Ruby had been involved in the plot and that she had seen Oswald at Ruby's club. Neither
the Dallas Police Department nor the Warren Commission were interested in her accounts.[56]

Like Kilgallen's close friend Pritchett Smith, pivotal conspiracy suspect David Ferrie also died of a cerebral hemorrhage, though under much
different circumstances. After Ferrie was publicly named as a defendant
in Garrison's conspiracy case, Ferrie told Garrison's aide, Lou Ivon, "You
know what this news story does to me? I'm a dead man. From here on,
believe me, I'm a dead man."[57] Before he could be brought to trial, Ferrie's
body was found in his New Orleans apartment next to two typed notes
suggesting suicide, both notes unsigned and undated.[58] Despite the notes,
New Orleans Coroner Nichols Chetta ruled that Ferrie had died of "natural causes" – a congenital brain aneurysm that ruptured under extreme
mental and emotional stress. James E. Files, the controversial self-pro-
claimed Kennedy assassin, has said the type of brain hemorrhage Ferrie
suffered could have been inflicted by piercing the roof of the mouth and
entering the brain with a very thin metal object, such as a nail file or ice
pick, leaving little evidence of a wound.[59]

Ferrie was at the nexus among the chief suspects in the assassination.
An anti-Castro extremist, Ferrie had known Oswald as a teenager and
had paid frequent visits with him in the months before the assassina-

tion to the office of anti-Communist zealot and former FBI agent Guy Banister; Ferrie had worked closely with Jack Ruby and New Orleans businessman Clay Shaw, the CIA informant some researchers suspect of payrolling the assassination; and he was employed by Louisiana crime syndicate lieutenant Carlos Marcello as both his personal pilot and private investigator.[60]

Anti-Warren researchers point out that many other witnesses were intimidated into conforming their testimony to the commission's official theory. An extreme example is Warren Reynolds, who had worked at a car lot a block from where Oswald allegedly shot Dallas police officer J.D. Tippit several hours after the assassination. Reynolds chased a gunman from the scene for a block and a half and claimed to have gotten a good look at him. Reynolds told the FBI that the man was not Oswald. Two days later, Reynolds was shot in the head while sitting in his basement office. Reynolds miraculously survived, only to receive telephone death threats to himself and his family. He changed his mind and identified Oswald as the gunman.[61]

Perhaps the best-known criticism of the Warren Report centers on The Single Bullet Theory, or as critics call it, The Magic Bullet – a theory developed by commission members Senator Arlen Specter and U.S. Representative Gerald Ford to explain how a lone gunman, using a Mannlicher-Carcano rifle like the one discovered at the scene, could have fired just three shots that accounted for all of the wounds in Kennedy and Connally.[62] In order to fit all three shots into the filmed sequence of the assassination captured on the Zapruder film, one of the three shots had to account for the 1.6 second difference in the reactions of Kennedy and Connally, since Oswald could not possibly have fired two separate shots in that time from his bolt-action rifle.[63]

The first bullet fired at Kennedy has never been found. A fragment discovered in the presidential limousine apparently was part of a second bullet that struck the fatal blow to Kennedy's head. Therefore, according to the Warren Commission, the third bullet, discovered on an empty stretcher in the basement of Parkland Hospital in nearly pristine condition, had to account for all seven of the other nonfatal wounds in Kennedy and Connally, including Connally's blown-out fifth rib and shattered wrist. Much debate has focused on the location of the entry wound in Kennedy's back and whether it was high enough to have exited his throat and then struck Connally in the torso, wrist, and thigh. But perhaps the strongest case against the Single Bullet Theory is that

X-rays showed more fragments were left in Connally's body than were missing from the almost immaculate bullet. (The fragments were never removed and weighed, however, even after Connally's death in 1993, per the wishes of his family.)[64]

While books questioning the Warren Report appeared within months of its release, including Mark Lane's groundbreaking *Rush to Judgment* (1966), the public's attention was not drawn to the assassination debate until 1967, when word leaked to the press that New Orleans District Attorney Jim Garrison was building a conspiracy case against two men seen by credible witnesses in the company of Oswald in Louisiana just months prior to the assassination.[65] One of the men was Ferrie, a middle-aged, gay pedophile who was hard to miss because he lavishly penciled in his eyebrows to cover a medical condition. When Ferrie died just hours before his scheduled arrest, Garrison was forced to prosecute a much weaker case against Shaw, a wealthy importer-exporter who had been seen in the company of both Ferrie and Oswald in Clinton, Louisiana less than three months before the assassination. The six witnesses who saw them included a deputy sheriff and a voting registrar.[66]

Garrison's prosecution of Shaw, uniformly condemned by the media as a witch hunt, was hampered by government officials who refused to extradite key witnesses to New Orleans and by the untimely deaths of several other witnesses, including Ferrie. One of the witnesses with perhaps the strongest ties to the CIA, Gordon Novel, fled to Columbus, Ohio, where he was protected from extradition by then-Gov. James Rhodes. Garrison charged Novel, a one-time New Orleans bartender, of conspiring with Ferrie in staging a munitions theft at an oil service company's bunker outside New Orleans to supply arms to CIA-backed, anti-Castro militants. Novel called Garrison's investigation a "fraud," but told a number of friends and associates that he was indeed a CIA agent. He also publicly called the phony arms heist "the most patriotic burglary in history" and said cryptically that "I think Garrison will expose some CIA operations in Louisiana."[67]

Shaw was acquitted after a brief jury deliberation, but was later revealed in CIA documents released in 1998 to be a long-time CIA informant.[68] Shaw was also a board member of Centro Mondiale Commerciale (CMC), a Rome-based trade promotion group that French President Charles de Gaulle publicly linked to attempts on his own life and that the Italian press linked to operatives at the CIA as well.[69] CMC and its Swiss-based subsidiary, Permindex, were expelled from their respective countries for failing to account for millions of dollars in funds and for suspicions of financing subversive tactics against leftist parties in Europe.[70] No mainstream U.S. newspaper or magazine has ever written about the potential links between CMC-Permindex and the assassination. But in a glowing account of the company's genesis published by the *Chicago Tribune* in 1960, William Clark wrote during a junket to Rome that Permindex was "organized with Italian, Swiss, Canadian, and United States capital. The trade center is a sort of operating subsidiary whose officials emphasize that it is a service organization in the field of international trade, not merely the producer of a fair." Shaw is mentioned in the story as the board representative for U.S. interests, which included 20 U.S. stockholders.[71]

After the ill-fated Shaw trial, the JFK assassination disappeared from the news agenda for nearly eight years until March 1975 when Americans saw the Zapruder film uncensored for the first time in a broadcast of ABC's *Good Night America*, hosted by Geraldo Rivera. The televised footage, which showed Kennedy's head and body jerking backward from the fatal shot, contradicted earlier reports by Dan Rather of CBS and *Life* magazine that the president's head had snapped forward from a rear shot by Oswald.[72] Rather had been the only journalist outside the *Life* newsroom to see the film, a privilege he held for nearly 12 years.[73]

By then, the media had exposed a number of illegal CIA activities, including the assassination of foreign leaders and the surveillance of domestic political activists. To look deeper into the allegations, the Senate formed an investigative committee in 1975, headed by Senator Frank Church and thereafter dubbed the Church Committee. Its members found that the CIA had withheld information from the Warren Commission about its plots to kill Fidel Castro and that both the CIA and FBI had lied to the commission about their monitoring of Oswald in the months prior to the assassination.[74] More than a half-century later, CIA historian David Robarge confirmed that CIA director John McCone did, in fact, lie on both accounts to the commission, but that it was part of a "benign cover-up" intended to prevent U.S. retaliation against Cuba or Russia. McCone believed at the time that the "best truth" was that Oswald had acted alone.[75]

The ensuing public outcry from the committee's findings as well as the broadcast of the Zapruder film led to the formation of the HSCA in 1976 and the reopening of government investigations into both JFK's murder and that of Martin Luther King Jr. in Memphis, Tennessee, in 1968.[76] The HSCA probe, however, was hampered from the beginning by internal squabbling, the deaths of more witnesses and, eventually, a lack of funding.[77] The primary impact of the HSCA investigation was to suggest that organized crime was complicit in the JFK assassination, pointing a finger primarily at Carlos Marcello in Louisiana and Santos Trafficante in Florida, as well as at certain anti-Castro activists, all of whom had "the motive, means and opportunity" to kill the president.[78] The motive cited for Marcello and Trafficante was the Kennedy brothers' crackdown on organized crime and, for anti-Castro activists, the perception that JFK had doomed the Bay of Pigs invasion of Cuba in 1961 by withholding air support from anti-Castro forces.[79] The committee, however, absolved the CIA and the FBI of any connection, even among possible rogue elements, a move that HSCA chief investigator G. Robert Blakey later regretted after learning that the CIA had withheld information from the committee about its involvement with the anti-Castro community and its possible ties to Oswald.[80]

Both the Warren Commission and the HSCA have been criticized by JFK researchers for their handling and interpretation of medical evidence in the assassination. Despite Blakey's outrage over the CIA's deception, critics accuse him and the HSCA of either ignoring or suppressing key evidence that casts doubts on JFK's official autopsy report. Questions about the chain of custody in handling the medical evidence began in earnest in 1980 with the publication of David Lifton's best-selling book, *Best Evidence*.[81] Lifton, a former NASA engineer and private researcher, was among the first authors to note the contradiction between the crater-like blow-out of the president's right temple in the Zapruder film with the eyewitness testimony of doctors and law enforcement officials who saw Kennedy's body at Parkland Hospital.[82] Dr. Charles Crenshaw, then a resident physician at Parkland and later the author of several books on the assassination, has been the most outspoken of the witnesses, insisting that JFK arrived at the hospital with a small entrance wound to his throat and a large exit wound in the right rear of his skull about the size of a baseball. Both are indications that he had been shot from the front.[83] Eight witnesses to the autopsy at Bethesda Naval Hospital testified to seeing a large exit wound at the back of the president's head – a wound that did not appear on the official photos released from the autopsy. Despite the conflicting testimony, Blakey's report said that all witnesses to the autopsy supported the official autopsy photos.[84] The HSCA then sealed the medical evidence in the case for the next fifty years.[85]

In his 700-page bestseller, Lifton meticulously documented the transit of the president's body from Parkland Hospital to its arrival at Bethesda

Naval Hospital, where an empty bronze casket was wheeled into the front of the hospital in view of TV camera crews at about 6:55 p.m. Unknown to the media and nearly everyone watching the solemn spectacle, Kennedy's body had been removed to another casket, a simple gray aluminum one, for shipping, and secretly delivered to the back entrance of the hospital about twenty minutes earlier. In a bizarre shell game worthy of a dark comedy, the military honor guard assigned to meet the coffin at the front entrance of the hospital was led on a wild-goose chase when the navy ambulance that had transported the bronze casket suddenly shot off at high speed. The honor guard tried to follow in a pick-up truck but lost the ambulance. At 7:17 p.m., two FBI agents witnessed the arrival of a navy ambulance and the bronze casket at the back of the hospital and assisted in moving the casket to an anteroom outside the morgue. However, the agents were blocked from following the casket into the morgue. If this weren't bizarre enough, the honor guard reported that they moved the bronze casket from the navy ambulance to the morgue at 8 p.m., or 40 minutes after the FBI agents had witnessed the earlier delivery of the same casket. Over a period of about ninety minutes, Lifton documented from official reports three deliveries to the Bethesda morgue at three different times in two different caskets for only one body.[86]

Lifton argues that the FBI agents were detained in the anteroom to keep them from discovering that Kennedy's body was already in the morgue, where it was transferred back to its original bronze casket before being delivered, a second time, to the autopsy room at 8 p.m. Morgue witnesses testified that when the president's corpse was removed from the cheap aluminum shipping casket in which it was originally delivered, it was encased in a rubber body bag even though it had been originally wrapped in a white sheet when it left Parkland Hospital. Lifton theorizes that all of these machinations were necessary to disguise the fact that Kennedy's wounds had been secretly altered prior to the autopsy to make it appear as though the fatal shot had been fired from the rear rather than from the front of the motorcade. However, his research could not confirm where or when this might have happened, although he documents a 14-minute period when the body was left unattended on Air Force One while the plane was delayed for takeoff. [87]

Lifton's theory has been given further credence and several additional twists in more recent years through the research of Douglas P. Horne, who was initially a senior analyst and later became the chief analyst for military records on the staff of the Assassination Records Review Board.

The ARRB was created by the JFK Records Act in 1992 to oversee the release of some 400,000 pages of internal documents in the case and to account for any missing or conflicting evidence. A Navy veteran and long-time Navy civil servant, Horne was charged with taking unsworn testimony and assisting the ARRB General Counsel in obtaining depositions from witnesses to the JFK autopsy at Bethesda Naval Hospital.[88]

Horne procured a copy of a report from the Marine sergeant-in-charge of the morgue security detail at the autopsy in Bethesda, which stated that the aluminum casket arrived at 6:35 p.m., twenty minutes prior to the motorcade from Andrews Air Force Base that delivered the original bronze casket. Three witnesses who saw the body at Bethesda prior to the commencement of the autopsy saw the same egg-sized right-rear exit wound in Kennedy's skull reported by all of the other witnesses at Parkland. Yet, ninety minutes later, when the body was wheeled into the morgue a second time in the ornamental bronze casket at 8:00 p.m. for the start of the "official" autopsy, most witnesses told the HSCA that they saw a large opening in the top-front of the skull – five times larger than the exit wound seen in Dallas. One FBI agent reported to the ARRB that nearly half the president's brain was missing, and that most of the missing mass was in the right rear of the brain.[89]

Horne argues that, during the ninety minutes when JFK's body is unaccounted for inside the naval hospital, his head wounds were altered to remove all evidence of bullet entries from the front – entrance wounds, bullet fragments, and brain tissue – and to roughly conform with a rear-entry shot. One witness, embalming technician Tom Robinson, testified to the ARRB staff that he saw doctors remove most of Kennedy's upper skull, and more than ten bullet fragments from his brain, inside the morgue shortly after the body arrived.[90] A corroborating witness, Navy X-ray technician Ed Reed, testified to the ARRB that he saw the chief pathologist, Dr. James J. Humes, commence the surgery to the top of JFK's skull before he was then summarily dismissed from the morgue.[91] Only two small bullet fragments were reported in the autopsy findings and given to the FBI, and their remains are still in the National Archives today. Missing are four larger bullet fragments seen by a Navy corpsman, Dennis David, who typed a receipt for them, as well as the ten smaller fragments seen by Tom Robinson.[92] After studying all the applicable Warren Commission, HSCA, and ARRB testimony and interviews, as well as noteworthy researcher interviews, and comparing them with what is in the National Archives, Horne concluded that at least eighteen autopsy photos, and two skull x-rays from angles that would have shown the blow-out at the back of JFK's head, are missing.[93]

In most of the autopsy photos, the back of the head is conveniently obscured by a metal rest support that several technicians and photographers at the photo shoot said was not present at the time.[94] The few autopsy photos that do show the back of JFK's head show it to be apparently intact, contradicting the testimony of witnesses at both Parkland and Bethesda who instead saw the egg-sized exit wound in the right-rear of the skull. The much larger dimensions of the damage seen at Bethesda to the top-front of the skull were recorded by the autopsy pathologists in their report and in a sketch made at the autopsy, which survives today. In 1993, physicist and radiologist David W. Mantik examined the three remaining X-rays of the skull in the National Archives and concluded that they had been altered, including the use of "light blasting" at the back of the head, to obscure evidence of missing brain tissue and bone.[95]

While Lifton's theory was that JFK's wounds had been altered prior to the body's arrival at Bethesda Naval Hospital, Horne is convinced that alterations occurred at Bethesda during the mysterious ninety-minute delay before the start of the official autopsy. Further supporting his argument was Horne's discovery of two separate brain examinations at Bethesda, one three days after the autopsy on November 25 and a second one a week later. The three pathologists present at the second exam, and the Navy photographer present at the first exam, have given conflicting testimony about the timing of the second exam, the people in attendance, and the methods used to dissect the brain.[96] Former FBI agent Francis X. O'Neill, who was present at the Bethesda autopsy prior to the first brain examination, testified in 1964 that when he saw doctors remove Kennedy's brain and place it in a jar, more than half of it was missing. But in 1997, when asked during his ARRB deposition to examine photographs of the brain in the official record at the National Archives, O'Neill said the specimen looked "almost like a complete brain."[97] John Stringer, the Navy photographer at the first brain exam on November 25, testified to the ARRB that the numerous photos he took of cross-sections of the brain are not in the National Archives, and that the brain photos in the archives are definitely recorded on a different kind of film.[98]

In a 32-page report completed by Horne in 1998 and released to the public by the National Archives that November, Horne argued that the brain removed from Kennedy at the autopsy could not have been the same brain photographed during the second examination on December 2, a redundant procedure that was highly unorthodox to begin with.[99] In his self-published,[100] five-volume set of books on the medical and forensic evidence in the JFK assassination, Horne devotes an entire chapter to evidence that he says supports his theory that another brain was substituted for Kennedy's during the second examination to eliminate evidence of a frontal wound and massively altered just prior to the start of the official autopsy.[101]

Horne's ARRB report in 1998 garnered just two stories in the media,[102] arousing only the faintest echo of the public outcry and media circus that attended the 1991 release of Oliver Stone's *JFK*. The three-hour film epic was based liberally on Jim Garrison's *On the Trail of the Assassins* and Jim Marrs' *Crossfire: The Plot That Killed Kennedy*, plus a good deal of Stone's own artistic and theoretical license. Stone, whose previous acclaimed films had dealt with the tragedy of the Vietnam War (*Platoon, Born on the Fourth of July*), pinned the blame for the murder on a military-industrial complex that had feared Kennedy would withdraw from Vietnam just as he had pulled away from an invasion of Castro's Cuba.[103]

As district attorney for New Orleans, Garrison had tried unsuccessfully in 1967 to convict New Orleans businessman and CIA asset Clay Shaw of conspiracy in the JFK assassination. Garrison was one of the first JFK researchers to suspect CIA involvement in the assassination, but turned a blind eye to organized crime, some critics say, because he was too closely tied to Louisiana's mob operation himself. He was later charged with but not convicted of taking bribes from pinball operators linked to Carlos Marcello's organization.[104] Marrs' book, released in 1989, was one of the first to explore the ties among organized crime, the CIA, the U.S. military, and anti-Castro activists in the slaying of Kennedy – the very same alliance responsible for the failed Bay of Pigs invasion.[105] A former reporter for the *Fort Worth Star-Telegram*, Marrs pointed out in his book that the HSCA had refused to investigate the Dallas police, elements of which may also have been involved in the conspiracy.[106]

Stone's film was pummeled by the mainstream media and, in particular, by the *Washington Post* and the *New York Times*, both of which printed articles critical of the film project months before its release.[107] Not content to confine their disdain to reviews and columns, the *Washington Post* printed two parodies of the film and the *New York Times* ran an interview with Jack Valenti, chief executive of the Motion Picture Association of America and a former aide to LBJ, calling the film a "hoax" and "a fraud."[108]

Communications professor Barbie Zelizer, author of 1992's nearly impenetrable book *Covering the Body: The Kennedy Assassination, the Media and the Shaping of Collective Media*, argues that the media attacks against *JFK* were vicious and widespread because Stone had dared, as a Hollywood filmmaker and "fictionalizer," to invade the turf of journalists "as preferred spokespersons of the assassination story."[109]

Why, then, have journalists in other English-speaking countries been far more sympathetic toward Stone and his film? A Lexis-Nexis search of *JFK* film reviews in major world publications shows that, while top U.S. newspapers mustered only one positive review of Stone's film against five negative, major foreign English-language newspapers produced nine positive reviews against three negative – three to one in favor of the film. (See Appendix F) As Catherine Dunphy wrote in the *Toronto Star*, *JFK* "may be [Stone's] most audacious movie to date; certainly *JFK* is the bravest thing Oliver Stone has ever done. He has delved headfirst into a nation's obsession, its shame and possibly its ugliest secret. He has given credence to, and delivered up, an audience of millions for a compressed and culled factual and fictional retelling of many of the paranoid whispers about what may be the ultimate conspiracy."[110] Dan McDonnell of Australia's *Sunday Herald Sun* praised Stone for "standing up manfully to the withering attacks on his credibility and that of former New Orleans district attorney Jim Garrison, played by Kevin Costner in the picture."[111]

If journalistic turf and pride alone were on the line, it seems the mainstream media would have been most predisposed toward books authored by other journalists. Yet the two media darlings in the JFK assassination pantheon that have received the most favorable reviews by far – Gerald Posner's *Case Closed* and Vincent Bugliosi's *Reclaiming History* – were penned by lawyers. The key here is that both books are elaborate defenses of the Warren Report.

Zelizer writes at great length about the ongoing battle among journalists, historians, and independent researchers over who should have the final authority on "retelling" the Kennedy assassination. But she never tells us why the mainstream media were so wedded to the Warren Commission report to begin with, or why the majority of Americans continue to doubt both the findings of the report and the media's "retelling" of the assassination story. As sociologist Todd Gitlin pointed out in his *Washington Post* book review, Zelizer "fails to ask, let alone explain, how a public flooded by credulous media could have ended up so skeptical of the official version."[112]

Despite the near-universal contempt of the U.S. mainstream media, *JFK* was a box office hit that set off a new wave of public debate over the assassination and led to demands for an earlier release of government documents to settle the issue once and for all.[113] Within a year of the film's release in 1991, Congress passed the JFK Records Act and handed over the government's archive to a five-member commission, the ARRB, to begin releasing top-secret intelligence documents related to the assassination. The president, however, would have the final say in any dispute between the ARRB and intelligence agencies.[114]

As new information has come to light, researchers have touched on a variety of possible motivations and potential conspiracy theories for the killing of the thirty-sixth president, and yet definitive answers have been hard to come by on all sides of the debate. Much of the original evidence was damaged, destroyed, or suppressed.[115] Many of the witnesses and potential conspirators are long dead.[116] And even if all information from government files is released by 2017, many researchers say it is unlikely that these last thousand pages or so will resolve the half-century dispute over lone-gunman versus conspiracy. As Lindsay Porter, author of *Assassination: A History of Political Murder,* told *USA Today* in September 2010: "The more alleged data that's accumulated, the more muddled things become. It is now become a dialogue separate to the event itself."[117]

Contrasting theories and heated debates have surged across the Internet and in non-mainstream publications with varying degrees of evidence and logic to support them.[118] Some of the more outlandish theories posited in the last fifty years include a gunman hiding in a sewer and a bystander with a poison-dart-shooting umbrella. The more plausible conspiracy theories do not deny Oswald's involvement in the assassination but question whether he may have been used, wittingly or unwittingly, as part of a larger conspiracy. Many researchers have zeroed in on the potential involvement of the CIA, military intelligence, and/or FBI in the assassination and its cover-up,[119] or of renegades from any of those agencies.[120] Many others also have cited the participation of organized crime figures and/or anti-Castro Cuban exiles, usually in tandem with the CIA.[121] A few have implicated right-wing Texas oil men and, with increasing frequency in recent years, JFK's successor, LBJ.[122] Still others have claimed a French connection via right-wing elements of France's military, again in tandem with the CIA and organized crime.[123] One highly contentious theory has been ignored by the mainstream media altogether – that the Mossad, Israel's equivalent of the CIA, may have been complicit in the conspiracy because of JFK's active opposition to Israel's development of nuclear weapons and his overtures toward Israel's nemesis, Egyptian President Gamal Nasser.[124] Kennedy, of course, was replaced by Vice President Johnson, long a friend of Israel and far less aggressive than Kennedy in pursuing a policy of nuclear nonproliferation. LBJ became the first U.S. president to supply Israel with offensive weapons.[125]

To say that every researcher brings his or her biases and preconceptions to the JFK assassination is a truism that fails to do justice to the complexity of the evidence and the social pressures that inevitably come to bear upon researchers. They not only find themselves hampered by the loss, distortion, and suppression of evidence but, depending on the investigative lens they choose, they risk being misdirected by disinformation and marginalized and even vilified as irrational and greedy "conspiracy buffs" by a mainstream media that holds to the narrowest and perhaps most filtered lens of all – that of Oswald as lone gunman. Those researchers who follow the advice of Gaddis and dare to widen and unfilter the lens to explore the fullest of possible antecedents to the assassination face the most perilous path of all – ostracism not only as crackpots but, as we shall see, anti-Semites.

Endnotes

1. David Von Drehle, "Broken Trust," *Time*, November 25, 2013, Academic Search Complete.

2. Mark Lane, *Rush to Judgment: Was the CIA Involved in the Assassination of JFK?* (New York: Thunder's Mouth Press, 1991), Kindle edition, Locations 7117-7118.

3. House Select Committee on Assassinations, Final Report, H.R. REP. NO. 95-1828 (1979), http://www.history-matters.com/archive/jfk/hsca/report/html/HSCA_Report_0005a.htm.

4. Larry J. Sabato, *The Kennedy Half Century: The Presidency, Assassination, and Lasting Legacy of John F. Kennedy* (New York: Bloomsbury, 2013), 243.

5. Michael Benson, *Who's Who in the JFK Assassination: An A-to-Z Encyclopedia* (New York: Citadel Press, 1993), xiv.

6. "The JFK Assassination Files," *ABC Nightline*, January 22, 1992, Lexis-Nexis Academic.

7. Nicholas M. Horrock, "Tracing Any Kennedy Conspirator Is Given Little Chance by Officials," *New York Times*, January 1, 1979, ProQuest Historical Newspapers.

8. David W. Belin, "The Case Against A Conspiracy," *New York Times*, July 15, 1979, ProQuest Historical Newspapers.

9. George Lardner Jr., "Assassinations Committee Turns to Tantalizing Leads," *Washington Post*, September 27, 1978, ProQuest Historical Newspapers.

10. See *HSCA Final Report*; Mark Lane, *Plausible Denial: Was the CIA Involved in the Assassination of JFK?* (New York: Thunder's Mouth Press, 1992); Sylvia Meagher, *Accessories after the Fact: The Warren Commission, the Authorities, and the Report* (New York: Vintage Books, 1976); John Newman, *Oswald and the CIA: The Documented Truth about the Unknown Relationship between the U.S. Government and the Alleged Killer of JFK* (New York: Skyhorse Publishing, 2008); and Harold Weisberg. *Never Again!: The Government Conspiracy in the JFK Assassination* (Ipswich, MA: Mary Ferrell Foundation Press, 2007).

11. See "The Assassination of John Kennedy," *CNN Live Event/Special,* November 23, 2013, LexisNexis Academic; and "Examining the Assassination of President Kennedy, Fifty Years Later," *48 Hours,* CBS, November 16, 2013, LexisNexis Academic.

12. "Lyndon Johnson Expresses Alarm and Disgruntlement Following Kennedy Assassination," *CBS Evening News,* April 15, 1994, LexisNexis Academic.

13. House Select Committee on Assassinations, "Testimony of James R. Malley," *Final Report, Volume III,* H.R. REP. NO. 95-1828, at 471 (1979), https://www.maryferrell.org/mffweb/archive/viewer/showDoc.do?absPageId=75237.

14. "Memorandum for Mr. Moyers," November 25, 1963, FBI 62-109060 JFK HQ File, Section 18, https://www.maryferrell.org/mffweb/archive/viewer/showDoc.do?absPageId=756877.

15. Ibid.

16. See John Simkin, *Assassination of John F. Kennedy* (Spartacus Educational, 2010), Kindle Edition, Locations 92435-92437; John Newman, *Oswald and the CIA* (New York: Skyhorse Publishing, 2008), 636-7; and Holzman, *James Jesus Angleton,* 193.

17. Lane, *Plausible Denial,* 43.

18. Larry J. Sabato, *The Kennedy Half Century: The Presidency, Assassination, and Lasting Legacy of John F. Kennedy* (New York: Bloomsbury, 2013), 253.

19. Ibid., 252; and Michael Benson, *Encyclopedia of the JFK Assassination* (New York: Checkmark Books, 2002), 47.

20. "Secretary John Kerry Doubts Kennedy's Assassination Is Solved," *Anderson Cooper 360 Degrees,* CNN, November 8, 2013, LexisNexis Academic; and "Conspiracy Theory; Speaking Out," *World News Saturday,* ABC, January 12, 2013. LexisNexis Academic.

21. "No Lone Gunman? New Details on JFK's Assassination," ABC *Good Morning America,* January 13, 2013, LexisNexis Academic.

22. Michael L. Kurtz, *The JFK Assassination Debates: Lone Gunman versus Conspiracy* (Lawrence: University Press of Kansas, 2006), 47.

23. Ibid., 27.

24. Ibid.

25. Ibid., 26-27

26. Ibid., 30.

27. Ibid., 50.

28. Benson, *Encyclopedia,* 280.

29. Sabato, *Kennedy Half Century,* 143.

30. Ibid., 145.

31. Seth Kantor, *Who Was Jack Ruby?* (New York: Everest House, 1978), 41.

32. Simkin, *Assassination of John F. Kennedy,* Kindle Locations 94801-94802.

33 Bill Kelly, "Journalists and JFK: The Real Dizinfo Agents at Dealey Plaza," Citizens for the Truth About the Kennedy Assassination, May 2011, ctka.net, accessed September 7, 2016.

34. Sabato, *Kennedy Half Century,* 149

35. Ibid.

36. David Talbot, *Brothers: The Hidden History of the Kennedy Years* (New York: Free Press, 2007), 387.

37. Kurtz, *JFK Assassination Debates*, 32.

38. Ibid., 33.

39. Ibid., 43-44

40. Ibid.

41. Ibid., 45.

42. David W. Mantik, "The Harper Fragment Revisited – and JFK's Head Wounds: A Final Synthesis – Part 1," Citizens for the Truth About the Kennedy Assassination website, www.ctka.org, posted Nov. 11, 2014.

43. David W. Mantik, "The Harper Fragment Revisited – and JFK's Head Wounds: A Final Synthesis – Part 2," Citizens for the Truth About the Kennedy Assassination website, www.ctka.org, posted Nov. 26, 2014.

44. "Columnist Jack Anderson Dies," Mary Ferrell Foundation website, December 2005, https://www.maryferrell.org/wiki/index.php/News_Archive_-_Dec_2005; and Church Committee, *Book V - The Investigation of the Assassination of President John F. Kennedy: Performance of the Intelligence Agencies*, S. REP. NO. 94-755, at 80 (1976), https://www.maryferrell.org/mffweb/archive/viewer/showDoc.do?absPageId=150540.

45. "Confession of Howard Hunt," Mary Ferrell Foundation website, accessed July 17, 2014, https://www.maryferrell.org/wiki/index.php/Confession_of_Howard_Hunt; and Talbot, Brothers, 402-404.

46. Richard Belzer and David Wayne, *Hit List: An In-Depth Investigation into the Mysterious Deaths of Witnesses to the JFK Assassination* (New York: Skyhorse Publishing, 2013).

47. Mark Lane, *Last Word: My Indictment of the CIA in the Murder of JFK*, New York: Skyhorse Publishing, 2012).

48. Michael Benson, *Who's Who in the JFK Assassination: An A-to-Z Encyclopedia* (New York: Citadel Press, 1993), 92.

49. Jim Marrs, *Crossfire: The Plot that Killed Kennedy* (New York: Basic Books, 2013), Kindle edition, Kindle location 13811.

50. John McAdams, *JFK Assassination Logic: How to Think about Claims of Conspiracy* (Washington, D.C.: Potomac Books, 2011), 105.

51. Benson, *Who's Who in the JFK Assassination*, 151, 388.

52. Lee Israel, *Kilgallen: A Biography of Dorothy Kilgallen* (New York: Delacorte Press, 1979), 396-9

53. Benson, *Who's Who in the JFK Assassination*, 111, 236.

54. Israel, *Kilgallen*, 420-1.

55. Belzer, *Hit List*, 47-52.

56. James DiEugenio and Lisa Pease, *The Assassinations: Probe Magazine on JFK, RFK, MLK and Malcolm X* (Los Angeles: Feral House, 2002), 225-228.

57. Jim Garrison, *On the Trail of the Assassins* (New York: Sheridan Square Press, 1988), 138; and Belzer, *Hit List*, 91.

58. Dick Russell, *The Man Who Knew Too Much* (New York: Carroll & Graf Publishers, 1992), 182.

59. Wim Dankbar, "JFK Murder Solved," accessed January 4, 2016, http:jfkmurdersolved. com/film/ferrie.wmv.

60. Belzer, *Hit List*, 172.

61. Belzer, *Hit List*, 94-95.

62. Benson, *Encyclopedia of the JFK Assassination*, xi.

63. Kurtz, *JFK Assassination Debates*, 56.

64. Benson, *Encyclopedia of the JFK Assassination*, xi, 47.

65. *HSCA Final Report*, 142-145, http://www.history-matters.com/archive/jfk/hsca/report/html/HSCA_Report_0086b.htm.

66. Ibid, 142.

67. Hoke May, David Snyder, Ross Yockey, Rosemary James and R.T. Endicott, "Evidence Links CIA to DA Probe: Novel Says Munitions Theft 'Set Up,'" *New Orleans States-Item*, April 25, 1967.

68. Central Intelligence Agency, "Memo: Clay Shaw's Connection with CIA," February 1978, Mary Ferrell Foundation website, https://www.maryferrell.org/mffweb/archive/viewer/showDoc.do?docId=4902&relPageId=2.

69. Marrs, *Crossfire*, Kindle locations, 12295-12330.

70. Paris Flammonde, *The Kennedy Conspiracy: An Uncommissioned Report on the Jim Garrison Investigation* (New York: Meredith Press, 1969), 219-21; Marrs, Crossfire, 500; and Alan J. Weberman and Michael Canfield, *Coup d'État in America: The CIA and the Assassination of John F. Kennedy* (San Francisco: Quick American Archives, 1992), 40.

71. William Clark, "Rome's Trade Center – How It Came to Be," *Chicago Daily Tribune*, September 17, 1960, ProQuest Historical Newspapers.

72. "How Geraldo Rivera Changed America (And Why That Is So Hard to Admit)," JFK-FACTS.org, http://jfkfacts.org/assassination/review/how-geraldo-rivera-changed-america-and-why-that-is-so-hard-to-admit/Ibid.

73. Marita Sturken, "Personal Stories and National Meanings," in *The Seductions of Biography*, eds. by Mary Rhiel and David Bruce Suchoff (New York: Routledge, 1996), 33.

74. Church Committee Final Report, *Book V - The Investigation of the Assassination of President John F. Kennedy: Performance of the Intelligence Agencies*, S. REP. NO. 94-755, at 6 and 95 (1976), https://www.maryferrell.org/mffweb/archive/docset/getList.do?docSetId=1014 and https://www.maryferrell.org/mffweb/archive/viewer/showDoc.do?absPageId=150555.

75. Philip Shenon, "Yes, the CIA Director Was Part of the JFK Assassination Cover-Up," *Politico*, October 6, 2015.

76. David E. Scheim, *Contract on America: The Mafia Murder of President John F. Kennedy* (New York: Zebra Books, 1991), 10.

77. Ibid., 11.

78. Kurtz, *JFK Assassination Debates*, 51.

79. Simkin, *Assassination of John F. Kennedy*, Kindle Locations 92115-92116.

80. G. Robert Blakey and Richard N. Billings, *Fatal Hour: The Assassination of President Kennedy by Organized Crime* (New York: Berkley Books, 1992), xliii; HSCA Final Report, 9-11; and "Interview: G. Robert Blakey," Frontline, PBS, November 19, 2019, http://www.pbs.org/wgbh/pages/frontline/biographies/oswald/interview-g-robert-blakey/#addendum.

81. David S. Lifton, *Best Evidence: Disguise and Deception in the Assassination of John F. Kennedy* (New York: McMillan, 1980).

82. Simkin, *Assassination of John F. Kennedy*, Kindle location 55443.

83. Ibid., Kindle locations 40164-40170.

84. Douglas P. Horne, interview by author, April 6, 2014.

85. "Freeing the JFK Files," Mary Ferrell Foundation website, accessed July 17, 2014, https://www.maryferrell.org/wiki/index.php/Freeing_the_JFK_Files.

86. Ed Magnuson, "Now, a 'Two-Casket' Argument," *Time*, January 19, 1981.

87. Magnuson, "Now, a 'Two-Casket' Argument," *Time*.

88. Horne interview.

89. Assassination Records Review Board, "ARRB Testimony of Francis X. O'Neill, Jr., 12 Sep 1997," 3, http://www.maryferrell.org/mffweb/archive/viewer/showDoc.do?docId=792.

90. ARRB, "ARRB Meeting Report Summarizing 6/21/96 In-Person Interview of Tom Robinson," 3, http://www.maryferrell.org/mffweb/archive/viewer/showDoc.do?docId=711&relPageId=3.

91, ARRB, "Testimony of Edward F. Reed, 21 Oct 1997," 7-8, http://www.maryferrell.org/mffweb/archive/viewer/showDoc.do?docId=794&relPageId=8.

92. ARRB, "ARRB Call Report Summarizing 2/14/97, Telephonic Interview of Dennis David," http://www.history-matters.com/archive/jfk/arrb/master_med_set/md177/html/md177_0001a.htm

93. Douglas P. Horne, *Inside the Assassination Records Review Board: The U.S. Government's Final Attempt to Reconcile the Conflicting Medical Evidence in the Assassination of JFK* (Falls Church, VA.: D.P. Horne, 2009), Chapters 4 and 5.

94. Allan Eaglesham, "Where Were the JFK Autopsy Photos Taken?" *JFK/Deep Politics Quarterly XI* no. 2 (2006): 30-36, http://www.manuscriptservice.com/AutopsyRoom/.

95. David W. Mantik, "Optical Density Measurements of the JFK Autopsy X-Rays," in *Assassination Science: Experts Speak Out on the Death of JFK*, ed. James H. Fetzer (Chicago: CatFeet Press, 1998), 153-8.

96. George Lardner Jr., "Archive Photos Not of JFK's Brain, Concludes Aide to Review Board; Staff Member Contends 2 Different Specimens Were Examined," *Washington Post*, November 10, 1998, LexisNexis Academic; and ARRB, "Questions Regarding Supplemental Brain Examination(s) Following the Autopsy on President John F. Kennedy," by Doug Horne, http://history-matters.com/archive/jfk/arrb/staff_memos/DH_BrainExams/html/d130_0001a.htm.

97. Lardner, "Archive Photos," *Washington Post*; and ARRB, "ARRB Testimony of Francis X. O'Neill."

98. Ibid; and ARRB, "Testimony of John T. Stringer, 16 Jul 1996," http://www.maryferrell.org/mffweb/archive/viewer/showDoc.do?docId=798

99. ARRB, "Questions Regarding Supplemental Brain Examination(s) Following the Autopsy on President John F. Kennedy," by Doug Horne, http://history-matters.com/archive/jfk/arrb/staff_memos/DH_BrainExams/html/d130_0001a.htm.

100. Horne said several publishers turned him down because he insisted on publishing all five volumes of his work.

101. Horne, *Inside the AARB*, Vol. 3, 777-844.

102. See Lardner, "Archive Photos Not of JFK's Brain"; and Deb Riechmann, "Newly Released JFK Documents Raise Questions about Medical Evidence," Associated Press, November 9, 1998, LexisNexis Academic.

103. Oliver Stone, "Who Is Rewriting History?" *New York Times*, December 20, 1991, LexisNexis Academic.

104. Blakey and Billings, *Fatal Hour*, 54.

105. Marrs, *Crossfire*, 169.

106. Ibid., 536.

107. Bernard Weinraub, "Substance and Style Criticized in 'JFK'," *New York Times*, November 7, 1991, LexisNexis Academic; and George Lardner Jr., "Oliver Stone's Version of the Kennedy Assassination Exploits the Edge of Paranoia," *Washington Post*, May 19, 1991, LexisNexis Academic.

108. See Art Buchwald, "Bugged: The Flu Conspiracy," *Washington Post*, January 14, 1992, LexisNexis Academic; Michael Isikoff, "H-e-e-e-e-r-e's Conspiracy!; Why Did Oliver Stone Omit (or Suppress!) the Role of Johnny Carson?" *New York Times*, December 29, 1991, LexisNexis Academic; and Bernard Weinraub, "Valenti Calls 'J.F.K.' 'Hoax' and 'Smear'," *New York Times*, April 2, 1992, LexisNexis Academic.

109. Barbie Zelizer, *Covering the Body* (Chicago: University of Chicago Press, 1992), 137.

110. Catherine Dunphy, "Gutsy Stone opens JFK assassination wounds," *Toronto Star*, Dec. 20, 1991, LexisNexis Academic.

111. Daniel McDonnell, "JFK : New Oliver Stone Film Causes A Storm," *Sunday Herald Sun*, Dec. 22, 1991, LexisNexis Academic.

112. Todd Gitlin, "JFK Slaying: Who Owns the Truth," *Washington Post*, November 13, 1992, LexisNexis Academic.

113. Robert O'Harrow Jr., "Conspiracy Theory Wins Converts; Moviegoers Say 'JFK' Nourishes Doubts That Oswald Acted Alone," *Washington Post*, January 2, 1992; and Esther B. Fein, "Book Notes," *New York Times*, January 8, 1992.

114. Jefferson Morley, "The Kennedy Assassination: 47 Years Later, What Do We Really Know?" *The Atlantic Monthly*, http://www.theatlantic.com/national/archive/2010/11/the-kennedy-assassination-47-years-later-what-do-we-really-know/66722/.

115. See Ross Frank Ralston, "The Media and the Kennedy Assassination: The Social Construction of Reality," (PhD diss., Iowa State University, 1999); and "Destruction of Records," Mary Ferrell Foundation website, accessed July 17, 2014, http://www.maryferrell.org/wiki/index.php/Destruction_of_Records.

116. Belzer, *Hit List, passim*.

117. Gregory Korte, "Conspiracy Theories over JFK's Assassination Thrive," *USA Today*, http://usatoday30.usatoday.com/news/washington/2010-09-26-jfk-assassination-conspiracy-theories_N.htm?csp=34.

118. James F. Broderick and Darren Miller, *Web of Conspiracy: A Guide to Conspiracy Theory Sites on the Internet* (Medford, N.J.: CyberAge Books, 2008); and Jack Zeljko Bratich, "Grassy Knoll-Edges: Conspiracy Theories and Political Rationality in the 1990s," (PhD diss., University of Illinois, 2001).

119. See Lane, *Plausible Denial;* John Newman, *Oswald and the CIA: The Documented*

Truth about the Unknown Relationship between the U.S. Government and the Alleged Killer of JFK (New York: Skyhorse Publishing, 2008); and Peter Dale Scott, *Deep Politics and the Death of JFK* (Berkeley: University of California Press, 1993).

120. Anthony Summers, *Conspiracy* (New York: McGraw-Hill, 1992).

121. See Blakey and Billings, *The Plot to Kill the President*; John H. Davis, *Kennedy Contract: The Mafia Plot to Assassinate the President* (New York: Harper Paperbacks, 1993); David E. Scheim, *Contract on America: The Mafia Murder of President John F. Kennedy* (New York: Shapolsky Publishers, 1988); John H. Davis, *Mafia Kingfish: Carlos Marcello and the Assassination of John F. Kennedy* (New York: McGraw-Hill, 1989); and Frank Ragano, *Mob Lawyer* (New York: Maxwell Macmillan International, 1994).

122. See Barr McClellan, *Blood, Money and Power: How LBJ Killed JFK* (New York: Hannover House, 2003); Phillip F. Nelson, *LBJ: The Mastermind of the JFK Assassination* (New York: Skyhorse Publishing, 2011); and Roger Stone and Mike Colapietro, *The Man Who Killed Kennedy: The Case Against LBJ* (New York: Skyhorse Publishing, 2013).

123. See Peter Kross, *JFK: The French Connection* (Kempton, Ill.: Adventures Unlimited Press, 2012); and Bradley S. O'Leary and L.E. Seymour, *Triangle of Death: The Shocking Truth about the Role of South Vietnam and the French Mafia in the Assassination of JFK* (Nashville, Tenn.: WND Books, 2003).

124. See Michael Collins Piper, *Final Judgment: The Missing Link in the JFK Assassination Conspiracy* (Washington, D.C.: Wolfe Press, 1993); Seymour M. Hersh, *The Samson Option: Israel's Nuclear Arsenal and American Foreign Policy* (New York: Random House, 1991); and Jacob Peter Hogan, "Democracy, Duplicity and Dimona: The United States of America, Israel and the Globe since 1949," (master's thesis, University of Ottawa, 2010).

125. Hersh, *The Samson Option*, 120-28.

Chapter 2

Marginalizing the "Conspiracy Buffs"

By now, we would expect the mainstream media to have rejected the Warren Commission's findings in favor of some other theory that better fits the known facts surrounding the case – what Thomas Kuhn in his seminal book, *The Structure of Scientific Theory*, calls a "paradigm shift."[1] And, yet, rather than transitioning to a more comprehensive and consistent theory as logic would demand, the media – especially those elements that JFK researcher Peter Dale Scott calls "the responsible media"[2] – seem stubbornly attached to the embattled, half-century-old notion of a lone disturbed assassin. In fact, there's no reason to use the word "seem" any longer. An analysis for this book of newspaper reviews, magazine articles, TV news broadcasts, and mainstream publishing trends related to the JFK assassination clearly shows a bias in the mainstream media in favor of the Warren Commission and against those who favor alternative theories.

"The historical consensus seems to have settled on Lee Harvey Oswald as the lone assassin," *New York Times* Executive Editor Jill Abramson decreed without argument or evidence in an editorial on the eve of the fiftieth anniversary of JFK's death, as though she and other elite media journalists have the final say on the nation's history.[3] At the other extreme, in his dissertation "Rendezvous with Death: The Assassination of President Kennedy and the Question of Conspiracy," history doctoral candidate Andrew Lee Dvorak needed 1,900 pages to argue that, despite the proliferation of conspiracy theories since the release of the Warren Report, "there is not one shred of evidence" to disprove its main conclusion – that Lee Harvey Oswald assassinated JFK.[4] But as we have seen, adjusting one's investigative lens can lead to very dramatic differences in what constitutes "evidence" in the JFK case. A better question might be, whose evidence are we talking about?

If nothing else, the Warren Report provides a clear benchmark for gauging the mainstream media's treatment of JFK assassination theories. By dint of its official status and its widely publicized and debated findings, the report forces anyone delving into the mysteries of the JFK assassination to take a defined stance on its findings. Generally speaking, those stances fall into one of the following three categories:

- Pro-Warren positions may criticize aspects of the Warren Report but support its chief finding that Oswald acted alone in killing JFK.

- Anti-Warren positions criticize the methods and findings of the Warren Commission and argue against its lone gunman theory.

- Mixed positions criticize the methods and/or findings of the Warren Report but argue there is not enough evidence to develop an alternative theory.

Hundreds of books of wildly varying quality have been written about the Kennedy assassination, from authors who have blamed the driver of JFK's limousine (*Behold a Pale Horse*) to JFK's interest in uncovering the truth about aliens (*A Celebration of Freedom: JFK and the New Frontier*). To narrow the sample to books worthy of analysis, I conducted a search of the holdings in the Library of Congress, the government research service that acquires materials "necessary to the Congress and the various officers of the Federal Government to perform their duties."[5] The search was restricted to the years 1988 through 2013 in order to limit the sample to a workable size while also including the findings from the 1979 report of the House Select Committee on Assassinations and from the release of millions of new records since the passage of the JFK Records Act in 1992. (See Appendices A and A-1 for details.) Of the eighty-seven books compiled, sixty-five were anti-Warren, eighteen were pro-Warren, and four were mixed. Anti-Warren books clearly dominate the field, outnumbering pro-Warren books by nearly four to one (3.6 to 1).

Classifying reviews of the JFK books required a more methodical approach. Reviews of twenty-eight of the eighty-seven listed books were found in the archives of the nation's two most influential newspapers, the *New York Times* and *Washington Post*. Using a coding template, each review was analyzed for its stance (1=positive, 2=negative, 3=mixed or 4=neutral/not applicable) toward the following components of the book – research, reasoning and organization/writing. The reviewer's overall opinion of the book – either positive or negative – was determined by evaluating the stances toward the three components as well as any generalized comments about the book. (See Appendix B for more details.)

For instance, in analyzing Bryan Burrough's *New York Times* review of Vincent J. Bugliosi's *Reclaiming History,* Burrough's stance toward the book's quality of reasoning was categorized as positive based on the following statement:

> It is in the arguing that Bugliosi, as a former prosecutor, truly shines. When he gets down to the sweaty business of wrestling the conspiracy buffs, he charges into the ring as a righteous avenger, body-slamming everyone from [Mark] Lane to Oliver Stone.[6]

In contrast, *New York Times* reviewer Michiko Kakutani's comments about the quality of research in Norman Mailer's *Oswald's Tale* were categorized as negative based on this supporting text:

> Much of this cumbersome volume consists of little but excerpts from earlier books and studies, cut and pasted together into an awkward collage. At the same time, Mr. Mailer declines to use his enormous gifts as a reporter and novelist to create an unvarnished portrait of his subject ...[7]

Pro-Warren books were five times more likely to be reviewed than anti-Warren – a clear indication that books opposing the Warren Report's lone gunman theory were not given the credence or importance of those supporting it. Even more telling of a pro-Warren bias is that nine of the fourteen reviews of pro-Warren books were positive (64 percent) while only one of the thirteen reviews of anti-Warren books was positive (less than 10 percent). Therefore, if selected for review, a pro-Warren book was six times more likely to receive praise than an anti-Warren book.

Although the sample is admittedly small, the academic and professional credentials of the authors were far less significant in determining whether a book was reviewed by the *Times* or the *Post* and whether the review was positive. (See Appendix A-1.) Although books by lawyers were most likely to be reviewed (three books of five reviewed, or 60 percent) as well as to receive a positive review (six positive of six reviews, or 100 percent), it should be noted that five of the six positive reviews were for just two books unequivocally supporting the Warren Report – Posner's *Case Closed* and Bugliosi's *Reclaiming History.*

Faring less well in the mainstream media were books by academic historians (three reviews of seven books, or 43 percent; one positive of three reviews, or 33 percent), by witnesses and official investigators (four reviews of sixteen books, or 25 percent; one positive of four reviews, or 25 percent), by independent researchers (eight reviews of forty-four books, or 18 percent; two positive of ten reviews, or 20 percent) and academics outside the history field (two reviews of 11 books, or 18 percent; no positive reviews, or 0 percent). A likely explanation is that advanced academic degrees are not highly valued in the U.S. media industry and are seldom a factor in hiring or promotion.

Contrary to Zelizer's argument in *Covering the Body* that journalists closed ranks around their "preferred" version of the assassination, JFK assassination books by working journalists fared worst of all in the elite media, with just one of four books receiving a review – Bill O'Reilly's *Killing Kennedy* – and a severely negative one at that.[8] Not even Jefferson Morley, who for years was a respected reporter with the *Washington Post* before starting his own website devoted to JFK research, could garner a review from his former employer or from the *New York Times* for his well-researched and engagingly written biography of Winston Scott, the CIA's bureau chief in Mexico City. Scott was in a key position to know whether the real Oswald or an impostor had shown up at the Cuban embassy in Mexico City seeking a visa to Cuba. His secret files, including a tell-all novel he had written, were personally removed from his safe soon after his death by the CIA's ubiquitous counterintelligence chief James Angleton.[9]

One reason the *Times* and the *Post* were more likely to notice and review pro-Warren books is that they were more often published by large corporate entities with considerable marketing resources and the advantage, in many cases, of being based in New York, the nation's top media center. Publishers of pro-Warren books on the sample list issued an average of 1,054 new titles per year, or more than six times the average of 166 new titles issued by publishers of anti-Warren books. Of the eighteen pro-Warren books, nine (50 percent) were published by imprints, divisions, or subsidiaries of large commercial firms based in New York. Of the sixty-five anti-Warren books, only four (16 percent) were published by New York-based corporate entities. (See Appendix C).

The corporate antipathy to publishing anti-Warren books would appear to be strong enough to overcome even the industry's profit motive, given that books questioning the Warren Report tend to outsell those supporting it, according to David Steele, editorial director of Chicago's Catfeet Press.[10] Catfeet publishes about twenty new titles each year, most of them dealing with philosophy, but decided to enter the JFK market in 1998 with the release of James H. Fetzer's *Assassination Science*, a collection of essays by experts questioning technical aspects of the Warren Report. Catfeet has since published two more books by Fetzer, which "have done very well for us by our modest standards," Steele said. "In that sense, I believe it has been a good decision." Steele said he personally agrees with the commission's lone gunman theory but that has not kept him from publishing alternative theories "because we are an open court and believe that competing views should be ventilated."[11]

Small, independent presses have stepped into the breach "because the publishing industry is not doing its job," said Kris Millegan, a musician/bibliophile who founded TrineDay in Walterville, Oregon, the publisher of this book. "We follow the Jeffersonian model of publishing all points of view in the interest of public dialogue. [Corporate publishers] have what I consider a propaganda model, where only those in power get to voice their views."[12]

Millegan said he borrowed $5,000 and launched TrineDay in 2001 after several of his friends were frustrated in getting books published by the mainstream industry, including Daniel Marvin, a former Green Beret captain who led a detachment of Special Forces on covert missions in Southeast Asia during the Vietnam War. In 2003, TrineDay published Marvin's *Expendable Elite: One Soldier's Journey into Covert Warfare,* a memoir that documents the team's CIA-sponsored assassination attempt on Cambodian Crown Prince Norodom Sihanouk in 1966. Members of the Special Forces Association sued TrineDay for libel and slander in 2004 in an effort, Millegan said, to keep the book off the market and to ruin TrineDay financially. TrineDay successfully fended off the suit in federal court in 2013, but at a cost of $150,000 in legal fees, Millegan said.[13]

"We stood up for our Constitution and, basically, people started throwing books at me" that they could not get published by larger commercial houses, he said. Among them were Saint John Hunt, son of CIA operative and Watergate conspirator E. Howard Hunt, as well as a key witness to the JFK assassination, James Tague, who was wounded by curb fragments from a shot that missed Kennedy's limousine. The Warren Commission never called Tague as a witness and was going to conclude that Oswald's three shots hit Kennedy twice and Texas Gov. John Connally once until Tague contacted Jim Lehrer, then a reporter for the *Dallas Times Herald,* who wrote a story about the missed shot.[14] Tague's minor facial wound forced the Warren Commission to adopt the Single Bullet Theory in order to explain how, with just three shots, Oswald could have struck Kennedy twice and inflicted wounds on both Connally and Tague.[15]

Tague's book, *LBJ and the Kennedy Killing*, was published by TrineDay in 2013. "This man's testimony totally changed the Warren Commission [report] and his book had to come out from me – a silly little hippie out in Oregon. It is ridiculous," Millegan said. "The New York publishing industry is part of the [information] control mechanism."[16]

News magazine articles and TV news transcripts from 1988 to 2013 also show a decided bias toward the Warren Report. A search using the keywords "Kennedy and assassination and conspiracy" was conducted for the nation's three major news magazines – *Time, Newsweek,* and *U.S. News & World Report* – on both LexisNexis Academic and Academic Search Complete. Nine articles and columns were found from 1988 to 2013, six of which were pro-Warren (66 percent), two anti-Warren (22 percent) and one mixed (11 percent). One of the two anti-Warren articles – a 2013 interview with filmmaker Oliver Stone – was relegated to *Time*'s website and did not appear in print.[17] (See Appendix D.)

A similar search was done on LexisNexis Academic of TV news transcripts from 1988 to 2013. Sources for each broadcast, including reporters who expressed their own opinions on the topic, were categorized as pro-Warren, anti-Warren or mixed, based on their on-air comments and/or history of publication. The 101 TV broadcasts related to JFK assassination theories aired the views of 154 pro-Warren sources versus 84 anti-Warren sources, for a ratio of nearly two to one (1.8). (See Appendix E.)

CNBC by far had the highest ratio of pro-Warren to anti-Warren sources, seven to one, but produced only three newscasts on the subject during the twenty-five-year period under study. The pro- to anti-Warren ratios for the other networks ranged from a low of 1.2 for CNN to a high of 2.6 for ABC. CNN also proved to be the least biased network in another category – none of its reporters, as opposed to its sources, expressed a pro-Warren opinion during the network's thirty newscasts on assassination theories. Fox reporters likewise remained neutral, but the network aired only three newscasts on the topic.

By comparison, the traditional TV networks – ABC, CBS, and NBC – often failed to maintain their neutrality on assassination theories. CBS reporters expressed ten pro-Warren opinions during thirty-three newscasts; ABC reporters tallied seven during fourteen newscasts; and NBC reporters lapsed twice in sixteen newscasts. In all, traditional TV journalists expressed twenty pro-Warren opinions in one-hundred-and-one broadcasts. None expressed an anti-Warren opinion.

Some TV journalists have stretched and even broken the truth in claiming that they were in key positions to better understand the events surrounding the assassination and its aftermath. In his biography, *The Camera Never Blinks*, Rather says it was his job that day to collect the film from the CBS truck crews near Dealey Plaza and run it to the local CBS affiliate station, KRLD, for editing. When the shots were fired in Dealey Plaza, Rather says he happened to be "on the other side of the railroad tracks, beyond the triple underpass, thirty yards from a grassy knoll that would later figure in so many conspiracy theories." That's where he was stationed to pick up the film from the camera truck for delivery to KRLD. Rather says he heard no shots, despite his proximity to the shooting. He heard nothing of what may have caused the commotion until he reached KRLD, running all the way, through Dealey Plaza: "The moment I cleared the railroad tracks I saw a scene I will never forget. Some people were lying on the grass, some screaming, some running, some pointing. Policemen swarmed everywhere and distinctly, above the din, I heard one shout, 'DON'T ANYBODY PANIC.' And, of course, there was nothing but panic wherever you looked."[18] Rather writes that he continued to run the five blocks to KRLD to deliver the film.[19]

But in a CNN Special for the 50th anniversary of the assassination, Rather narrates himself into the scene as eyewitnesses storm the grassy knoll moments after the shots were fired.

> RATHER: I saw some police run up this grass. I thought they're chasing the gunman. I run with them.
>
> UNIDENTIFIED MALE: They report here that the attempted assassin … we now hear it was a man and a woman.
>
> RATHER: They got to the top, looked around. A policeman went over the fence so I went over the fence, too. There was nothing there.[20]

Rather was not only in two places at once in the immediate aftermath of the shooting, he also failed to run into the bogus Secret Service agents that many eyewitnesses said showed their badges and prevented anyone, even the police, from venturing past the grassy knoll.[21]

Bill O'Reilly was too young to have reported on the Kennedy assassination, but makes a specious claim to having been the reporter whose knock on the door was enough to drive a beleaguered George de Mohrenschildt to suicide. In his decidedly pro-Warren book, *Killing Kennedy*,

O'Reilly builds the phony suspense by calling himself "the reporter" and writes that he "traced de Mohrenschildt to Palm Beach, Florida and traveled there to confront him. At the time de Mohrenschildt had been called to testify before a congressional committee looking into the events of November 1963. *As the reporter knocked on the door of de Mohrenschildt's daughter's home, he heard the shotgun blast* [Emphasis added] that marked the suicide of the Russian, assuring that his relationship with Lee Harvey Oswald would never be fully understood."

Then he added: "By the way, that reporter's name is Bill O'Reilly."[22]

Really? The same Bill O'Reilly?

O'Reilly's phone call that day to congressional investigator Gaeton Fonzi confirms that O'Reilly was in his office in Dallas at the time, some 1,200 miles away.[23] But the story does serve to show how O'Reilly dramatically changed his mind about the JFK assassination from the time he was a young reporter to his decidedly pro-Warren stance as a celebrity commentator on Fox News.[24] Fonzi, who was convinced Kennedy had been murdered by conspirators, was one of the young O'Reilly's chief sources for reporting that the CIA was involved in the murder. [25]

Barbie Zelizer argues that TV journalists like Rather and O'Reilly are trying to reinforce their credibility as the "preferred storytellers" in the JFK Assassination by dint of their being eyewitnesses. Other tools for reinforcing their credibility, Zelizer writes, are claims to having investigated the assassination or simply "being there" in Dallas on the day of the murder. "These roles allowed journalists a repertoire of ways to situate themselves in association with Dallas," she writes, "providing different foundations for the claim to be legitimate tellers of this story." [26] That claim, she argues, was enhanced by "the persistent emphasis on television as the medium that most effectively memorialized Kennedy."[27]

But she assumes that TV reporters are somehow working in a power vacuum without oversight and the more subtle pressures to conform from editors, managers and owners. An equally logical argument is that the reporters were trying to please their superiors. Those reporters in Dallas who were either disinclined or unwilling to criticize the Warren Report rapidly advanced their mainstream media careers, especially in the TV industry. The list of celebrity TV journalists with roots in the Dallas JFK coverage includes Dan Rather, Peter Jennings, Bob Schieffer, Robert MacNeil, and Jim Lehrer. Only MacNeil, a Canadian-born NBC correspondent and later an anchor for PBS, would go on in his career to question the Warren Report.

Unlike Rather, who by one of his accounts had raced off to the nearest CBS affiliate when the shots in Dealey Plaza rang out, MacNeil had been the only reporter to run from the press bus and sprint toward the scene of the crime, trailing after police onto the grassy knoll. (He later regretted not having interviewed witnesses there.) Soon after, in search of a telephone, MacNeil had gone up the stairs in the Texas School Book Depository where he encountered a young man in shirt sleeves coming down. MacNeil asked where he could find a phone. The young man briefly replied: "You better ask inside." That young man may have been Oswald, but even MacNeil has said he can't be sure.[28] MacNeil, who had been the first reporter to arrive at the epicenter of the action, expressed doubts years after the tragedy that Oswald acted alone. "When the Warren Commission report came out," he said in a 2013 CNN interview, "I believed it. We were still in a time when you tended to believe what officials told you."[29]

By contrast, reporters critical of the Warren Report realized that, if they were to continue to investigate the assassination, they would have to leave behind their mainstream media jobs and strike out on their own. On that list are Jim Marrs of the *Fort Worth Star-Telegram*, Josiah Thompson of *Life* magazine, Martin O. Waldron of the *New York Times,* and Jefferson Morley of the *Washington Post.*

The tallies of all these media formats – books, reviews, magazine articles, and TV broadcasts – clearly show that the nation's mainstream media have developed a consensus (one might also say bias) in favor of the findings of the Warren Report. But that comes as no surprise to authors whose books question the Warren Commission findings, most of whom say the mainstream media have either ignored or panned and ridiculed their work, and in some cases impugned their character and motives as well.

To illustrate this bias, James Fetzer, a JFK researcher and professor of philosophy at the University of Wisconsin, pointed out the contrast in the media treatment of two important press conferences in the early 1990s, one that endorsed the Warren Commission's medical evidence and another that found evidence that the official autopsy X-rays had been altered. *The Journal of the American Medical Association* (JAMA) announced at a May 19, 1992 press conference the publication of an article that claimed to have resolved the inconsistencies surrounding the president's autopsy, including the location and direction of his wounds, based on interviews with two autopsy physicians at Bethesda and several other physicians at Parkland who had seen the president's body earlier in the day. The *JAMA* article concluded that JFK had been shot twice from above and behind, in line with the Warren Commission findings. The press conference and article received widespread national media attention, including a front page story in the *New York Times* and a *Times* editorial the next day arguing that *JAMA* had presented "irrefutable proof" of the Warren Report's accuracy.[30]

At the press conference, *JAMA* Editor-in-Chief George Lundberg singled out for attack the 1990 book, *Trauma Room One*, by Dr. Charles Crenshaw, an attending physician at Parkland who has consistently maintained that he saw an entry wound to Kennedy's throat and an exit blow-out at the back of his head. Lundberg called Crenshaw's book a "sad fabrication based on unsubstantiated allegations" and characterized the motives of Crenshaw and other conspiracy theorists as "paranoia, desire for personal recognition and public visibility, and profit."[31] Crenshaw sued Lundberg and *JAMA* for slander and settled out of court for $213,000.[32] Lundberg was fired in 1999 as *JAMA*'s editor-in-chief for timing the release of a journal article about college students' perceptions of what constitutes having sex to strengthen the impeachment hearings against President Bill Clinton, whose definition of sex with White House intern Monica Lewinsky had been a focus of the hearings.[33]

Nearly a year after the *JAMA* release, on November 18, 1993, Fetzer held his own press conference in New York to publicize the findings of a panel of national experts he had assembled to examine the forensics and medical evidence in the JFK assassination. The strongest finding against the Warren Report was the discovery by respected physicist and radiologist David Mantik that the Kennedy autopsy X-rays had been altered to hide the massive blow-out at the back of his head and to position a 6.5-millimeter metal object that makes it appear as though Kennedy's skull had been pierced from behind by a bullet from Oswald's rifle.[34] The press conference was sparsely attended by U.S. media and garnered only two sentences from CNN headline news the next morning.[35] "What needs to be understood is that there is a very active disinformation community [supporting the Warren Report] that appears to be rooted in the CIA," Fetzer said. "They are looking to eliminate and control information that contradicts the official version of a lone gunman getting off three lucky shots."[36]

Peter Dale Scott said his 1993 conspiracy book, *Deep Politics and the Death of John F. Kennedy*, "got the treatment I had expected from the media," especially since it was released at the same time as Gerald Posner's much-heralded defense of the Warren Commission, *Case Closed*, a finalist for a Pulitzer Prize.[37] In a *Washington Post* review that also included Posner's book and Gaeton Fonzi's *The Last Investigation*, staff writer Jeffrey A. Frank dismissed Scott's book in the final eight sentences, concluding that "ultimately, Scott appears to go around the bend."[38] In addition to his being characterized as "a nut case" in the mainstream media, Scott said, reviewers in academic journals attacked the University of California Press "four or five times for publishing my book" as a sign of "the scandalous decline of UC Press." [39]

For his book *Mary's Mosaic*, about the mysteries surrounding the 1964 murder of JFK mistress Mary Pinchot Meyer on a secluded canal towpath in Georgetown, author Peter Janney mounted his own expensive publicity campaign with disappointing results. The book failed to get a mention from either the *Washington Post* or the *New York Times* even though (or perhaps because) Janney presents strong evidence that *Washington Post* editor Ben Bradlee helped the CIA confiscate Meyer's sensitive diary on the night after her death. [40] Bradlee was married at the time to Meyer's sister, Toni, and was also part of the CIA's Operation Mockingbird, which recruited prominent journalists to promote the agency's views.[41] "Not one mainstream media outlet would touch [the book]," Janney said. "All the press I got was in the alternative media."[42]

Investigative journalist Russ Baker had the good fortune to land a contract with Bloomsbury Press – the powerful publisher of J.K. Rowling's Harry Potter books, the top-selling series of all time – for his carefully researched exposé of the Bush dynasty in American politics, *Family of Secrets*, released in 2009. The promotional department at Bloomsbury had lined up interviews on *The Today Show*, NPR, PBS "and on and on and on, and in major glossy magazines," Baker said. "And low-level people at all these places read the book and got very, very excited."[43] But when editors and managers at the higher levels of those organizations became aware that Baker's book included three chapters on the whereabouts of George H.W. Bush before and during the Kennedy assassination and raised questions about the CIA's involvement in the murder, "somehow or other ... I didn't appear on any of those things."

David Talbot's book, *Brothers*, about the hidden history of the relationship between JFK and RFK, got a similar love-gone-bad reception once he began turning in pages to his New York publisher at Free Press. "They were liking it and liking it, until I hit a certain point that began to alarm them," Talbot said. "And I'll never forget the words that were said to me by my editor. He said, 'Now, David, this is terrific work. Keep going. It's going to be a best-seller. Just don't go all Oliver Stone." Talbot said he did go "all Oliver Stone," and the book ended up a bestseller. But when *Brothers* was optioned by Lionsgate, the producers of the hit TV series *Mad Men* at the time, Stone warned Talbot it would never be made into a film. Stone was right, despite initial support from some of the biggest names in Hollywood. "They had high hopes of turning *Brothers* into a mini-series. They had John Hamm from *Mad Men*, apparently, interested in playing JFK. It looked like all systems were go. They went to every network in Hollywood, and every network in Hollywood turned us down, even ones who initially went for it." One of them was Chris Albrecht, the TV executive who made HBO a major Hollywood player with its production of *The Sopranos*, Talbot said. Albrecht "was all excited about this until a few days later, he was not, for reasons that went unexplained."[44]

Mainstream journalists continue to marginalize opponents of the Warren Commission by a variety of fallacious means, including *ad hominem* attacks, loaded words, and broad-brush criticisms. Abramson's fiftieth anniversary editorial for the *New York Times* couldn't resist such attacks:

> ...Conspiracy speculation abounds – involving Johnson, the C.I.A., the mob, Fidel Castro or a baroque combination of all of them. Many of the theories have been circulating for decades and have now found new life on the Internet, in websites febrile with unfiltered and at times unhinged musings.[45]

In a *Washington Post* review of historian Larry J. Sabato's book *The Kennedy Half Century*,[46] released in 2013, David Greenberg chided Sabato for having devoted several chapters to the JFK conspiracy debate:

> While the book's first section is perfunctory, the second part, which deals with the assassination, is somewhat wearying and likely to interest only those hard-core buffs – I realize there are many – who wallow in outraged speculation about who was behind Kennedy's murder.[47]

The nation's major news magazines have been no less wedded to the simplicity of the Warren Report and no less fierce in attacking its critics. *Newsweek* in 1998 called the report "the official version of what happened in Dallas on November 22, 1963," slighting the "official" report issued in 1979 by the House Select Committee on Assassinations that criticized the work of the Warren Commission.[48] In a 1991 review of Oliver Stone's *JFK*, *Newsweek* savaged the film as "a piece of propaganda for a huge conspiracy theory of the Kennedy murder" while defending the Warren Commission as "the imperfect but painstaking government investigation that concluded that Oswald murdered Kennedy acting on his own."[49]

Not to be outdone, a *U.S. News* cover story in 1993 blamed conspiracy "hobbyists" and "profiteers" for destroying the nation's faith in the Warren Report, and, ultimately, in government itself. "Fully seven out of ten American think a nameless, craftily concealed conspiracy did Kennedy in – and why would they not? For three decades, harum-scarum conspiracy theories have come not as single spies but in battalions, marching at us out of 200 books and a Hollywood blockbuster."[50] And while *Time* has been the most restrained among the three major news magazines in its criticism of "conspiracy theorists," its fiftieth anniversary coverage of the assassination profiled one of the chief defenders of the Warren Commission, historian John McAdams, under the headline "Debunker among the Buffs."[51]

Of the nine articles in major news magazines devoted to JFK assassination theories from 1988 to 2013, only two questioned the Warren Report – a *Time* interview with anti-Warren filmmaker Oliver Stone and a column by anti-Warren journalist, David Talbot, whose views were safely juxtaposed in the same *Time* article with pro-Warren author Vincent J. Bugliosi.[52] A single news magazine article, appearing in *Time* on the fiftieth anniversary of the assassination in 2013, somehow managed to remain neutral in the debate, declaring the mystery of JFK's murder forever insoluble.[53]

Book reviews in the *New York Times* and the *Washington Post* have overwhelmingly defended the conclusions of the Warren Report against alternative assassination theories. The reviewers often resorted to broad criticism of conspiracy researchers as paranoid, obsessed, or just plain mercenary. In a 2007 *Washington Post* review of Vincent Bugliosi's pro-Warren *Reclaiming History*, Alan Wolfe wrote that "Bugliosi is right that this case is, and ought to be, closed. And I share his distaste for the wild finger-pointing and often paranoid reasoning of the Warren Report's critics, from the overweening New York State Assemblyman Mark Lane in the 1960s to the irresponsible filmmaker Oliver Stone in the 1990s."[54]

In another largely positive review of Bugliosi's book for the *New York Times*, Bryan Burrough told readers to "go ahead and buy this book if you feel the need to poke the conspiracy-mongers in the eye."[55]

Bugliosi got a drive-by rave from historian Tim Naftali as part of a scathing but not very detailed review in the *Washington Post* of David Kaiser's *The Road to Dallas*. Kaiser's argument that Oswald may have led a double life as a Castro supporter while working for either the Mafia or the CIA was dismissed simply as "manic and unreadable."[56] Naftali went on to say that:

> Kaiser borrows from Jim Garrison's hoary theories of the role of the right-wing New Orleans demimonde in recruiting Oswald and adds touches of the Mafia-did-it theory to explain why Jack Ruby silenced Oswald. Readers interested in why this concoction of hearsay and irrelevancies does not add up cannot do better than to read Vincent Bugliosi's encyclopedic *Reclaiming History: The Assassination of President John F. Kennedy* or Max Holland's extensive work on the subject.[57]

In one of two *New York Times* reviews of Norman Mailer's pro-Warren *Oswald's Tale: An American Mystery*, Thomas Powers lauded Mailer for delving into Oswald's psyche and compared his work favorably to Priscilla Johnson McMillan's book, *Marina and Lee*, the latter having "made no deep impression on the public, which was unready to recognize, much less accept, Oswald's humanity, while the professional assassination scholars darkly suspected that Marina (and perhaps even Ms. McMillan!) might be part of the plot."[58]

Reviewers saved their choicest words for conspiracy researchers in their reviews of Gerald Posner's apologia for the Warren Commission, *Case Closed,* released before the thirtieth anniversary of the assassination in 1993. In his *New York Times* review, Geoffrey C. Ward praised Posner for his detailed footnotes:

> He offers a devastating record of the lengths to which sensationalists have gone to sow suspicion and sell books – omitting inconvenient facts, misrepresenting testimony, favoring stories grown more gaudy with the passing years over those first told when details were fresh, libeling the safely dead. Shame is out of fashion these days, but perhaps it's not too much to hope that one or two of the authors Mr. Posner exposes – along with the editors and publishers who have profited from peddling their irresponsible wares – might suffer at least a momentary pang of embarrassment.[59]

Veteran *New York Times* book reviewer Christopher Lehmann-Haupt credited Posner with refuting "the mounting welter of conspiracy claims

... involving the Federal Government, the K.G.B., the Central Intelligence Agency, the Federal Bureau of Investigation, Cuba, opponents of Fidel Castro's Cuba, a cabal of Corsican assassins and, of recently fashionable vintage, members of organized crime."[60]

Rather than selecting individual books for more detailed reviews, the *New York Times* and *Washington Post* often collectively dismissed the whole range of anti-Warren books in overview columns, sometimes in tongue-in-check treatments. In his column "All the President's Triggermen," published for the thirtieth anniversary of the assassination, *Washington Post* staff writer Charles Paul Freund compiled a laundry list of books that speculate on different gunmen who may have been involved in the assassination, starting with the wackiest theories that Oswald was robotized by the Soviets and Jack Ruby was hypnotized.[61] For the fiftieth anniversary, *New York Times* writer Gregory Cowles slammed the anti-Warren best seller *They Killed Our President* by sneeringly referring to its co-author as "the renowned historian and investigative journalist Jesse (the Body) Ventura."[62] Cowles pitted Ventura's book against Bill O'Reilly's pro-Warren best seller, *Killing Kennedy*, and concluded that he was amazed that "O'Reilly has found a debate where he looks like the non-bullying, rational party."[63]

In a 1992 *Washington Post* column, "Historians, Buffs and Crackpots," freelance writer John G. Leyden burned through nearly thirty years of assassination books, writing off whole categories of them in a sentence or two: "Most of the contemporary crop of assassination writers have a more global view and tend to mix and match their conspiracy theories according to the latest fashion. The only consistent element throughout is the alleged involvement of the CIA."[64] Leyden reserved a special venom for David Lifton, author of *Best Evidence* "as the most imaginative among the current crop, although some might argue that the plot for *Best Evidence* was borrowed from the cult film *Invasion of the Body Snatchers*."[65] He continued:

> Rather than arguing that the official autopsy photos and X-rays are fakes, as others have done, Lifton alleges that Kennedy's body was taken from Air Force One, surgically altered to make it look as if the fatal shots came from the rear, and then put back in the casket at Bethesda Naval Hospital before the autopsy began. However, in 1988, when the PBS *Nova* series brought four of the doctors who treated Kennedy at Dallas Parkland Hospital to Washington to

view the official X-rays and autopsy photos, none could find any evidence of altered wounds.[66]

But a careful viewing of the *Nova* broadcast shows that the interviews with the four Parkland physicians were far from conclusive.[67] Prior to viewing the autopsy photos (the physicians didn't view the X-rays, as Leyden claims), all four doctors described a wound farther to the rear of the head than that shown in the autopsy photos. But they emerged after their private viewings of the photos to say they saw no discrepancies with their memory of the wound. Why? Perhaps because they were too embarrassed to admit in front of a national TV audience that they had made a mistake at Parkland. Or perhaps because they didn't want to appear skeptical or belligerent by protesting that the photos had been altered. Few things intimidate a candid answer more than the intruding lens of a national TV camera.

The TV interviews aside, the program ultimately failed to make its case about the location of JFK's head wound. Host Walter Cronkite pointed out that six physicians at Parkland Hospital, including a neurosurgeon, testified to the Warren Commission that Kennedy's damaged cerebellum, located at the rear and base of the brain, could be seen through his head wound, indicating a shot from the front. Yet the autopsy photos show no evidence of a wound anywhere near that part of the brain. The two Parkland physicians interviewed for the show admitted they must have made a mistake in the emergency room in identifying the type of brain matter. But that still leaves four other Parkland physicians, including a neurosurgeon highly trained in observing and treating all parts of the brain, who testified that they saw Kennedy's cerebellum.

Joel Achenbach's 1992 *New York Times* column, "JFK Conspiracy: Myth vs. Facts," managed to take the numerous doubts about the lone gunman theory and, in a sophomorically flippant style, reduce them to absurdities.

> Like, the brain disappeared after the autopsy! Doesn't that mean something? Maybe. But while a brain itself is surely evidence, the fact that a brain is missing isn't necessarily evidence of anything.
>
> Conspiracy theorists exploit doubt. Like, how could Oswald have fired three shots from a bolt-action rifle in merely 5.6 seconds, the interval between Kennedy's wounds? One possible answer: "Easily." The gun requires about 2.3 seconds between shots. Figure it out. Boom, reload, boom, reload, boom. You need 4.6 seconds. Amazingly, this is still cited as evidence of a conspiracy.

Then there's the "single-bullet theory," another doubt-sower. The Warren Commission said there was "persuasive evidence" that a single bullet caused the nonfatal neck wound to Kennedy and the wounds to Gov. John Connally. But the Zapruder film seems to contradict the idea, and Connally says he was hit by a separate shot. What does this mean? Maybe it means that the single-bullet theory is wrong. But the flimsiness of the official theory is not itself evidence of a second gunman. Pony up an actual name, an actual gun, an actual bullet, an actual eyewitness, then we'll talk.[68]

The flip side of Achenbach's argument, of course, is that conspiracy theories are also hard to prove. Conspirators do not generally leave evidence, or "doubt-sowers," around to implicate themselves.

TV coverage of JFK assassination theories, especially by the "responsible" journalists at ABC, CBS, and NBC, has also skewed in favor of the Warren Report. CBS anchor Bob Schieffer has been one of the most vocal on-air Warren supporters, expressing his bias during four separate newscasts since 1988. As the host of a fiftieth anniversary special on *Face the Nation*, Schieffer led into a question asking his panelists why 61 percent of Americans still think that Oswald had not acted alone by first declaring, "I think the evidence is overwhelming that he did."[69]

A month earlier, while introducing JFK author Philip Shenon for a segment on *CBS This Morning*, Schieffer lauded Shenon for having done "a magnificent job of ... connecting the dots of how the Warren Commission investigated this thing." He then added, "And, you know, he doesn't dispute their conclusion that Lee Harvey Oswald was the lone gunman and he again underlines what the rest of us have been saying for years. There is no evidence to suggest that there was a conspiracy or anybody else was involved."[70] *CBS Early Show* co-host Harry Smith also has declared his pro-Warren bias on air, signing off on a fortieth anniversary segment by telling viewers, "Did Oswald act alone? I think so."[71]

In an informal but wide-ranging analysis of the U.S. and U.K. media in the months leading up to the 50th anniversary of the assassination, JFK researcher Pat Speer carefully examined the bias in more than 60 newspaper and magazine articles, cable and TV productions (both fiction and non-fiction) and Web postings. The final tally? Media support for the Warren Report outgunned conspiracy theories 44 to 18, or more than two to one.[72] Among Speer's many interesting findings were:

- An October 9, 2013 George Will column blames the decline of the Left on its refusal to acknowledge Oswald as the lone commie nut who killed their beloved leader and "by giving birth to a destructive narrative about America."

- Barnes & Noble, the largest bookstore chain in America, promotes only two assassination-related books in the month before the anniversary, both pro-lone nut, the Time/Life box and Philip Shenon's *A Cruel and Shocking Act*.

- *The Daily Beast*, the employer of Warren Report defender-in-chief Gerald Posner before his firing in 2010 for plagiarism, runs at least four anti-conspiracy articles leading up to the anniversary, including an article by Shanin Specter, son of Warren Commission Counsel Arlen Specter. The younger Specter reveals that U.S. Rep. Robert Edgar, then a member of the HSCA, asked his father's help during the committee's investigation. The elder Specter obliged by volunteering his son, who fails in the article to explain why anyone involved in the Warren Report would have been asked to help with the HSCA's investigation.

- Despite the HSCA findings in 1975 and the release of millions of documents since Congress passed the JFK Records Act in 1992, *U.S. News & World Report* re-publishes on November 13, 2013 an article by Arlen Specter defending the Warren Commission, originally published in October 1966.

- A special anniversary edition of *TV Guide* titled "John F. Kennedy, Remembering Jack 50 Years Later," provides a timeline for readers identifying Oswald as "the assassin" with no mention of the HSCA findings.

- The same day *Newsweek* republishes the Specter defense, CNN premieres a two-hour documentary based on *Reclaiming History*, Vincent Bugliosi's 1,800-page rant against the JFK research community, whom Bugliosi blames in the film for persuading gullible Americans that their government can no longer be trusted. The production parades a news celebrity list of Warren Report supporters before the camera, including Walter Cronkite, David Susskind, Eric Sevareid and Dan Rather, who scold Americans for not believing what they've been told by the media. CNN will show the film six times before the anniversary date.

The mainstream media's response to what was supposed to be the final release of thousands of JFK files in the fall of 2017 was to call on three of their favorite lone gunman proponents for comment – political science professor Larry J. Sabato and authors Gerald Posner and Philip Shenon. Posner has long been the top cheerleader for the Warren Report and Sabato and Shenon have argued that the CIA cover-up in the JFK assassination is a "benign" ploy aimed at hiding the agency's failure to keep tabs on Oswald in the weeks leading up to the assassination.[73] Why the agency should fear the shaming of agents and investigators long dead is perhaps a mystery of its own.

A Lexis-Nexis search of the *New York Times* and *Washington Post* as well as six network and cable news channels (CNBC data wasn't available after 2012) produced a total of 196 news stories between Oct. 15 and Nov. 15 of 2017 on the final document releases. Shenon led the pack as a source in 23 of those stories, followed by Sabato with 17, and Posner with 16. Jefferson Morley – a former *Washington Post* reporter, founder of JFKFacts.org, and a researcher who carefully eschews any theory related to the assassination – was a source in four stories, one each for the *New York Times* and his alma mater *Washington Post,* and twice for CNN. John Newman, a former Army intelligence analyst and a leading critic of the Warren Report best known for having meticulously documented the CIA's tracking of Oswald, managed a single appearance on CNN just prior to the release. No other Warren critics were consulted.

It's no wonder that JFK researcher Jim DiEugenio has dubbed the media coverage leading up to and after the 2017 records dump as "The Larry and Phil Show." The summer before the release, Sabato and Shenon co-authored columns in the *Washington Post* and *Politico* reiterating their two signature arguments – one, that somehow "21st-century forensic science has proven" that Oswald was the lone assassin, even if he was part of a conspiracy; two, the CIA had no active role in a cover-up but only later came to realize that Oswald had mysteriously passed under their radar, an oversight that was all the more egregious because Oswald had been under their surveillance while making visits to the Cuban and Soviet embassies in Mexico City just weeks prior to the assassination.[74] As for the duo's first point, forensic pathologist Cyril Wecht has repeatedly challenged the two researchers to say exactly what 21st-century forensic science they're referring to.[75] As for their second point, DiEugenio notes there are at least three documented examples of the CIA obstructing the JFK investigation, beginning with the Warren Commission, the Garrison trial, and the House Select Committee on Assassinations.[76]

Morley, in a column for the progressive alternative news website Alternet, was even more scathing of the *Politico* column, arguing that the CIA didn't simply botch or bungle the JFK investigation but that the documented evidence shows they controlled it.[77]

> If no one in the ranks of the CIA or FBI followed up obvious questions raised by Oswald's trip to Mexico City and other key issues, it was because Deputy Director Richard Helms and Counterintelligence Chief James Angleton made sure they didn't. Helms and Angleton were the second and third ranking officials in the agency in 1963. They proceeded to crush colleagues like John Whitten, chief of the agency's Mexico desk, who dared to seek a real investigation of Oswald.
>
> Helms, who served as CIA director from 1967 to 1973, was the first director to be convicted of a crime. In 1978, he pleaded guilty to a misdemeanor charge of lying to Congress about an assassination plot in Chile. Helms died in 2002. Angleton was fired as counterintelligence chief in December 1974 after the *New York Times* revealed he had presided over a massive program to spy on opponents of the Vietnam War. He died in 1987.
>
> The new documents show how these two spymasters relied on a series of deceptive memoranda to steer investigators away from evidence that indicated a possible prior anti-Castro Cuban conspiracy. If the official investigation was botched, it was because Helms and Angleton intended it to fail.

Shenon and Sabato come close in their *Politico* column to reviving the much-discredited connection between Castro and Oswald, a propaganda ploy that was floated within hours of the assassination by the Cuban Student Directorate – a CIA-financed, anti-Castro group in Miami whose members declared that Oswald and Castro were the "presumed assassins."[78] If nothing else, the authors argue, Oswald may have been enraged enough to kill Kennedy after reading a story in the *New Orleans Times-Picayune* detailing Kennedy's efforts to assassinate his alleged hero in Cuba. (This is at least a step beyond the Warren Commission, which concluded that Oswald had no discernible reason for murdering the president.) Not until 1975, Shenon and Sabato claim, did the CIA discover that "no one had properly followed up on clues about an especially mysterious chapter in Oswald's life – a six-day, apparently self-financed trip to Mexico City." It was because of this lapse that the agency failed to investigate Oswald's ties to Cuban intelligence.

But as Morley points out, the new records at the National Archives show that Helms and Angleton covered up their own roles in monitoring Oswald and misled JFK investigators through a series of memos in which they lied about: 1) the agency's efforts to assassinate Castro in 1962-63, 2) the date that the CIA first opened a file on Oswald, 3) what they knew about Oswald's contacts with a CIA-backed anti-Castro group in New Orleans the summer before the assassination and, 4) what they and other top officials knew about Oswald's visit to the Cuban Consulate in Mexico City.[79] In his groundbreaking book published in 1995, *Oswald and the CIA*, Newman was able to show through CIA memo routing codes that all the early intel on Oswald, beginning in December of 1959, went straight to Angleton and his stalwart aide Ann Egerter, and no one else. It wasn't until a year later that Egerter opened a public file on Oswald, and only after Oswald showed up on a State Department list of known defectors to the Soviet Union, forcing her hand.[80] Even then Egerter closely monitored all materials going in and out of Oswald's file.

The obvious, and unanswered, question is why Angleton held his information on Oswald so close to the vest from 1959 until after the assassination, then lied to the Warren Commission about how much he knew about Oswald and when.[81]

Regardless of what journalists may tell them, the majority of Americans continue to doubt the Warren Report, although the lone gunman theory is slowly regaining favor. Skepticism reached its highest point in 1985, when 80 percent of Americans did not believe the Warren Commission. Surveys show the margin has been declining gradually ever since. A 2003 Gallup poll found that 75 percent of Americans felt there was a conspiracy.[82] By 2013, in an Associated Press-GfK poll, the portion of Americans who believed in multiple assassins had slipped to 59 percent while 24 percent thought Oswald had acted alone. That was the highest percentage of Warren Commission supporters since the mid-1960s, when 36 percent of Americans supported the lone gunman theory.[83]

Pro-Warren journalists and researchers often resort to a kind of mantra in explaining the disconnect between the views of the mainstream media versus the majority of Americans on the JFK assassination. The mantra argues that Americans are psychologically resistant to believing that a loser like Oswald could have single-handedly vanquished a president of such charismatic and mythical proportions as JFK. The notion that Americans will not accept that a peasant brought down the King of Camelot was cited at least twenty times by sources and reporters in the hundred-and-one

TV newscasts on assassination theories from 1988 through 2013. What is so maddening about the mantra to many JFK researchers is that the majority of Americans believed the lone nut theory (56 percent) when the Warren Report was first released in September 1964. It was only after critics began to poke holes in the theory that public trust in the commission's findings began to drop.

An ABC special report on the fortieth anniversary recited the mantra four separate times during an hour-long broadcast. "In all these years," ABC anchor Peter Jennings said in a voiceover, "there hasn't been a single piece of credible evidence to prove a conspiracy." So why do so many Americans refuse to believe the Warren Report? Historian Robert Dallek told Jennings, "Because I think it's very difficult for them to accept the idea that someone as inconsequential as Oswald could have killed someone as consequential as Kennedy." And if the audience missed the point after three repetitions of the same idea, Jennings concluded the broadcast by quoting William Manchester, author of *Death of a President*: "If you put the murdered president on one side of the scale and that wretched waif, Oswald … on the other, it doesn't balance. You want to add some weight to Oswald. It would invest the president's death with meaning. Kennedy would have died for something…. A conspiracy would do the job nicely."[84] Interestingly, anti-Warren sources have never once been given the opportunity to respond to the mantra on air.

The mantra, however, does raise an important question: Why is there such a wide and obstinate divergence of opinion on the Warren Report between the mainstream media and the American public? Perhaps even more curious, why is the same gap widening between the mainstream media and the majority of JFK researchers? The next chapter will examine some of the possible answers.

Endnotes

1. Thomas Kuhn, *The Structure of Scientific Theory* (Chicago: University of Chicago Press, 1962).

2. Edward S. Herman and Noam Chomsky, *Manufacturing Consent: The Political Economy of the Mass Media* (New York: Pantheon Books, 2002), xvii. Scott lists among the responsible media the major newspapers and major TV networks whom local and regional journalists look to as both professional models and as news agenda setters – *New York Times*, *Washington Post* and ABC, CBS and NBC news.

3. Jill Abramson, "The Elusive President," *New York Times*, October 27, 2013, LexisNexis Academic.

4. Andrew Lee Dvorak, "Rendezvous with Death: The Assassination of President Kenne-

dy and the Question of Conspiracy" (PhD diss., Illinois State University, 2003).

5. "Introduction to Collections Policy Statements," Library of Congress website, last modified November 2008, http://www.loc.gov/acq/devpol/cps.html.

6. Bryan Burrough, "Conspiracy… Or Not?" review of *Reclaiming History*, by Vincent Bugliosi, *New York Times,* May 20, 2007, LexisNexis Academic.

7. Michiko Kakutani, "Books of the Times; Oswald and Mailer: The Eternal Basic Questions," review of *Oswald's Tale*, by Norman Mailer, *New York Times*, April 25, 1995, LexisNexis Academic.

8. Barbie Zelizer, *Covering the Body: The Kennedy Assassination, the Media, and the Shaping of Collective Memory* (Chicago: University of Chicago Press, 1992), p. 198.

9. Jefferson Morley, *Our Man in Mexico: Winston Scott and the Hidden History of the CIA* (Lawrence: University Press of Kansas, 2008).

10. David Steele, interview by author, April 8, 2014.

11. Steele interview.

12. Kris Millegan, interview by author, May 23, 2014.

13. Millegan interview; and *Tuttle v. Marvin*, No. 204094818 (filed in U.S. District Court in South Carolina, Charleston Division, 2004).

14. Jason Sickles, "James Tague, Key JFK Assassination Witness, Dies," Yahoo News, March 1, 2014, http://news.yahoo.com/james-tague-key-jfk-assassination-witness-dies-175758762.html; and James T. Tague website, accessed July 17, 2014, http://jtague.com, accessed May 24, 2014.

15. Ibid.

16. Millegan interview.

17. Jack Dickey, "Interview: Oliver Stone Keeps Rolling," Time.com, November 15, 2013, Academic Search Complete.

18. Dan Rather and Mickey Herskowitz, *The Camera Never Blinks: Adventures of a TV Journalist* (New York: William Morrow and Company, 1977), 111-115.

19. Rather and Herskowitz, *The Camera Never Blinks*, 115.

20. "The Assassination of John Kennedy," CNN, November 23, 2013, LexisNexis Academic.

21. Michael T. Griffith, "The Man Who Wasn't There, Was There: Phony Secret Service Agents in Dealey Plaza," *JFK Lancer*, 1996, http://www.jfklancer.com/ManWho.html

22. O'Reilly, *Killing Kennedy*, 300.

23. Jefferson Morley, "Investigator's Tape Exposes Bill O'Reilly's JFK Fib," JFK Facts, January 30, 2013, http://jfkfacts.org/assassination/news/reporters-tape-exposes-bill-oreillys-jfk-fib/

24. "Bill O'Reilly Reports On CIA Connection to JFK Assassination," YouTube.com, uploaded April 5, 2007, http://www.youtube.com/watch?v=tvdS-1dcVxw&feature=player_embedded

25. Ibid.

26. Zelizer, *Covering the Body*, 131.

27. Ibid., 130.

28. Michelle McQuigge, "Did Canadian-Born Robert McNeil Meet Lee Harvey Oswald

After JFK Shooting?" Global News.com, November 21, 2013, http://globalnews.ca/news/981131/did-canadian-born-robert-macneil-meet-lee-harvey-oswald-after-jfk-shooting/

29. "The Assassination of John F. Kennedy," *CNN*, Nov. 14, 2013, LexisNexis Academic.

30. James H. Fetzer, "Prologue: The Death of JFK," in *Assassination Science: Experts Speak Out on the Death of JFK,* ed. James H. Fetzer (Chicago: Catfeet Press, 1998), 6-7.

31. D. Bradley Kizzia, "On the Trail of the Character Assassins," in *Assassination Science*, 67.

32. Ibid., 61-83; and Crenshaw v. Sutherland, U.S. Dist., LEXIS 19610 (1993).

33. Suzanne W. Fletcher and Robert H. Fletcher, "Medical Editors, Journal Owners, and the Sacking of George Lundberg," *Journal of General Internal Medicine* 14, no. 3 (1999): 200-2, MDhttp://www.ncbi.nlm.nih.gov/pmc/articles/PMC1496545/.

34. David W. Mantik, "The JFK Assassination: Cause for Doubt," in *Assassination Science,* 124.

35. Fetzer, Prologue, *Assassination Science*, 17.

36. James H. Fetzer, interview by author, April 2, 2014.

37. "1994 Finalists," The Pulitzer Prizes website, accessed July 17, 2014, http://www.pulitzer.org/finalists/1994.

38. Jeffrey A. Frank, "Who Shot JFK? The 30-Year Mystery," *Washington Post*, October 31, 1993, LexisNexis Academic.

39. Peter Dale Scott, interview by author, April 19, 2014.

40. Peter Janney, interview by author, April 4, 2014.

41. John Simkin, "Operation Mockingbird," Spartacus Educational website, accessed May 27, 20, http://spartacus-educational.com/JFKmockingbird.htm14.

42. Janney interview.

43. "The JFK Assassination and The Media," Passing the Torch conference, Senator John Heinz History Center, Pittsburg, Pennsylvania, October 17, 2013. Video download.

44. Ibid.

45. 34. Abramson, "The Elusive President."

46. Larry J. Sabato, *The Kennedy Half Century: The Presidency, Assassination, and Lasting Legacy of John F. Kennedy* (New York: Bloomsbury, 2013).

47. David Greenberg, "Every President Wants That JFK Magic," review of The Kennedy Half Century, by Larry J. Sabato, *Washington Post*, October 27, 2013, LexisNexis Academic.

48.. David Gates, "The Kennedy Conundrum," *Newsweek*, November 28, 1988, LexisNexis Academic.

49. Kenneth Auchincloss, "Twisted History," *Newsweek*, December 23, 1991, Academic Search Complete.

50. Gerald Parshall, "The Man with the Deadly Smirk," *U.S. News & World Report* , August 30, 1993, Academic Search Complete.

51. Jack Dickey, "Debunker among the Buffs," *Time*, November 25, 2013, Academic Search Complete.

52. David Talbot, "The Assassination: Was It a Conspiracy?: Yes," *Time*, July 2, 2007, Academic Search Complete.

53. David Von Drehle, "Broken Trust," *Time*, November 25, 2013, Academic Search Complete.

54. Alan Wolfe, "Goodbye, Grassy Knoll," review of *Reclaiming History,* by Vincent Bugliosi, *Washington Post*, May 27, 2007, LexisNexis Academic.

55. Bryan Burrough, "Conspiracy ... Or Not?" *New York Times*, May 20, 2007, LexisNexis Academic.

56. Tim Naftali, "A Complex Journey to the Grassy Knoll," review of *The Road to Dallas*, by David Kaiser, *Washington Post*, January 15, 2009, LexisNexis Academic.

57. Ibid.

58. Thomas Powers, "The Mind of the Assassin," review of *Oswald's Tale*, by Norman Mailer, *New York Times*, April 30, 1995, LexisNexis Academic.

59. Geoffrey C. Ward, "The Most Durable Assassination Theory: Oswald Did It Alone," review of *Case Closed*, by Gerald Posner, *New York Times*, November 21, 1993, LexisNexis Academic.

60. Christopher Lehmann-Haupt, "Books of The Times: Kennedy Assassination Answers," review of *Case Closed*, by Gerald Posner, *New York Times*, September 9, 1993, LexisNexis Academic.

61. Charles Paul Freund, "All the President's Triggermen," *Washington Post*, November 22, 1992, LexisNexis Academic.

62. Gregory Cowles, "Inside the List," *New York Times*, October 27, 2013, LexisNexis Academic.

63. Ibid.

64. John G. Leyden, "Historians, Buffs and Crackpots," *Washington Post*, January 26, 1992, LexisNexis Academic.

65. Leyden, "Historians, Buffs and Crackpots," *Washington Post*.

66. Ibid.

67. "Who Shot President Kennedy?" *Nova*, PBS, November 15, 1988, http://dvp-potpourri.blogspot.com/2010/02/who-shot-president-kennedy.html.

68. Joel Achenbach, "JFK Conspiracy: Myth vs. the Facts," *Washington Post*, February 28, 1992, LexisNexis Academic.

69. "A Special on the Assassination of John F. Kennedy," CBS *Face the Nation*, November 17, 2013, LexisNexis Academic.

70. "Talking About a New Book on the Kennedy Assassination," CBS *This Morning*, October 25, 2013, LexisNexis Academic.

71. "Overview of Investigation into Conspiracy Theory about JFK's Death," CBS *The Early Show*, November 21, 2003, LexisNexis Academic.

72. Pat Speer, "The Onslaught: the Media's Response to the 50th Anniversary of the JFK Assassination," patspeer.com, http://www.patspeer.com/the-onslaught, accessed September 14, 2016.

73. "Andrew Krieg, Wecht, CAPA Challenge Warren Report Defenders Sabato, Shenon," Justice Integrity Project, September 22, 2017, http://www.justice-integrity.org/1311-wecht-capa-challenge-warren-report-defenders-sabato- shenon.

74. Philip Shenon and Larry J. Sabato, "How the CIA Came to Doubt the Official Story of JFK's Murder," Politico.com, August 3, 2017.

75. "Andrew Krieg, Wecht, CAPA Challenge Warren Report Defenders Sabato, She-non," Justice Integrity Project, September 22, 2017, http://www.justice-integrity.org/1311-wecht-capa-challenge-warren-report-defenders-sabato- shenon.

76. James DiEugenio, "The Larry and Phil Show, Part 3," Kennedys and King, October 18, 2017, https://kennedysandking.com/john-f-kennedy-articles/the-larry-and-phil-show-part-3.

77. Jefferson Morley, "New Files Confirm the JFK Investigation Was Controlled by the CIA – Not 'Botched' as Some Pretended," Alternet.org, August 11, 2017, https://www.alter-net.org/media/new-files-confirm-jfk-investigation-wasnt-botched-it-was-controlled-top-cia-officials.

78. Ibid.

79. Ibid.

80. John Simkin, "Oswald's 201 Files," The Education Forum, September 28, 2006, http://educationforum.ipbhost.com/topic/8038-oswald%E2%80%99s-201-cia-file/.

81. Morley, "New Files."

82. Lydia Saad, "Americans: Kennedy Assassination a Conspiracy," November 21, 2003, Gallup website, http://www.gallup.com/poll/9751/americans-kennedy-assassina-tion-conspiracy.aspx.

83. Associated Press, "Poll: Belief in JFK Conspiracy Slipping Slightly," *USA Today* website, May 11, 2013, http://www.usatoday.com/story/news/nation/2013/05/11/poll-jfk-con-spiracy/2152665/.

84. "Special Report," *ABC News*, November 20, 2003, LexisNexis Academic.

Chapter 3

Consensus through Propaganda and Fear

T he mainstream media's support for the Warren Report – despite early and growing evidence of its numerous omissions, misdirections, and unanswered questions – no doubt has many possible causes, some less damning of the profession than others. Time constraints and the sheer volume of documents and conflicting research surrounding the JFK assassination no doubt has kept the vast majority of deadline-oppressed journalists from plunging into a deeper look at the Warren Report. When JFK researcher Lisa Pease began digging into the JFK documents in the late 1970s, "it became clear to me that the notion that Oswald acted alone simply wasn't supported by the evidence," she said during a 2013 panel discussion on the JFK assassination and the media. "I read (Warren Commission member) Arlen Specter's questioning of Dr. Malcolm Perry (who saw JFK in the emergency room at Parkland Hospital in Dallas immediately after the shooting) and was shocked to find Specter leading the witness. Perry clearly thought the wound was an entrance wound in his neck, and Perry indicated that, and Specter clearly didn't want Perry saying that. My first thought was that Specter's agenda was so obvious that no serious journalist could have missed it. My second thought was, no serious journalist ever read this."[1]

In his book *Conspiracy*, author Anthony Summers mentions "one eminent commentator (who) declined to accept the evidence for a second gunman, yet admitted that he hadn't written post-study of the commission's volumes of evidence. 'It would have taken too long and I had a deadline,' he told me."[2] Investigative reporter Jerry Policoff said Summers later identified the journalist as legendary *New York Times* political reporter and columnist Tom Wicker.[3]

Other JFK researchers on the 2013 panel, including Pease and Salon.com founder David Talbot, argued that most journalists are by nature passive creatures and that only the rare exceptions – "a freak like Glenn Greenwald," Talbot said – try to pierce the veil of the spinmeisters. As Pease told a reporter in the audience, "I call you guys repeaters, not reporters, because you repeat what (national security authorities) say; you don't challenge it."[4] Russ Baker, who once was a member of the Washington press corps himself, was a bit more forgiving in his comments during the same panel discussion. "My experience is that we all stay with the pack. It's okay to get a little ahead of the pack, if you figure out where the pack is heading… You don't want to get way ahead and cut your head off."[5] But panelist Jerry Policoff came closest to a theoretical perspective on the timidity of most journalists. "When you talk about the Kennedy assassination, you're talking about America's basic institutions. And the fact is, the U.S. corporate media – and I think it's important to include that word when you talk about the media – sees its role as protecting American institutions, and that's what this case is all about."[6]

Policoff would get no argument from Edward S. Herman and Noam Chomsky, authors of *Manufacturing Consent: The Political Economy of the Mass Media*. In their groundbreaking book, they argue that "the media serve, and propagandize on behalf of, the powerful societal interests that control and finance them."[7] Normally, they note, such control is not exercised through direct intervention, "but by the selection of right-thinking personnel and by the editors' and working journalists' internalization of priorities and definitions of newsworthiness that conform to the institution's policies."[8]

Reporters who aren't "right-thinking," such as Earl Golz of the *Dallas Morning News*, eventually find themselves without a job. Golz wrote more than a hundred stories on the JFK assassination during his tenure at the *Morning News* during the 1970s, discovering many new eyewitnesses to the shooting, including several who said men impersonating Secret Service agents had blocked their advance on the grassy knoll soon after shots rang out.[9] On January 22, 1976, Golz's editor sent him a letter saying his work on the assassination had become "a personal crusade" and should be "put on a back burner" so that his "time and energy be turned to something that is more immediately productive."[10] Golz kept writing about the assassination and was fired in the early 1980s.

The propaganda model includes structural factors that also influence news coverage, including ownership and control, funding from major advertisers, and "mutual interests and relationships between the media and those who make the news and have the power to define it and explain what it means."

If all else fails, Herman and Chomsky argue, powerful interests can use "flak" to discipline and intimidate journalists who dare to stray from the dominant ideology. Flak "may take the form of letters, telegrams, phone calls, petitions, lawsuits, speeches and bills before Congress, and other modes of complaint, threat, and punitive action. It may be organized centrally or locally, or it may consist of the entirely independent actions of individuals. If flak is produced on a large scale, or by individuals or groups with substantial resources, it can be both uncomfortable and costly to the media."[11]

It's not surprising then that "right-thinking" journalists, especially among the elite of the profession, could be recruited to do the bidding for "powerful societal interests" such as the CIA. Ties between the mainstream media and the American intelligence community stretch back to the early years of the Cold War. Alpha 66, a dangerous anti-Castro group that was violently anti-Kennedy in 1963, had the support of Henry and Clare Booth Luce and their publishing empire at *Time-Life*.[12] *Life* reporters routinely accompanied Alpha 66 combatants in their attacks on Soviet targets in Cuba in order to publicize their successes.[13] Several JFK researchers, including former military intelligence officer John Newman, say there is evidence that Alpha 66 had backing and guidance from the CIA.[14] Luce's widow, Clare Booth Luce, sponsored one of the speedboats used by exiles to gather intelligence along the Cuban coast and would later claim that it was "my boys" who first spotted the missile sites in Cuba.[15]

JFK researcher James DiEugenio, drawing on internal CBS documents obtained by onetime CBS assistant news producer Roger Feinman, provides a striking example of how "powerful societal interests" were able to stifle and redirect a newsroom push to take a critical look at the Warren Commission findings in 1967. CBS, then the top-rated TV news network in the country, had the chance to redirect the nation's discourse at a crucial time when most of the witnesses and suspects in the assassination were still alive, when critics of the Warren Report such as Sylvia Meagher and Mark Lane were gathering public momentum and when prosecutor Jim Garrison announced he was reopening the JFK case in New Orleans. Instead, under pressure from top CBS executives, and with the clandestine assistance of Council on Foreign Relations chairman and Warren Commission member John McCloy, CBS broadcast a four-hour, four-night special in which the producers bent and fudged the facts to make the commission's findings seem plausible.[16]

Late in the summer of 1966, after doubts about the Warren Report had spread through the CBS news ranks, including correspondent Daniel Schorr and Washington Bureau chief Bill Small, CBS News vice president Gordon Manning sent a proposal to CBS News president Richard Salant for a fair and critical examination of the commission's methodologies and findings. Salant declined, and declined again in October of 1966 when Manning suggested an open debate between critics of the report and former commission attorneys moderated by a neutral legal expert. In November, a few days after *Life* magazine published its front-page story questioning the Warren Report based on key frames in the Zapruder film, Manning tried a third time for a CBS special, this time with a panel of law school experts conducting a mock trial of Lee Harvey Oswald with evidence from both the Warren Report and its critics. Backing him on the third attempt was top prime-time producer Les Midgley, who suggested a three-night, three-hour series with the first night devoted to commission defenders, the second to overlooked or discounted witnesses, and the final night to an Oswald verdict decided by legal experts.

At this point, the Big Guns at CBS manned their battle stations. To handle the newsroom coup, Salant turned to John Schneider, president of CBS Broadcasting group, telling him in a memo he might refer the proposal to the secretive CBS News Executive Committee (CNEC), formed in response to the controversies generated by departing investigative reporter Edwin R. Murrow, who had the audacity to take on Sen. Joe McCarthy's communist witch hunt and the mistreatment of migrant farm workers. Harvard-educated Salant, an attorney with no previous journalistic experience, had been handpicked for the news management team by CBS President Frank Stanton, a former chairman of Rand Corporation, a CIA-associated think tank. Salant was on the RAND corporate board.

Besides Stanton, the other two members of CNEC were Sig Mickelson, the previous CBS News president who had gone on to be director of Time-Life Broadcasting, and CBS founder Bill Paley, who was already part of the CIA's Operation Mockingbird. Salant informed the CNEC about the proposed JFK assassination special and, a day later, told Manning he wasn't keen on the mock trial. He then sent both Manning and Midgely on a trip to California, ostensibly to talk to a couple of lawyers about the project, but in reality, to be intimidated into changing their minds about the Warren Report. One of the attorneys, Edwin Huddleson, had attended Harvard Law with Salant and was on the Rand board with him, and the other was Bayless Manning, dean of Stanford Law School. The two attorneys advised the newsroom representatives against the project on the grounds of "the national interest" and because of its political repercussions.[17]

Manning, who saw the light on what CBS executives really wanted, changed the title of the proposed new series to "In Defense of the Warren Report" and rewrote the plan to dismiss "the inane, irresponsible, and harebrained challenges of Mark Lane and others of that stripe." But Midgely, who was either clueless about the pressure from above or obstinate, circulated a memo on the project proposing that CBS run experiments more credible than "the ridiculous ones run by the FBI" and asking again for a mock trial to expose the "almost incredibly inadequate" methods of the commission.[18]

In a thinly-disguised newsroom spanking of Midgely, Salant circulated an anonymous, undated, blow-by-blow rebuttal to Midgely's proposal, which Feinman later discovered had been written by Warren Commissioner McCloy, who also happened to be the father of Ellen McCloy, Salant's administrative assistant. Throughout the development of the 1967 JFK assassination special, Ellen McCloy received most of the memos on the project, acting as a secret go-between for CBS executives and her father. But rather than twisting Midgley's arm, CBS executives found a better way to convert him to "right thinking" – a promotion – elevating him to executive editor of *The CBS Evening News*, the top-rated news broadcast in America. At last, Midgely, too, saw the light and the 1967 CBS special was an unquestioning defense of the Warren Report that also ridiculed and marginalized its critics.[19]

Collaboration with intelligence officials did not stop with publishers and TV news executives. The Church Committee in 1976 found that the CIA had recruited and used hundreds of academics, editors, and reporters during the 1960s and 1970s. According to the committee's report:

> The Central Intelligence Agency is now using several hundred American academics, who in addition to providing leads and occasionally making introductions for intelligence purposes, occasionally write books and other materials to be used for propaganda purposes abroad. ... These academics are located in over one hundred American universities, colleges, and related institutions.
>
> Prior to 1967, the Central Intelligence Agency sponsored, subsidized, or produced over 1,000 books.... For example, a book written for an English-speaking audience by one CIA operative was reviewed favorably by another CIA agent in the *New York Times*.
>
> Until February 1976, when it announced a new policy toward U.S. media personnel, the CIA maintained covert relationships with about 50 American journalists or employees of U.S. media organizations. They are part of a network of several hundred foreign individuals around the world who provide intelligence for the CIA and at times attempt to influence foreign opinion through the use of covert propaganda.[20]

Investigative journalist Carl Bernstein, in an article published in *Rolling Stone* in 1977, found CIA documents showing that the agency and the House Select Committee on Assassinations had hidden the full extent of the CIA's involvement with major media during the Cold War, and perhaps beyond. As part of the CIA's Operation Mockingbird, more than four hundred American journalists, including Pulitzer Prize winners, "provided a full range of clandestine services – from simple intelligence gathering to serving as go-betweens with spies in Communist countries. Reporters shared their notebooks with the CIA. Editors shared their staffs … . In many instances, CIA documents show, journalists were engaged to perform tasks for the CIA with the consent of the managements of America's leading news organizations."[21] In return, journalists were often supplied with classified documents, as long as they guaranteed the agency's spin on the news.[22]

The list of news executives who collaborated with Operation Mockingbird reads like a Who's Who of "responsible" U.S. media. They included William Paley of CBS, Henry Luce of *Time-Life*, Arthur Hayes Sulzberger of the *New York Times*, Barry Bingham Sr. of the *Louisville Courier-Journal*, Philip L. Graham and Alfred Friendly of the *Washington Post*, and James Copley of the Copley News Services. Among the more than twenty-five news organizations that cooperated with the CIA were ABC, NBC, the Associated Press, UPI, Reuters, Hearst Newspapers, Scripps-Howard, *Newsweek* magazine, the Mutual Broadcasting System, the *Miami Herald*, and the now-defunct *Saturday Evening Post* and *New York Herald-Tribune*. "By far the most valuable of these associations, according to CIA officials, have been with the *New York Times*, CBS and Time Inc.," Bernstein wrote.[23]

Harold "Hal" Hendrix, a Scripps-Howard News Service editor in Florida who won the Pulitzer Prize for his reporting on the Cuban Missile Crisis, was one of many journalists who worked directly for David Atlee Phillips as part of Operation Mockingbird. At the time of the assassination, Phillips was working for the CIA in Mexico City, where he monitored the Cuban and Russian embassies during Oswald's alleged visits there seeking a visa to Cuba. His other duties included keeping tabs on the Fair Play for Cuba Committee, the pro-Castro group for which Oswald ostensibly organized a chapter in New Orleans with himself as sole member. In August 1963, Oswald was seen with Phillips, who was using the name of "Maurice Bishop," in the lobby of a Dallas hotel shortly before Oswald left for Mexico City. From his office in Florida, Hendrix supplied Scripps' Dallas reporter Seth Kantor with information on Oswald within minutes of the assassination – more than Kantor could gather at the crime scene in Dallas. That call was classified for reasons of national security until Kantor filed a Freedom of Information Request in 1975.[24]

Richard Billings, son of *Life* magazine's first managing editor and a staff writer for the magazine at the time, was directly involved in the CIA operations to overthrow Fidel Castro in Cuba. In June of 1963, he was part of a small anti-Castro group that made a secret trip to Cuba in order to bring back several defecting Soviet officers to the U.S. who claimed Castro still had nuclear weapons on the island despite the Cuban missile agreement. The group failed to find the officers and returned to Miami, although one member went missing and may have been captured and executed.[25]

After the assassination in 1963, Billings was a member of the *Life* magazine team that purchased the Zapruder film, which *Life* then kept from public access for 12 years, and successfully negotiated the exclusive rights to Marina Oswald's story, which never appeared in print.[26] In November 1966, Billings learned from another journalist, David Chandler, that Jim Garrison was preparing a case against Clay Shaw. In January 1967, Billings arranged a meeting with Garrison and told him that the executives at *Life* had concluded that Kennedy's assassination had been a conspiracy and that Garrison's "investigation was moving in the right direction". And according to Garrison, Billings suggested that "the magazine would be able to provide me with technical assistance, and we could develop a mutual exchange of information."[27]

Garrison agreed to this deal and Billings was introduced to staff member, Tom Bethal, who was assigned the story. In his diary Bethal reported: "In general, I feel that Billings and I share a similar position about the Warren Report. He does not believe that there was a conspiracy on the part of the government, the Warren Commission or the FBI to conceal the truth, but that a probability exists that they simply did not uncover the whole truth."

Billings had no trouble persuading Bethal that the target of Garrison's investigation – Clay Shaw – was innocent. Later it was revealed by W. Penn Jones in his book *Forgive My Grief* that "Bethal made the entire trial plan, a complete list of State's witnesses and their expected testimony and other materials available to the Shaw defense team."[28]

Less is known about the CIA's inroads into the book publishing industry, but a well-documented example involves Cord Meyer, the head of the CIA's Operation Mockingbird, who insisted on, and got, the right from publishing giant Harper & Row in 1972 to preview an upcoming book, *The Politics of Heroin in Southeast Asia*.[29] Author Alfred McCoy had obtained on-the-record interviews with key figures in the heroin trade detailing how American intelligence had partnered with the drug trade going as far back as World War II.[30] In the end, McCoy's book was published mostly intact, in large part because of the public furor created by media coverage of the CIA's request for prior review.[31]

Mark Lane, author of the bestseller *Rush to Judgment*, which generated the first widespread doubts about the Warren Report in 1966, more recently obtained a series of CIA memos to its station chiefs detailing the agency's efforts to sway public opinion toward the official theory of the assassination. One of those documents, titled "Countering Criticism of the Warren Report" and dated April 1, 1967, reads in part:

> 3. Action. We do not recommend that discussion of the assassination question be initiated where it is not already taking place. Where discussion is active, however, addresses are requested:
>
> a. To discuss the publicity problem with liaison and friendly elite contacts (especially politicians and editors), pointing out that the Warren Commission made as thorough an investigation as humanly possible, that the charges of the critics are without serious foundation, and that further speculative discussion only plays into the hands of the opposition. Point out also that parts of the conspiracy talk appear to be deliberately generated by Communist propagandists. Urge them to use their influence to discourage unfounded and irresponsible speculation.
>
> b. To employ propaganda assets to answer and refute the attacks of the critics. Book reviews and feature articles are particularly appropriate for this purpose ... [32]

At least one mainstream journalist went beyond propagandizing for intelligence officials to collaborating with them to thwart those who dared to discredit the Warren Commission. While covering the Garrison investigation for *Newsweek*, reporter Hugh Aynesworth fed inside information on Garrison's strategy and his list of witnesses to the intelligence unit of the Dallas Police Department.[33] Aside from the scathing reports he filed for *Newsweek* on Garrison, Aynesworth played a key role in sabotaging his investigation. Records released under the 1992 JFK Act reveal that Aynesworth had applied to work for the CIA in 1963, just six weeks prior to JFK's assassination.[34] Nothing in the CIA documents show that Aynesworth was hired, but he was caught trying to silence witnesses in the Garrison investigation by offering them jobs with the CIA. According to Joan Mellen's *A Farewell to Justice*, one of those he tried to buy off, Sheriff John Manchester of Clinton County, declined the offer in very colorful terms by telling Aynesworth: "I advise you to leave the area. Otherwise, I'll cut you in a new asshole." [35] Many of the CIA documents related to Aynesworth are still being withheld.[36]

A journalist even closer to the events immediately after the assassination was Dallas radio mogul Gordon McLendon, a rabid anti-communist who had also been considered for employment by the CIA but turned down. McLendon denied to HSCA investigators that he knew Jack Ruby very well, even though Ruby had listed McClendon as one of his closest friends. Ruby often visited McLendon's radio stations and made frequent phone calls to his unlisted home phone number. On the day of the assassination, Ruby had visited McLendon's KLIF radio, arranged interviews for reporters there with Dallas police officials and again called McLendon's home number. Many of McLendon's CIA records, like those of Aynesworth, are still sealed.[37]

A heavily redacted 18-page CIA document released in 2017 shows that the agency requested a covert security clearance for McLendon on February 11, 1953 but closed the case on July 17, 1953 since it had "no further interest in the subject."[38] McLendon, who had been a Japanese translator for the Office of Naval Intelligence during World War II, owned a company in Japan in the 1950's when the CIA launched a massive covert operation to support the conservative Japanese party that dominated the country against the Left for a generation. The CIA spent millions of dollars in pay-offs to party officials.[39]

In the immediate aftermath of the assassination, Aynesworth demonstrated an uncanny ability to be in the right place at the right time while reporting for the two major Dallas dailies. From the *Dallas Morning News* newsroom, where Aynesworth and Jack Ruby said they were together during the assassination, Aynesworth arrived within minutes at the book depository where Oswald allegedly had fired the shots at JFK. He was also at the Texas Theater when Oswald was arrested and in the basement of Dallas police headquarters when Ruby gunned down Oswald.[40] Aynesworth's serendipitous reporting led to his hiring at *Newsweek*, and later at *Life* magazine, *US News & World Report*, and CBS. He went on to work for the arch-conservative *Washington Times*.[41]

Mainstream journalists cling to the official version of the Kennedy assassination for reasons that aren't necessarily political or economic but rather spring from the profession's easy deference to authority. Government reports and experts are lent an instant credibility and prestige that critics and even eyewitnesses are denied. As Mark Fishman writes in *Manufacturing the News*, news workers are predisposed to treat bureaucratic accounts as factual because news personnel help uphold a normative order of "authorized knowers" in society.

> Reporters operate with the attitude that officials ought to know what it is their job to know.... In particular, a news worker will recognize an official's claim to knowledge not merely as a claim, but as a credible, competent piece of knowledge. This amounts to a moral division of labor: officials have and give the facts; reporters merely get them.[42]

This presumption that government sources are honest and accurate not only makes the job of journalists easier – i.e., they don't have to investigate and confirm whatever "facts" officials serve up – but it enables journalists to claim that they are "objective" conduits of the news. On the other hand, to report on the claims of critics and detractors requires time-consuming and costly digging to confirm and, even then, can still lead to criticism and threats.[43]

As we'll examine later, foreign journalists and news operations have been far less subservient to official pronouncements of the U.S. government. While America's mainstream media have never reported on the money connections among the international trade group Permindex, New Orleans businessman Clay Shaw, and the CIA-backed anti-Castro groups linked to Oswald, Canadian papers have at least reported on those who have raised questions about those connections. In 2007, both the *National Post* and the *(Montreal) Gazette* wrote stories about the efforts of Montreal researcher Maurice Phillips to unseal the papers of the late Louis M. Bloomfield, a prominent Montreal attorney and the largest shareholder in Permindex, which was accused of having ties to the CIA.[44] Shaw, whom Jim Garrison suspected was part of a CIA-backed conspiracy, was a board member of Permindex at the time of the JFK assassination.

One way mainstream American journalists have closed ranks around the government version of the JFK assassination has been to label those opposed to the Warren Report as "conspiracy theorists" and "assassination buffs." Russ Baker, a veteran journalist and author of the Bush family exposé, *Family of Secrets*, said he once confronted a fellow journalist at an international conference who had asked him if he was a conspiracy theorist. "What you're actually saying is... 'Are you crazy?'" Baker replied.

"And this person admitted, 'Yes, that's basically what it means.'"[45] JFK researcher Lisa Pease says when she's asked whether she's a conspiracy theorist, "I say I'm a conspiracy realist – conspiracies happen. And because that's not a phrase they're programmed for, they listen."[46]

By questioning the rationality of conspiracy theorists, the mainstream media sidestep the examination of the evidence and "jam" the machinery of public discourse, argue Ginna Husting and Martin Orr in "Dangerous Machinery," a seminal paper that appeared in *Symbolic Interaction* in 2007.[47] The term "conspiracy theorist" reframes the debate by disparaging those with opposing views as unworthy of consideration while, at the same time, protecting mainstream views from closer examination. Husting and Orr say the label can call into question a critic or claim in three different ways. First, the label may be directly linked to pejorative words like those cited in book reviews in the previous chapter – "unhinged musings," "hard-core buffs," "conspiracy-mongers," "mounting welter of conspiracy claims," and "outraged speculation." Secondly, "it can be attached to a caricature or misstated claim," as in Charles Paul Freund's "All the President's Triggermen" parody column in the *Washington Post*.[48]

Finally, Husting and Orr write, "the label can challenge a claim by equating it with another taken or implied to be patently absurd," as in Thomas Powers' parenthetical comment in his review of Norman Mailer's *Oswald's Tale* that "perhaps even [JFK researcher] Ms. [Priscilla] McMillan!" is part of the cover-up plot.[49] "In all three of these ways, 'conspiracy theorist' allows a respondent to shift concern from the truth or falsehood of a claim onto the character, quality, or competence of the claim or claimant."[50]

In fact, despite Powers' ridicule of the idea that McMillan was part of the cover-up, official records released under the 1992 JFK Act show that she applied for employment with the CIA in 1952 and was granted a conditional clearance in 1956. She was later hired by the North American Newspaper Alliance, owned by American and British intelligence officers, and was working for NANA in Moscow at the time she interviewed Oswald as an ex-Marine defector in 1959. After the JFK assassination, she would obtain exclusive rights to interview Oswald's widow Marina. A CIA memo declassified in August 1993 noted: "I think that Miss Johnson [McMillan] can be encouraged to write pretty much the articles we want. It will require a little more contact and discussion, but I think she could come around … It would be important to avoid making her think that was being used as a propaganda tool and expected to write what she is told." Not surprisingly, many of the pages in McMillan's file are still being withheld by the CIA.[51]

In June of 1999, when newly released documents from the National Archives revealed that JFK's original bronze coffin had been drilled with holes and dumped secretly at sea in 1965,[52] CBS reporter Eric Engberg saw nothing suspicious about the government's action, which the documents said had been done to prevent "morbid curiosity" among the public. Instead, Engberg's chief concern was that "all this only fuels the JFK conspiracy industry. And it is puzzling the new documents don't show anyone worrying that a secret coffin-sinking might raise just the kind of questions the government was trying to put down."[53] Earlier on the same day on the *CBS Morning News*, reporter Bob Orr also fretted that "the latest revelation is sure to rekindle conspiracy theories. Assassination buffs are anxious to get a hold of the latest Kennedy documents."[54]

Orr failed to mention that several JFK researchers, beginning with David Lifton in 1980, have uncovered evidence that the president's wounds were secretly altered before the official autopsy was performed at Bethesda Naval Hospital. Witnesses have testified the body was delivered to naval physicians in a different coffin than the one that left Parkland Hospital in Dallas on the day of the assassination.[55] The original coffin had been significantly damaged, according to JFK historian William Manchester, one of the few people who had viewed the bronze casket prior to its disposal.[56]

On the day the coffin disposal document was released, Lifton was interviewed on *CBS This Morning* and lamented the loss of one more key piece of evidence in the case. "What we're dealing with here is the issue of whether the body was removed from this coffin. That's what makes the damage to the coffin relevant. And the fact that this coffin was dumped secretly in the ocean thirty-four years ago is really bizarre."[57] Casting doubt on the government's explanation, Lifton pointed out that other graphic materials held by the National Archives, including Kennedy's blood-soaked clothing and other items of potential "morbid" public interest, have never been available for public viewing. The coffin could have been treated in the same manner.

The fear of being labeled a conspiracy theorist can lead some researchers and journalists to hedge their bets in both directions. After more than a hundred pages in which he weighs the latest evidence for and against a conspiracy in his book *The Kennedy Half Century*, historian Larry J. Sabato concludes in dramatic but waffling fashion that "whether one embraces a conspiracy theory or prefers the lone gunman explanation, there is simply no question that – at the very least – negligence and deception among some officials contributed to the death of a president and the incomplete public explanation of his demise that followed. This is no minor matter, but some have treated it like a typographical error, to be overlooked without full accountability."[58]

As a frequent guest historian on TV news shows, Sabato has played both sides of the issue. On an October 14, 2013, segment of CBS *This Morning*, he expressed numerous doubts about the Warren Report, including this:

> When you really get into the details, it is amazing how many pieces don't fit. Just to cite one, right after the President was shot, some Dallas policemen ran up the Grassy Knoll and they encountered people who had Secret Service credentials. They let them go. They had their guns drawn. They let them go. You know what we found out since? There were no Secret Service agents in Dealey Plaza. They were all with the motorcade and they went with the motorcade to Parkland [Hospital].[59]

A month later, on CBS *Face the Nation*, Sabato made no mention of why the public might be skeptical of the Warren Report, and fell in line with pro-Warren news anchor Bob Schieffer by reaffirming the tiresome peasant-versus-king mantra:

> People look at this as one of the most terrible things that had ever happened in American history; it was. It was so big, how could you balance it with a loser, a total loser, who had failed at everything, as Lee Harvey Oswald had? There had to be more meaning in it. And they tried to invest it with meaning by saying, it is the CIA, it is the anti-Castro Cubans, it is LBJ. It is this one. It is that one.[60]

The mainstream media have never labeled as "theorists" those researchers who have devoted themselves to framing and filtering the evidence to fit the needs of the Warren Report. Nor has the media accused them or their "industry" of being driven by fame or fortune, despite evidence in some cases to the contrary. Sales of Gerald Posner's pro-Warren *Case Closed* were "boosted by a steady stream of publicity orchestrated by the indefatigable Harold M. Evans, president and publisher of Random House's adult trade group," noted Sarah Lyall in her column in the *New York Times*, adding that *Case Closed* "spent five weeks on the *New York Times* best-seller list, reaching No. 8 before falling off."[61]

A *Newsweek* cover story on Posner and *Case Closed* was hard-pressed to find enough superlatives to describe the book. "Brilliant," "airtight," and "unshakable," the magazine said, arguing that it destroyed all the conspiracy theories "with impressive finality."[62]

More than any other single book about the assassination, *Case Closed* has garnered by far the most attention from the *New York Times* and *Washington Post*. A LexisNexis search of the two papers found thirty stories or references to Posner's book since its release, many of them describing it as "definitive" or "the gold standard" for all JFK assassination research. (An interesting side note: *Case Closed* was a finalist for a Pulitzer Prize in history during a year in which the selection committee declined to choose a winner in that category, including Posner's "brilliant" achievement.)[63] The second-highest number of newspaper references, eight in all, went to another pro-Warren book, Vincent J. Bugliosi's *Reclaiming History*.

Foreign media, on the other hand, have been far less impressed with either book and more likely to consider alternative theories of the assassination. (See Appendix G.) Only two major English-language foreign newspapers bothered to review Posner's book – the *Toronto Star* and the *(Montreal) Gazette* – and both reviewed it negatively. "Once again, the U.S. corporate media are calling for a return to a long-discredited status quo," poet and novelist Douglas Fetherling wrote in the *Toronto Star*. "They've done so by boosting Gerald Posner's book *Case Closed: Lee Harvey Oswald and The Assassination of JFK*, whose enthusiastic reception has included everything from a virtually unprecedented special double issue of *U.S. News & World Report* (the newsmagazine with the best sources inside the intelligence community) to a long excerpt in *Penthouse*."[64]

Fetherling went on to write that "Posner must play down or ignore decades of criticism about the (Warren) commission's investigative procedures, charges that it took into evidence only what fed its preconceptions, ignoring, refusing, dismissing or distorting what it knew existed but didn't wish others to hear.... (And) he wanders through the supermarket of evidence, picking and choosing what suits his argument, disputing the eyewitnesses and 'ear-witnesses' who disagree with him while supporting those who don't. He condemns photo-enhancement techniques when it suits his purpose but not when it doesn't. He criticizes the 1970s House Select Committee on Assassinations except when he agrees with its findings, and he takes every opportunity to slam those who have written books which suggest or endorse conclusions contrary to his own."[65]

In his review in *The Gazette*, freelance writer and JFK researcher Ulrich Shannon is far more detailed in his criticism of Posner:

Much of Posner's portrait of (Oswald during) the 17 months preceding the assassination is drawn from Marina Oswald's Warren Commission testimony. Posner even repeats without qualification her story about Oswald trying to kill Richard Nixon - a story so implausible it led one Warren Commission attorney to write, "Marina Oswald has lied to the Secret Service, the FBI and this commission repeatedly on matters which are of vital concern to the people of this country."

On another critical point – Oswald's association with David Ferrie, an investigator for Louisiana crime boss Carlos Marcello and a rabid Kennedy-hater – Posner states that the evidence for such a connection is not worthy of belief. In doing so, he ignores documentary evidence that Ferrie was Oswald's Civil Air Patrol squadron leader, as well as the half-dozen witnesses who have independently linked the two in that context.

When Posner's attention turns to the actual shooting in Dallas, he becomes even more selective in the evidence he chooses to present.

For example, he frequently quotes Howard Brennan, a Dallas steamfitter who identified Oswald as the man he saw fire three shots from the sixth floor of the Texas School Book Depository. But he does not mention that Brennan also testified that the man in the window lingered for a time, observing the aftermath of the shooting. This is incompatible with the fact that Oswald was seen by a policeman on the second floor only 75 to 80 seconds after the shooting.[66]

Bugliosi's *Four Day's in November* garnered only one review from an English-language foreign newspaper, the *Daily Telegraph*, although British historian Dominic Sandbrook leaps from superlative to superlative in his review:

> It is a minute-by-minute, sometimes second-by-second narrative of what happened in Dallas, from the moment Kennedy arrived until he was finally laid to rest in Arlington National Cemetery.
>
> Many readers will be familiar with the elements of the case, but I have never seen them presented with such forensic precision and power, each impression building on the next.
>
> The sheer density of human detail brings home the tragedy of the assassination like no other book I have read, and some images - Jackie Kennedy cradling bits of her husband's brain in her hands, or Lee Harvey Oswald pumping bullets into the helpless policeman J. D. Tippit, his "other" victim – are hard to forget.

Beyond that, the meticulous accumulation of detail hammers home the central and incontrovertible point that Lee Harvey Oswald did it, and he acted alone. He was a loner, a loser, moody and unstable, desperate for attention, classic assassin material.[67]

Most independent JFK researchers in the U.S. have been scathing in their criticism of *Case Closed*, including former military intelligence analyst John Newman, who called the media hype for the book a form of "collective insanity," since Posner claimed to have had the final word on the subject just months before the Assassinations Records Review Board began releasing millions of pages of formerly classified documents.[68] In a review for *The Southern Journal of History*, historian David Wrone argued that Posner's book is suffused "with a massive number of errors" and "asserts simple factual answers to explain complex problems that have plagued the subject for years. In the process [Posner] condemns all who do not agree with the official conclusions as theories driven by conjectures. At the same time, his book is so theory driven, so rife with speculation, and so frequently unable to conform his text with the factual content in his sources that it stands as one of the stellar instances of irresponsible publishing on the subject."[69] Author Peter Dale Scott took Posner to task as well for stating that the psychiatrist for the Warren Commission and two Soviet psychiatrists had determined that Oswald was psychotic when, in fact, all three had concluded he was not.[70]

JFK researcher Jim DiEugenio has perhaps been Posner's most aggressive critic, charging that he obtained CIA clearance to speak to sources no other researchers have had access to. DiEugenio also points out that Posner's editor at Random House, Robert Loomis, was once married to the personal secretary of James J. Angleton, head of counterintelligence at the CIA for twenty years and "also the man who many writers and researchers, like John Newman and Lisa Pease, believe was handling the Oswald file in the CIA."[71]

There is no question that sensationalized and misleading books and films about the Kennedy assassination have been issued for commercial gain – a list that contains both pro-Warren and anti-Warren titles. As Carol Publishing chief executive Paul Schragis told *Washington Post* reporter David Streitfeld not long after the release of Oliver Stone's film *JFK*:

"If we didn't have at least one JFK book, I don't think we'd be worthy of calling ourselves trade publishers."
What if you have two?

"It might mean you're not quite as serious," Schragis says with a laugh. Nevertheless, Carol acquired two weeks ago *Passport to Assassination: The Never-Before-Told Story of Lee Harvey Oswald by the KGB Colonel Who Knew Him*. "There is a huge market for these books," says Schragis. "That's been proven as recently as a few months ago."[72]

Nor can it be dismissed that some assassination books may have been written and published as part of a disinformation campaign to mislead the public and confuse the issues, a documented argument advanced by many JFK researchers, including Scott.[73] Disinformation is a common technique employed by intelligence agencies the world over. CIA documents released through the JFK Records Act show that the agency launched a disinformation campaign of its own soon after the Kennedy assassination in order to tie Oswald to Castro.[74] Within hours of the assassination, CIA officer George Joannides began working with Cuban exiles to brand Oswald as a Communist. By the night of the assassination, Oswald's alleged pro-Castro activism had hit the airwaves and, by morning, both the *Miami Herald* ("Oswald Tried to Spy on Anti-Castro Exile Group") and the *Washington Post* ("Castro Foe Details Infiltration Effort") ran stories to that effect.[75]

Twenty-five years later, Joannides was hauled out of retirement to act as the CIA liaison to the House Select Committee on Assassinations, despite a CIA agreement with the committee's chief counsel, Robert Blakey, that no one who had any connections to Oswald or activities related to the assassination would be part of the investigation.[76] The CIA withheld information from Blakey and the committee that Joannides had been the agency's handler in the early 1960s of a CIA-financed group of anti-Castro students in the U.S. known as the DRE (Directorio Revolucionario Estudiantil).[77] Oswald had crossed paths with the militant right-wing group in New Orleans in the summer before the assassination. Days before his encounter with DRE, Oswald wrote a letter to the Fair Play for Cuba Committee in New York, a pro-Castro group under the careful watch of the FBI, asking to start a chapter of the FPCC in New Orleans and boasting, falsely, that he had fought in the streets with anti-Castro activists. Several days later, Oswald did an about-face and tried to ingratiate himself with the DRE by walking into a Canal Street store owned by the group's chief spokesman in New Orleans, Carlos Bringuier, and offering his services to train anti-Castro commandos.[78]

Oswald's flip-flopping between pro- and anti-Castro forces culminated in a staged street "fight" a week later with members of the CIA-backed anti-Castro group DRE. On August 9, 1963, Oswald began passing out pamphlets for the FPCC on Canal Street just blocks from Bringuier's store. When Bringuier and two other members of the DRE confronted Oswald about his duplicity and knocked the pamphlets out of his hands, Oswald dared them to punch him. A police officer happened on the scene and issued summonses, but a New Orleans police lieutenant later wrote in his report that he thought the fight was contrived: "[Oswald] seemed to have set them up, so to speak, to create an incident, but when the incident occurred he remained absolutely peaceful and gentle."[79]

The bizarre story does not end there. When Oswald and Bringuier appeared in court, local TV crews were there. Robert Stuckey, host of a local radio talk show and a friend of Bringuier, then invited the two apparent adversaries to engage in an on-air debate about Cuba. During the debate, Oswald revealed he had once lived in the Soviet Union. Bringuier followed up on the debate by releasing an open letter to the media, part of which called on Americans to write their congressmen "asking for a full investigation on Mr. Lee H. Oswald, a confessed 'Marxist.'"[80]

Joannides and other CIA officials involved in the post-assassination disinformation effort answered to the CIA's chief of counterintelligence, James J. Angleton, who himself had served as the CIA's liaison to the earlier Warren Commission investigation. Hundreds of the CIA's documents on Joannides' activities are still sealed and are the target of a decade-long legal battle by former *Washington Post* reporter and JFK researcher Jefferson Morley, who wrote the original story on Joannides and the DRE for the *Miami New Times* in 2001.[81] Both elite newspapers have ignored the progress of Morley's lawsuit, although in 2009, the *New York* Times ran a page 11 story that managed to cast doubt on the importance of the suit while also pointing out the CIA's resistance to opening the Joannides files. Under a headline that read "CIA Is Cagey about '63 Files Tied to Oswald," reporter Scott Shane wrote this strangely tortured lead: "Is the Central Intelligence Agency covering up some dark secret about the assassination of John F. Kennedy? Probably not. But you would not know it from the CIA's behavior."[82]

In *Family of Secrets*, veteran journalist and author Russ Baker has drilled down into another intriguing possible connection to the CIA – the whereabouts of former president, vice president and CIA chief George H.W. Bush on the day Kennedy was killed. The elder Bush, known as "Poppy" to his family members, supposedly wasn't part of the CIA in 1963 at the time of the assassination, though he was named chief of the agency in 1976. But while researching a book on film director Frank Capra in 1985, a former *Daily Variety* writer, Joseph McBride, stumbled upon a memo from FBI director J. Edgar Hoover, dated November 29, 1963, with the subject heading "Assassination of President John F. Kennedy." Hoover recorded in the memo that the bureau had briefed two individuals on the day after Kennedy's murder – "Captain William Edwards of the Defense Intelligence Agency" and "Mr. George Bush of the Central Intelligence Agency."[83] In response to McBride's 1988 story in *The Nation* about his discovery, CIA officials told the media the FBI memo "apparently" referred to a George William Bush who had worked the night shift at the Langley, Va. headquarters in 1963, which "would have been the appropriate place to have received such an FBI report."[84] The agency said the "other" George Bush left the CIA in 1964 for the Defense Intelligence Agency but, for reasons never explained, they had not been able to locate him. Through a White House spokesperson, Bush, who was then president, told McBride that he was not the man mentioned in the FBI memo. "I was in Houston, Texas, at the time and involved in the independent oil drilling business. And I was running for the Senate in late '63. I don't have any idea of what he's talking about."

Aside from the curious fact that an intelligence agency with a worldwide reach can't locate a former employee, Baker thought it was even more curious that Bush has trouble recalling exactly where he was on the day JFK was murdered.

> I was writing my book about the Bush family, nothing about the Kennedy assassination, and I came across the odd assertion that George H.W. Bush once was asked, "What do you remember about the day Kennedy was shot and where were you?" And he kind of froze and he claimed he couldn't remember where he was. And I thought that was odd.
>
> I do a lot of traveling and public speaking and I always like to ask audiences, "How many of you were five years old and over on that day?" And people raise their hands. And then I ask, "How many of you can't remember where you were when John F. Kennedy was shot, and no hand ever goes up.... So his claiming he didn't know where he was, was very strange. And so I said, "I'm going to figure out where he was." I began looking into it, and five years later, I'm still looking into it now.[85]

What Baker has learned thus far is that Bush went to elaborate lengths immediately after the assassination to create a record that he was not in Dallas at the time of the shooting. However, records show Bush had been in Dallas the previous evening and probably on the morning of the assassination. On the evening of November 21, 1963, Bush spoke to a convention of the American Association of Oil Drilling Contractors at the Sheraton Hotel in Dallas. He had hopped a ride there on the plane of Joe Zeppa, a former president of the AAOC. Baker says it's likely that Bush left with Zeppa the morning after the conference to speak at the Kiwanis Club in Tyler, Texas, where Zeppa's oil drilling company was based. None of this would seem interesting if Bush hadn't made a call less than two hours after the assassination to the FBI headquarters to report a possible suspect in the shooting – a reclusive man named James Parrot who worked in the Harris County Republican headquarters in Houston. After clearly identifying himself as George H.W. Bush, Bush made two interesting points during his conversation with the FBI: 1) he was calling from Tyler, Texas and 2) he would probably spend the night in Dallas.[86] The "tip" that Bush left with the FBI, of course, proved fruitless and he later acknowledged that he had no personal knowledge of Parrot but was relying on what other Republican party workers had told him.

Bush's connections to key players surrounding the JFK murder are just as intriguing, Baker found. Allen Dulles, whom Kennedy fired as head of the CIA after the failed Bay of Pigs invasion, was a close family friend. George de Mohrenschildt, widely believed to be Oswald's CIA handler prior to the assassination, was the uncle of Bush's prep school roommate at Andover. Nor were Dulles and de Mohrenschildt strangers to one another. Italian journalist Michele Metta has found CIA documents showing that Dulles asked de Mohrenschildt (using the code name Philip Harbin) in 1954 to mentor a CIA recruit, Herbert Itkin, who turned up in Haiti in 1963 as part of an anti-Castro operation.[87] After his final contact with Oswald in the spring of 1963, de Mohrenschildt met in New York and Washington with a number of CIA and military intelligence officials. Among them was Thomas Devine, then Bush's oil business partner in Zapata Offshore and a CIA agent.[88] A decade after the assassination, when de Mohrenschildt felt he and his wife were being bugged and followed by unknown vigilantes and shadowy operatives, he sent a letter asking for help directly to Bush, who was then chief of the CIA. Six months later, de Mohrenschildt was found dead, ruled officially as a suicide by shotgun. Among his effects was an old address book dating back to the 1950s that included Bush's address in Midland, Texas.

In addition to the suffused influences of the intelligence community, the mainstream media have also been known to bow to pressure from organized crime, one of the more frightening examples of "flak." Scott noted that Random House, owned at the time by the Newhouse newspaper empire, published two of the books that have most kept the Warren report alive in the media – Posner's *Case Closed* and Mailer's *Oswald's Tale*. In 1981, influenced by syndicate lawyer and close friend Roy Cohn, publisher S.I. Newhouse ordered a front-page retraction in Cleveland's Newhouse paper of an accurate story detailing Jackie Presser's criminal activities in the Teamsters and his role as an FBI informant.[89] Scott says it is little wonder that Newhouse would have published Posner's assurances in *Case Closed* that Ruby "was not a gangster."[90]

In his 1999 dissertation, "The Media and the Kennedy Assassination," Ross Frank Ralston discovered a media consensus supporting the Warren Report, but not one based on evidence alone. Ralston concluded that the media had adopted a Hegemony Approach to the tragedy in order to "dissipate the greatest possible doubt of a conspiracy … to create the impression that the political structure was secure and legitimate [and] … to create an image of the stable institution of government."[91] Cultural Hegemony, a theory first developed in the early twentieth century by Italian sociologist and Marxist Antonio Gramsci, describes how the dominant class uses cultural institutions to maintain power in capitalist societies. By dint of their privileged access to major ideological institutions, including religion, education, and the media, those in power are able to employ ideology as a dominant, unifying force to reinforce their positions.[92]

Gramsci's idea that hegemony enables the powerful to limit the boundaries of debate and the legitimacy of alternative views was elaborated on by Chomsky in a series of interviews in the mid-1990s for the book *The Common Good*. Chomsky argues that postmodern democratic societies manufacture a consensus by allowing lively debate but over a narrowed range of issues.[93] Gatekeepers in the media keep the public debate focused only on those issues and their solutions that do not pose a serious threat to people in power. Outliers are ignored or labeled as crackpots and social deviants – or in the case of the JFK assassination, "conspiracy theorists" – whose findings and opinions hold no weight in the mainstream discourse. Ironically, Chomsky himself has narrowed the debate over who killed JFK by declaring the subject no longer worthy of time and attention.[94] He thinks it is unlikely that Kennedy was killed for his policies in Cuba and

Vietnam because they were no different from his successors, but he will not venture any other possible motivation for a conspiracy.[95]

But while Ralston's thesis may well explain why the media feared a collapse of government in the early years after the assassination and perhaps through the tumultuous decades of the 1960s and 1970s, it is hard to see how the Warren Report could have retained favor with the media during the relatively calm decades that followed. There appears to be a deep-seated fear among some elements in power that straying too far and too deep into the mysteries of the Kennedy assassination could jeopardize something that is perhaps more powerful than government itself – what Scott calls "the deep political system." Deep politics "habitually resorts to decision-making and enforcement procedures outside as well as those publicly sanctioned by law and society. In popular terms, collusive secrecy and law-breaking are part of how the deep political system works."[96] As we will see in later chapters, deep politics creates a natural and mutually beneficial alliance among intelligence communities and organized crime operatives across national boundaries.

Researchers who have dared to look at the transnational connections in the JFK assassination are often those most virulently attacked by supporters of the Warren Commission. One plausible theory that has been shunted aside by the mainstream media and largely ignored by even the most iconoclastic JFK researchers is that Israel's foreign intelligence service, Mossad, was complicit in JFK's death because he had tried to block Israel's path to nuclear armament. That theory was first developed in 1994 in *Final Judgment*, a controversial book by Michael Collins Piper, a journalist with ties to The American Free Press, an ultraconservative media outlet. Both Piper and the AFP have been accused of being anti-Semitic by the Anti-Defamation League of B'Nai Brith.[97] Piper, who died in 2015, denied the charges and argued that his critics had taken his character and his affiliations to task, but not the findings in his book.[98]

Piper garnered the mixed support of Israeli investigative journalist Barry Chamish, whose 1998 book *Who Killed Yitzhak Rabin?* attacks the widely held view that a lone Zionist gunman assassinated the moderate Israeli prime minister. Chamish reviewed Piper's book in 1999 from the self-described point of view "of a Zionist committed to the strength and survival of Israel."[99] In summary, he wrote, "Piper gets lots right and lots wrong. What is bothersome is it doesn't take much of what he gets right to make a case for Israeli involvement in the murder [of JFK]."[100] While Chamish believes that Piper relied too much on circumstantial evidence, he does not attack Piper personally for his work. "All in all, Piper doesn't sound like an anti-Semite and I can spot one. I believe he is a sincere truth seeker."[101]

Whatever his motivations, Piper was no less careful in his research than many other JFK researchers – enough so that his book is among the nearly two hundred publications and films on the assassination to be included in the Library of Congress. And without a mainstream publisher or media attention, *Final Judgment* has sold more than 40,000 copies.[102] Piper called it the bestselling banned book of all time.

A more recent book, Phillip F. Nelson's *LBJ: From Mastermind to Colossus*, has looked at the possibility of Israeli involvement in the JFK assassination, but from an angle that pins the blame primarily on an egomaniacal Lyndon Baines Johnson, who, the author argues, would have stopped at nothing to become president of the United States. Nelson writes that, by 1949, LBJ had "already become very close to a number of people who were dedicated, zealously strident, militant Zionists. Some of these people had connections with Irgun, the same organization behind the documented assassination attempt of Ernest Bevin," the British Foreign Secretary who was opposed to the formation of Israel.[103] Like Piper, Nelson points out JFK's intense opposition to Israel's development of nuclear weapons and his refusal to supply Israel with offensive weapons, in particular the vaunted F-4 Phantom fighter jets that were then state-of-the-art.[104] All that changed when LBJ ascended to power.

But Nelson argues it was LBJ who manipulated Israelis, not vice versa, in the plot to murder Kennedy. "It is important for the reader to understand that there were a number of ardently committed Zionists – people representing points on both ends, and different positions within that spectrum – who became chessmen on a gigantic chessboard being played by Lyndon Johnson as he advanced himself (all while he played the "king") up the political ladder. Lyndon Johnson's skill set – developed over the first three decades of his life, built around his life-long obsession to become president and targeted to any person or group that could help him advance toward that goal – inexorably led him to seek the support of Jewish leaders, whose agendas in post-WWII America were formed in the wake of Hitler's holocaust."[105]

Nelson devotes a single paragraph in his book to Permindex and its possible ties to the assassination, excusing any Mossad involvement to "its undeniably close connection to James J. Angleton, 'Israel's best friend' as noted elsewhere.... (His) involvement would have been inherently dependent upon the existence of the 'driving force,' for which the chief driver and the only man who had the power to bring all the other disparate forces together … was Lyndon B. Johnson."[106]

Nelson's book was published in 2014 by Skyhorse Publications, an alternative press that has published numerous books examining different JFK conspiracy theories. But the book's cover, and even its foreword by an adjunct professor of education, makes no mention of Israeli complicity in the assassination. Like Piper's book, it was ignored by the mainstream media.

None of the established JFK researchers, even those most opposed to the findings of the Warren Commission, have commented publicly on Piper's book. In the case of Piper's theory, the Chomsky propaganda model may not be enough to explain what is holding back debate. What is more likely at play is self-censorship – a fear that even broaching the possibility that Mossad or Israeli leaders were involved in JFK's assassination will lead to charges of anti-Semitism and bigotry.

Self-censorship and political correctness theory tell us that, once an unpopular opinion is viewed as likely to lead to an attack questioning the motives of the sender, those who hold the unpopular belief are likely to be silenced or to express themselves in indirect or ambiguous ways to avoid censure. As social beings, most people are afraid of becoming isolated from their social environment; they would like to be popular and respected. Therein lies the psychological basis for both self-censorship and the Spiral of Silence theory, as first explicated by Elisabeth Noelle-Neumann in 1977.[107] Spiral of Silence maintains that a person becomes less comfortable voicing an opinion that is perceived as uncommon or losing ground "for fear of being socially isolated or otherwise negatively evaluated for supporting an unpopular idea," which, in turn, leads to a downward spiral of fewer and fewer people openly supporting the idea until it is silenced altogether.[108]

In 1994, Glenn C. Loury of Boston University went a step further in explaining self-censorship by examining the complex interaction between message sender and receiver on sensitive issues. Loury advanced what he called a "theory of political correctness" that compels "people whose beliefs are sound but who nevertheless differ from some aspect of communal wisdom … to avoid the candid expression of their opinions."[109] Loury turns to earlier theories by sociologist Erving Goffman to help explain the interaction between sender and receiver as an "expression game" in which the sender expresses himself in some way and the receiver, who takes in and reacts to the expression, forms an impression of the sender.[110] Hence, in addressing a controversial topic, the sender risks exposing himself to receivers as either "a friend" or "an enemy" of the community's shared values.[111]

A regime of political correctness may be viewed as an equilibrium pattern of expression and inference within a given community, where receivers assign undesirable qualities to senders who express themselves in an "incorrect way" and, as a result, learn to avoid such expressions.[112] Once the practice of punishing those who express certain ideas is well established, the only people who will risk social isolation by speaking recklessly are those who place so little value on sharing in the community that they must be presumed not to share its dearest common values.[113] These social pressures, then, have a self-fulfilling effect – only those who have already been outcast dare to express an outcast point of view. Hence, political correctness theory informs us that researchers who have already been labeled as anti-Semitic are most likely to explore the possibility of Israeli/Mossad complicity in the JFK assassination, thus reinforcing in circular fashion the notion that those who go down that path are anti-Semitic.

JFK researchers who seek not to be "smeared" as an enemy of politically correct communal values must avoid certain sensitive issues altogether or speak on those issues in only the most circumspect, ambiguous, or indirect ways – what Loury calls "strategic imprecision" that allows for "plausible deniability" if the sender's motives are questioned or attacked.[114]

It is important to note here that social isolation and political correctness are not part of some monolithic effort to censor the media. As Herman and Chomsky point out in the introduction to *Manufacturing Consent*, those constraints and fears are more often internalized by journalists and academics who themselves "police the boundaries of what can legitimately be articulated in public arenas."[115]

Chomsky offers a practical and pungent example of how this micro-political power works in public discourse:

> If you're down at a bar ... and you say something that people don't like, they'll ... shriek four-letter words. If you're in a faculty club or an editorial office, where you're more polite – there's a collection of phrases that can be used which are the intellectual equivalent of four-letter words and tantrums. One of them is "conspiracy theory" ... [part of] a series of totally meaningless curse words, in effect, which are used by people who know that they cannot answer arguments, and that they cannot deal with evidence. But ... they want to shut you up.[116]

As any investigative journalist will attest, it is those areas of query where the pressure to "shut up" is strongest that often lead us to the truth.

Endnotes

1. "The JFK Assassination and the Media," Passing the Torch conference, Senator John Heinz History Center, Pittsburg, Pennsylvania, October 17, 2013. Video download.

2. Summers, *Conspiracy*,

3. "The JFK Assassination and the Media," Passing the Torch conference, Senator John Heinz History Center, Pittsburg, Pennsylvania, October 17, 2013. Video download.

4. Ibid.

5. Ibid.

6. Ibid.

7. Edward S. Herman and Noam Chomsky, *Manufacturing Consent: The Political Economy of the Mass Media* (New York: Pantheon Books, 2002), xi.

8. Ibid.

9. Asher Price, "Journeyman reporter who worked as a Statesman editor dies," MyStatesman.com, January 11, 2014, http://www.mystatesman.com/news/local-obituaries/journeyman-reporter-who-worked-statesman-editor-dies/vFnnTM5ZlQGqNx-PmsB5w5I/.

10. "The JFK Assassination and the Media," Passing the Torch conference, Senator John Heinz History Center, Pittsburg, Pennsylvania, October 17, 2013. Video download.

11. Herman and Chomsky, *Manufacturing Consent*, Kindle locations 1811-1815.

12. Peter Dale Scott, *Deep Politics and the Death of JFK* (Berkeley: University of California Press, 1993), 254.

13. Michael Benson, *Who's Who in the JFK Assassination: An A-To-Z Encyclopedia* (Secaucus, N.J.: Carol Publishing Group, 1993), 5.

14. John Newman, *Oswald and the CIA: The Documented Truth about the Unknown Relationship between the U.S. Government and the Alleged Killer of JFK* (New York: Skyhorse Publishing, 2008), 110.

15. Bill Kelly, "The Real Dizinfo Agents at Dealey Plaza, Part 2," Citizens for the Truth About the Kennedy Assassination, May 11, ctka.net, accessed September 7, 2016.

16. Jim DiEugenio, "How CBS News Aided the JFK Cover-up," April 22, 2016, Consortiumnews.com, accessed August 21, 2016, https://consortiumnews.com/2016/04/22/how-cbs-news-aided-the-jfk-cover-up/

17. DiEugenio, "How CBS News Aided the JFK Cover-Up," p. 4.

18. Ibid, 4.

19. Ibid, 5.

20. Church Committee Final Report, *Book V - The Investigation of the Assassination of President John F. Kennedy: Performance of the Intelligence Agencies*, S. REP. NO. 94-755, 452, 453-54, 192, https://archive.org/stream/finalreportofsel01unit#page/n3/mode/2up.

21. Carl Bernstein, "The CIA and the Media," *Rolling Stone*, October 20, 1977, http://danwismar.com/uploads/Bernstein%20-%20CIA%20and%20Media.htm.

22. John Simkin, *The Assassination of John F. Kennedy* (Spartacus Educational, 2010), Kindle Location 115781.

23. Bernstein, "The CIA and the Media."

24. Bill Kelly, "Journalists and JFK: Real Dizinfo Agent at Dealey Plaza," JFKcountercoup, May 24, 2011, http://jfkcountercoup.blogspot.com/2011/05/journalists-and-jfk-real-dizinfo-agents.html

25. John Simkin, "Richard (Dick) Billings," Spartacus Educational, http://spartacus-educational.com/JFKbillings.htm

26. Simkin, "Billings."

27. Ibid.

28. Ibid.

29. Alfred W. McCoy, *The Politics of Heroin: CIA Complicity in the Global Drug Trade* (Brooklyn: Lawrence Hill Books, 1991).

30. Peter Janney, *Mary's Mosaic* (New York: Skyhorse Publishing, 2102), 195.

31. Janney, *Mary's Mosaic*, 195.

32. Mark Lane, *Last Word: My Indictment of the CIA in the Murder of JFK* (New York: Skyhorse Publishing, 2012), 115; and National Archives and Records Administration, "Countering Criticism of the Warren Report," Record Number: 104-10009-10022, https://www.maryferrell.org/mffweb/archive/viewer/showDoc.do?docId=53510&relPageId=2.

33. Ray and Mary La Fontaine, *Oswald Talked: The New Evidence in the JFK Assassination* (Gretna, Louisiana: Pelican Publishing, 1996), 342.

34. James DiEugenio and Lisa Pease, *The Assassinations: Probe Magazine on JFK, MLK, RFK and Malcolm X* (Los Angeles: Feral House, 2002), 25.

35. Mellen, *Farewell to Justice*, 235.

36. Bill Kelly, "Part 3 , Citizens for the Truth About the Kennedy Assassination, July 2011, ctka.net

37. Ibid.

38. "CIA File on McLendon, Gordon Barton," National Archives, RIF: 104-10177-10220.

39. Tim Weiner, "CIA Spent Millions to Support Japanese Right in 50's and 60's," *New York Times*, October 9, 1994, http://www.nytimes.com/1994/10/09/world/cia-spent-millions-to-support-japanese-right-in-50-s-and-60-s.html?pagewanted=all

40. La Fontaine, *Oswald Talked*, 341.

41. Gary King, "Journalists and JFK: How to Succeed in the News Media," May 2011, *Citizens for the Truth in the Kennedy Assassination*, http://www.ctka.net/2011/journalist_&_JFK_King.html

42. Mark Fishman, *Manufacturing the News* (Austin: University of Texas Press, 1980), 143.

43. Gaye Tuchman, "Objectivity as Strategic Ritual: An Examination of Newsmen's Notions of Objectivity," *American Journal of Sociology* 77, no. 2 (1972), 662-64.

44. Elizabeth Thompson, "Do Lawyer's Files Hide JFK Secrets?: Bloomfield Papers. Montreal Lawyer's Widow Asks Federal Archives to Seal Husband's Documents for at Least 25 More Years," *Gazette* (Montreal), January 27, 2007, ProQuest Historical Newspapers; and Elizabeth Thompson, "JFK Confidential?: A Montrealer's Private Documents May Shed

Light on One of the Great Mysteries of Our Time--If They Can Be Released," National Post, January 27, 2007, ProQuest Historical Newspapers.

45. "The JFK Assassination and the Media," Passing the Torch conference, Senator John Heinz History Center, Pittsburg, Pennsylvania, October 17, 2013. Video download.

46. Ibid.

47. Ginna Husting and Martin Orr, "Dangerous Machinery," *Symbolic Interaction*, Vol. 30, no. 2 (2007): 127-50.

48. Charles Paul Freund, "All the President's Triggermen," *Washington Post*, November 22, 1992, LexisNexis Academic.

49. Thomas Powers, "The Mind of the Assassin," review of *Oswald's Tale*, by Norman Mailer, *New York Times*, April 30, 1995, LexisNexis Academic.

50. Husting and Orr, "Dangerous Machinery," 133-4.

51. Bill Kelly, "Part3 -Journalists and JFK – The Real Disinformation Agents at Dealey Plaza."

52. National Archives and Records Administration, "Documents Relating to the Disposition of the Kennedy Ceremonial Casket," http://www.maryferrell.org/mffweb/archive/viewer/showDoc.do?mode=searchResult&absPageId=70603.

53. "Documents Release Show What Happened to JFK's Original Bronze Casket," CBS Evening News, June 1, 1999, LexisNexis Academic.

54. "Government Releases New Information about Events Surrounding the Assassination of President John F. Kennedy," CBS *Morning News*, June 1, 1999, LexisNexis Academic.

55. "David Lifton, Author, *Best Evidence,* Discusses the Importance of the Newly Released Documents Related to the Assassination of President Kennedy," CBS *This Morning*, June 1, 1999, LexisNexis Academic.

56. Ibid.

57. Ibid.

58. Larry J. Sabato, *The Kennedy Half Century: The Presidency, Assassination, and Lasting Legacy of John F. Kennedy* (New York: Bloomsbury, 2013), 253.

59. "Larry Sabato Talks about His Book on the Kennedy Assassination," CBS *This Morning,* October 14, 2013, LexisNexis Academic.

60. "A Special on the Assassination of John F. Kennedy," CBS *Face the Nation*, November 17, 2013, LexisNexis Academic.

61. Sarah Lyall, "Book Notes," *New York Times*, December 1, 1993, LexisNexis Academic.

62. William F. Powers, "The Kennedy Assassination: Last Word?" *Washington Post,* August 24, 1993, LexisNexis Academic; and Lyall, "Book Notes," December 1, 1993.

63. "1994 Winners and Finalists," The Pulitzer Prizes website, accessed March 17, 2013, http://www.pulitzer.org/awards/1994.

64. Douglas Fetherling, "Dallas: Myth and Memory," *Toronto Star*, November 20, 1993, ProQuest Historical Newspapers.

65. Ibid.

66. Ulrich Shannon, "Case Closed?" *Gazette*, September 11, 1993, ProQuest Historical Newspapers.

67. Dominick Sandbrook, "Dallas '63: The Sad, Chilling Truth," *Daily Telegraph*, June 21,

2008, ProQuest Historical Newspapers.

68. Newman, *Oswald and the CIA*, 420.

69. David R. Wrone, "Review of Gerald Posner, Case Closed," *The Journal of Southern History* 6 (1995): 186-88.

70. Scott, *Deep Politics*, xix.

71. Jim DiEugenio, "How Gerald Posner Got Rich and Famous: Or, Bob Loomis and the Anti-Conspiracy Posse," *Citizens for Truth about the Kennedy Assassination* website, accessed March 17, 2014, http://www.ctka.net/posner_jd4.html.

72. David Streitfeld, "Book Report," *Washington Post*, June 13, 1993, Lexis Nexis Academic.

73. Scott, *Deep Politics*, xix; and Church Committee Final Report, *Book V - The Investigation of the Assassination of President John F. Kennedy: Performance of the Intelligence Agencies*, S. REP. NO. 94-755, 452, 453-54, 192, https://archive.org/stream/finalreportofsel01unit#page/n3/mode/2up.

74. Sabato, *Kennedy Half Century*, 180-1.

75. Jefferson Morley, "Revelation 19.63," *Miami New Times*, April 12, 2010, http://www.miaminewtimes.com/2001-04-12/news/revelation-19-63/7/; and Sabato, *Kennedy Half Century*, 182.

76. Sabato, *Kennedy Half Century*, 182.

77. Ibid.

78. Jefferson Morley, *Our Man in Mexico: Winston Scott and the Hidden History of the CIA* (Lawrence: University Press of Kansas, 2008), 171.

79. Ibid., 172.

80. Ibid., 174.

81. Jefferson Morley, "Morley v. CIA: Why I Sued for JFK Assassination Records," JFKFacts.org, February 21, 2013, http://jfkfacts.org/assassination/news/morley-v-cia-why-i-sued-for-jfk-assassination-records/; and Morley v. CIA, 2006 U.S. Dist., LEXIS 6858.

82. Scott Shane, "CIA Is Cagey about '63 Files Tied to Oswald," *New York Times*, October 17, 2009, LexisNexis Academic.

83. Judyth Vary Baker, Edward T. Haslam and Jim Marrs, *Me & Lee: How I Came to Know Love and Lose Lee Harvey Oswald*. (Walterville, OR: Trine Day, 2010), 7.

84. Ibid., 10

85. "The JFK Assassination and the Media," Passing the Torch conference, Senator John Heinz History Center, Pittsburg, Pennsylvania, October 17, 2013. Video download.

86. Baker, *Me & Lee,* 59

87. Michele Metta, "Thanks to CIA Documents, New Light on the Borghese Coup and the Connection between the JFK Assassination and the 'Strategy of Tension'," Kennedys and King website, https://drive.google.com/file/d/0B00c8f7eWLved3lzSThBOHNJbE-FROFM1RXhYakJfbW81TjVV/view)

88. Baker, *Me & Lee,* 70

89. Scott, *Deep Politics*, xxi

90. Ibid.

91. Ross Frank Ralston, "The Media and the Kennedy Assassination: The Social Construction of Reality" (PhD diss., Iowa State University, 1999), vii.

92. Ralston, "Media and Kennedy," 13.

93. Noam Chomsky, *The Common Good* (Canada: Odonian Press, 2001), 43.

94. Jim DiEugenio, "Noam Chomsky's Sickness unto Death," Citizens for Truth about the Kennedy Assassination website, accessed July 17, 2014, http://www.ctka.net/reviews/Chomsky_Sickness_DiEugenio.html, accessed July 17, 2013.

95. On the earth production, "Noam Chomsky Talks about the CIA and Other Topics," YouTube video, 12:32, uploaded April 13, 2009, http://www.youtube.com/watch?v=lXcL5o55q8s.

96. Scott, *Deep Politics*, xi-xii.

97. "Anti-Semites Attempt to Exploit Anti-Government Conspiracy Theories," The Anti-Defamation League archive website, April 5, 2010, http://archive.adl.org/nr/exeres/c2bcb515-c582-49d0-b936-9ead0eccdda0,0b1623ca-d5a4-465d-a369-df6e8679cd9e,-frameless.html.

98. Michael Collins Piper, *Final Judgment: The Missing Link in the JFK Assassination Conspiracy* (Washington, D.C.: Wolfe Press, 1993), 541.

99. Barry Chamish, "A Zionist Looks at *Final Judgment*," Rense.com, December 14, 1999, http://www.rense.com/politics5/zionist.htm.

100. Chamish, "A Zionist Looks at *Final Judgment*," Rense.com.

101. Ibid.

102. Piper, *Final Judgment*, "A Note from the Publisher," no page number.

103. Philip F. Nelson, *LBJ: From Mastermind to "The Colossus"* (New York: Skyhorse Publishing, 2015), Kindle edition, Locations 5128-5130.

104. Nelson, *LBJ*, Location 5342.

105. Ibid., Locations 4747-4751.

106. Ibid., Locations 5381-5385.

107. Elisabeth Noelle-Neumann, "Turbulences in the Climate of Opinion: Methodological Applications of the Spiral of Silence Theory," *Public Opinion Quarterly* 41, no. 2 (1977): 143-58.

108. Andrew F. Hayes, "Exploring the Forms of Self-Censorship: On the Spiral of Silence and the Use of Opinion Expression Avoidance Strategies," *Journal of Communication* 57, no. 4 (2007): 785.

109. Glenn S. Loury, "Self-Censorship in Public Discourse: A Theory of 'Political Correctness' and Related Phenomena," *Rationality and Society* 6, no. 4 (1994): 430.

110. Ibid., 432.

111. Ibid., 435.

112. Ibid., 437.

113. Ibid., 444.

114. Ibid.

115. Herman and Chomsky, *Manufacturing Consent*, xii.

116. Noam Chomsky, "On Historical Amnesia, Foreign Policy, and Iraq," interview by Kirk W. Johnson, February 17, 2004, http://www.chomsky.info/interviews/20040217.htm.

Chapter 4

The Lens Is Everything

If history proceeds from multiple causes and their intersections, as historian John Lewis Gaddis tells us,[1] then JFK researchers must be careful not to exclude pieces that may fit the larger puzzle of who killed John F. Kennedy and why. Widening and unfiltering the investigative lens to consider all the legitimate facts and possible connections would seem logically preferable to a more restrictive lens that may miss key evidence and linkages, thus keeping the puzzle from ever being solved. Yet so much of the perspective on the JFK assassination has been limited or distorted by secrecy, propaganda, disinformation, self-censorship, and political correctness that piecing together the larger picture is perhaps most daunting for those who have immersed themselves in the full spectrum of the debate. It may help, then, to begin the process with a lens that nearly everyone can agree on.

Any good detective knows that the strength of a suspect must be measured by three factors – motive, means, and opportunity. Part of the challenge in investigating the Kennedy murder is that JFK managed in his shortened presidency to create a large number of powerful and potentially violent enemies, both domestic and international, with the motives and means to assassinate him. Certainly, all modern American presidents have created powerful enemies by dint of their own power and by the global reach of U.S. foreign policy. But in the case of JFK, many of the plausible suspects for removing him from office were part of the deep political system that respects neither law nor national boundaries. The list of suspects includes:

- Organized crime, for Robert Kennedy's crackdown on the National Crime Syndicate while serving as JFK's Attorney General.[2]

- The CIA, or rogue elements within the agency, for JFK's vow to rein in its covert operations after the Bay of Pigs fiasco.[3]

- Elements of the CIA and anti-Castro Cubans, for his refusal to supply air support to the ill-fated Bay of Pigs invasion and his promise to Soviet Premier Nikita Khrushchev to never again invade Cuba as part of the agreement ending the Cuban Missile Crisis.[4]

- The U.S. Mafia, the Marseille Mob, and the South Vietnamese government, for his crackdown on organized crime and the U.S. heroin trade through The French Connection, and his assassination of South Vietnamese President Ngo Dinh Diem.[5]

- Right-wing oil interests, in particular Texas oil baron H.L. Hunt, for his willingness to reach out to the Soviet Union and for his plans to eliminate the oil depletion allowance.[6]

- The French secret army (OAS), as well as Israel, for his support of French President Charles de Gaulle's moves to withdraw militarily from Algeria and grant independence to the Arab nation. The OAS (*Organisation de l'armée secrète*) was a rebellious secret faction of the French military determined to assassinate de Gaulle for his anti-colonialist policies.[7]

- The military-industrial complex, for his peace and disarmament overtures to Khrushchev and for his intentions to wind down the war in Vietnam. (The latter, however, is one of the most hotly contested of the assassination motives. Many historians and analysts believe that Kennedy would have escalated the war in Vietnam if he had remained in office.)[8]

- President Lyndon Johnson, for JFK's plans to replace him as the vice presidential nominee in the 1964 election and for his brother Robert's role in leaking information to *Life* magazine that would have exposed Johnson's involvement in the Bobby Baker congressional bribery scandal, thus ending LBJ's political career and possibly sending him to prison.[9]

- Israel, and its supporters within the CIA and OAS, for his active opposition to Israel's development of nuclear weapons and for his overtures to pan-Arabist and Soviet ally Egyptian President Gamal Abdul Nasser.[10]

- The CIA, Right-Wing elements in the U.S., the French OAS, and Israel all shared a deep fear of Kennedy's overtures toward the Soviet Union in the wake of the Cuban Missile Crisis, which Kennedy had seen first-hand bring the world to the brink of nuclear disaster. All four groups viewed the Soviet Union, and communism, as an implacable foe that could not be negotiated with.[11]

The Warren Commission's lone gunman theory is, of course, the view through the narrowest of investigative lenses with all the seeming advantages of simplicity and "authoritative" fact: Unstable leftist malcontent Lee Harvey Oswald shoots president to make name for himself;

unstable small-time thug Jack Ruby shoots assassin to avenge president and family. But the commission's lens fails to capture the known historical context because it ignores the considerable ties that both Oswald and Ruby had to what JFK researcher Peter Dale Scott calls "the deep politics" of America's power base where "political and criminal activities interface."[12] The theoretical foundation of Scott's book *Deep Politics and the Death of JFK* is based on demonstrable historical realities: Intelligence organizations use organized crime to do their illegal dirty work, including gun-running, money laundering, and assassinations, while, at the same time, organized crime interpenetrates those government agencies and uses them to sustain their own illegal operations. Deep politics is a symbiotic underworld where distinguishing the good guys from the bad becomes murky and ill-defined.

The financial machinations behind this trans-national world of shadows is even murkier and more complex, and there is perhaps no better example than Permindex, the phony world trade promotion group at the heart of the JFK conspiracy and the likely funding source for the murder operation. Yet the mainstream media, in defiance of its decades-old adage of "follow the money," has done nothing to investigate Permindex, its operations, or its origins. In fact, it has failed to report even what has already been revealed about its connections through the efforts of international media and JFK researchers.

Geneva-based Permindex (short for PERmanent INDustrial EXposition), and its Rome-based parent company, Centro Mondiale Commerciale (Italian for World Trade Center), was a labyrinthine money laundering and transfer scheme for tens of millions of dollars, with ties to any number of international counter-intelligence operatives and their supporters, from ex-Nazis to Zionists. Here, the lens used to investigate those links is all-important because they spin off in so many different political and international directions.

The Montreal paper *Le Devoir* and the Italian leftist newspaper *Paesa Sera* were the first to report on the workings of CMC-Permindex in articles published in March 1967, not long after Garrison arrested Shaw. *Le Devoir* wrote that CMC "was the creature of the CIA ... set up as a cover for the transfer of CIA ... funds in Italy for illegal political-espionage activities."[13] Both Permindex and CMC were expelled from their respective countries after French President Charles de Gaulle learned that they were involved in plots in 1961 and 1962 to assassinate him.[14] The book and subsequent movie, *The Day of the Jackal,* is loosely based on one of those attempts.

Le Devoir wrote:

The [CMC] and Permindex got into difficulties with the Italian and Swiss governments. They refused to testify to the origins of considerable amounts of money, the sources of which are, to say the least, uncertain, and they never seemed to engage in actual commercial transactions. These companies were expelled from Switzerland and Italy in 1962 and then set up headquarters in Johannesburg.[15]

The two newspapers noted that the board of directors for CMC-Permindex included New Orleans businessman Clay Shaw, who had recently been arrested as part of Jim Garrison's investigation into the Kennedy assassination.[16] Also listed on the board was an intriguing array of politicians, bankers, businessmen, landowners, and royalty: respected Italian leaders Mario Ceravolo, a Christian Democrat, and Corrado Bonfantini, a Social Democrat; Carlo D'Amelio, lawyer and administrator of the former royal family's interests and president of the board; Swiss Minister Ernest Feisst; Swiss Professor Max Hagemann, owner-editor of the newspaper *National Zeitung*; Hans Seligman, Basel banker; Professor Edgar Salin, president of the faculty of economics at the University of Basel; Dr. Enrico Mantello, brother of George Mandel, a key figure in the Societa Italo-Americana; Ferenc Nagy, president of Permindex, former Hungarian premier and later leader of the anti-Communist Countryman's party; Prince Gutierez di Spadafora, industrialist and landowner, related through his daughter-in-law to Adolf Hitler's Minister of Finance, Hjalmar Schacht.[17]

The major shareholder for both CMC and Permindex was Louis Mortimer Bloomfield, who held half the shares, or $250 million, "for party or parties unknown."[18] Singled out by many JFK researchers as a central figure in the assassination, Bloomfield was a prominent Montreal lawyer, a U.S. intelligence agent, a fundraiser for Israel, and a banker who was reputed to control Le Credit Suisse of Canada, Heineken's Breweries, Canscot Realty, the Israel Continental Company, the Grimaldi Siosa Lines, Ltd., and more. In fact, CMC was founded in Montreal and moved to Rome in 1962. *Paesa Sera* accused, and Garrison had suspected, that CMC was a cover for transferring CIA money for covert operations.

The major U.S. newspapers ignored CMC-Permindex and its link to Shaw, but not radio producer and author Paris Flammonde, perhaps the first to explore the many tentacles of the shadowy organization in his 1969 book, *The Kennedy Conspiracy: An Uncommissioned Report on the Jim Garrison Investigation*. Flammonde's lens examined the fascist, anti-Communist underpinnings of CMC-Permindex and, in particular, Ferenc Nagy, the former premier of Hungary, and his business partner Giorgio Mantello. Both men had been accused of "criminal activities" by the Swiss and French press for their highly secret financial-political dealings supporting far-right political movements while subverting those on the left.[19] Nagy had been a generous contributor to the fascist movement of Jacques Soustelle and the French rebel secret army OAS. Of all places, Flammonde pointed out, Nagy ended up moving in 1963 to the city where JFK was about to be assassinated.[20]

William Torbitt, the pseudonym for the author of the 1970 book *Nomenclature of an Assassination Cabal*, instead focused on the CMC-Permindex links to the FBI, Pentagon, and munitions makers and expanded the conspiracy to include organized crime, rocket scientist Werner von Braun, and LBJ.[21] Torbitt argues that Permindex was the front for five different organizations that furnished personnel and resources for the assassination, including the Defense Industrial Security Command, an espionage agency for U.S. munitions makers. He says the assassination was organized by J. Edgar Hoover and his espionage chief William Sullivan and planned by Bloomfield, whom he accused of being the mastermind behind the plot.[22]

Maurice Philipps, a French Canadian who has researched the assassination's ties to Montreal, has been a defender of Bloomfield, while also arguing for the unrestricted release of Bloomfield's private papers. The author of *De Dallas a Montreal (From Dallas to Montreal)*, published in 1996, Philipps has argued in his blog that the Bloomfield papers released so far by the Library and Archives of Canada (LAC) show that Bloomfield often quarreled with and was put in his place by more powerful Permindex board members, in particular Nagy, Swiss banker Seligman, and especially Georges Mantello, whom Philipps repeatedly identifies in his blog as a 33rd-degree Freemason. Philipps believes that, by releasing all the Bloomfield papers, the LAC will absolve Bloomfield and point the finger at others. In 2005, he filed suit in Canadian federal court to open Bloomfield's archives, which his will stipulated would be opened to the public 20 years after his death. Bloomfield died in 1984, but LAC has kept the vast majority of the collection under wraps, initially at the request of Bloomfield's now-deceased widow, Justine Stern Bloomfield Cartier. Bloomfield's nephew, Harry, has supported Philipps' request, likewise arguing that the papers will prove his uncle innocent of conspiracy theories that place him at the center of the assassination. Philipps also believes that the release of the papers could clarify the relationship between Permindex and Clay Shaw.[23]

Perhaps no one has looked more deeply into the linkages of CMC-Permindex than Michael Collins Piper, whose lens has focused on the possible collaborative involvement of the CIA, Israel's Mossad, and Meyer Lansky's national crime syndicate. Unlike other researchers, Piper notes that one of the chief shareholders in the Permindex holding company was Banque de Credit International (BCI) in Geneva, Switzerland, founded by Tibor Rosenbaum, the longtime director for finance and supply of Israel's Mossad. BCI also served as both Meyer Lansky's chief money laundering bank in Europe and as a depository for the Permindex account.[24] According to investigative reporter Jim Hougan: "After Israel became a state, almost 90 percent of its purchases of arms abroad was channeled through Rosenbaum's bank. The financing of many of Israel's most daring secret operations was carried out through the funds in [BCI]."[25]

Piper preferred not to mention Mantello's status as a Freemason but rather his ties to Israel. Mantello established CMC, the parent company of Permindex, to serve as an international trade promotion organization aimed at creating a permanent worldwide network of trade expositions, little of which happened.[26] As a Jew originally from Eastern Europe, Mantello had changed his name from Georges Mandel. He and his brother Ernst Mandel had been instrumental in secret operations to channel European Jewish refugees to what would later become the state of Israel.[27] Piper writes that Hans Seligman, another Permindex board member, was involved with the Jewish Colonization Association, an Israeli-backed Zionist organization, although Piper's source is *Dope, Inc.*, a book sponsored by the arch-conservative U.S. Labor Party of Lyndon LaRouche.[28] Another key financial backer of Permindex, Piper notes, was Dr. David Biegun, secretary of the National Committee for Labor Israel, Inc., based in New York, which ex-CIA man Philip Agee has said was often used as a CIA cover.[29] Biegun oversaw the liquidation of CMC-Permindex after it was expelled from Switzerland and Italy in 1962 and relocated to South Africa.[30]

Piper likewise links Bloomfield, perhaps the most intriguing player in the Permindex operation, to Israel. Bloomfield, Piper notes, was not only a devoted and influential supporter of Israel as a chief fundraiser for its national labor union, but had links to Lansky's crime syndicate as well as to the FBI and CIA. Bloomfield founded the law firm that represented the interests of the Canadian-based Bronfman family, which built its fortune with Lansky's syndicate through the illegal liquor trade.[31] Members of the Bronfman family have been key supporters of Israel and at the forefront of the Zionist cause.[32] At least one independent researcher, Brian Dowling Quig, says Ruby was on the Bronfman family payroll, citing an interview with Al Lizanetz, the long-time public relations agent for Kemper Marley, Sam Bronfman's mobster protégé.[33]

Although a Canadian by birth, Bloomfield's links to U.S. intelligence go back to his days during World War II when he served in the Office of Strategic Services, the predecessor to the CIA. J. Edgar Hoover later hired Bloomfield as a recruiting agent for Division Five, the FBI's counterespionage group.[34] In that role, Bloomfield worked closely with the head of the division, William Sullivan, who was a close friend of Angleton, the Mossad's CIA ally. Sullivan, in turn, was Angleton's liaison to the FBI. [35]

Because Garrison had stumbled on to Shaw's connections to the CIA, Piper argues that the investigation had to be shut down before it took a closer look at his links to Permindex. Denver oil man John King showed up at Garrison's office and offered him an appointment to a federal judgeship if he would abandon his investigation. King's interests included oil drilling off the coast of the Sinai peninsula on Arab territory seized by Israel in 1967.[36]

Oswald, too, is an excellent example of the murky, ill-defined interface among intelligence agencies and organized crime. Consider Oswald's connection to gangster and sometimes CIA operative John Martino, who was ignored by both the Warren Commission and the House Select Committee on Assassinations.[37] In August 1963, Martino was seen several times in a New Orleans sports betting bar accompanied by associates of Louisiana mob boss Carlos Marcello.[38] Two of those associates were Dutz Murrett and Emile Bruneau, both of whom employed Oswald to run errands from the bar. Murrett was Oswald's uncle and, many researchers say, surrogate father in the absence of his real father. Bruneau was the man who bailed Oswald out of a New Orleans jail after he was arrested for that very public and, some observers say, contrived altercation with anti-Castro leader Carlos Bringuier.[39]

In the mid-1950s, Martino worked for Santos Trafficante and Meyer Lansky in a Havana casino. When Castro came to power in 1959, Martino was caught and jailed for trying to sneak out of Cuba with a large bundle of cash. After his release three years later, Martino returned to the United States and was quickly recruited for the CIA-organized plots to assassinate Castro. Martino also joined the anti-Castro operations in New Orleans. According to JFK researcher and Pulitzer Prize finalist Anthony Summers, Martino had inside knowledge of the assassination. Summers disclosed that Martino had told a business associate in Texas that the "anti-Castro people put Oswald together. Oswald didn't even know who he was working for."[40] When Oswald failed to shake the Dallas police before his rendezvous with the conspirators at the Texas Theater, Martino said, "they [organized crime] had him killed."[41] In 1963, Martino was a roommate of Johnny Roselli, who also had connections to both the CIA and organized crime.[42] Roselli's mutilated body was found floating in an oil drum in Miami's Dumfoundling Bay after he talked to investigative journalist Jack Anderson and before he could be called to testify before the Church Committee in 1976.[43]

Ruby's connections are just as tangled and suspicious. A hot-headed syndicate gangster by way of the Teamsters and the Chicago underworld, Ruby was by no means the "small-time pawn" dismissed by the Warren Commission. In the mid-1950s, Ruby (who went by Jack Rubinstein at the time) was running guns to anti-Batista forces in Cuba with the backing of National Crime Syndicate boss Meyer Lansky. With the outcome of the revolution uncertain, Lansky was hedging his bets by supporting both Cuban dictator Fulgencia Batista and rebel leader Fidel Castro to protect his gambling interests in Cuba.[44] After Castro's takeover in 1959, CIA files show that Ruby visited Trafficante in a Havana jail at the bidding of Lansky. According to Lansky biographer and investigative journalist Hank Messick, Lansky "pulled the strings in every important move made by the National Crime Syndicate" before and after the JFK assassination.[45]

At the time of his visit to Trafficante, Ruby was a Potential Criminal Informant for the FBI and was interviewed eight times by federal agents over a seven-month period.[46] HSCA investigators found that Ruby had made twelve phone calls to five organized crime figures in the weeks leading up to the assassination. Seven of those calls were to one individual – Lewis McWillie.[47] In the pre-Castro days, McWillie had run one of Lansky's casinos in Havana and, at the time of the assassination, was working at the Thunderbird hotel and casino in Las Vegas, where Meyer Lansky and his brother Jake had an interest.[48] In June 1963, Ruby visited New Orleans, where he recruited a stripper known as Jada. Three months later, he fired her, adding to his problems with the American Guild of Variety Artists, the union representing his workers. Warren Report defenders say Ruby was seeking advice on how to handle the union when he contacted mobsters Carlos Marcello and Santos Trafficante during the summer of 1963.[49] On November 17, 1963, just five days before the assassination, Ruby made a trip to Las Vegas, FBI records show, although it is not known whether he visited with McWillie.[50]

Shortly before killing Oswald, Ruby had talked on the phone with Al Gruber, a henchman for Mickey Cohen, Lansky's West Coast operative.[51] After Ruby was arrested, he told his lawyer Tom Howard that the one person who could hurt his defense as a patriotic avenger was his former business associate, Thomas Eli Davis III, a gun-runner to Cuba and to the French OAS.[52] As head of the syndicate in Dallas, Ruby had considerable influence in the Dallas Police Department, working for them as a narcotics informant and, if rumors at the time were true, also supplying their parties with prostitutes.[53] The HSCA conceded that someone, possibly members of the Dallas police, may have helped Ruby gain access to the Dallas jail basement to shoot Oswald.[54]

If one goes further into the history of Oswald's and Ruby's connections and up the chains of command, the deep politics grow deeper and more unsettling. Lansky's ties to U.S. intelligence operatives go back to World War II, when the Office of Naval Intelligence struck a secret deal with Lansky and business partner Lucky Luciano to use their union control to ferret out enemy saboteurs among the dock workers in New York harbor, where they were doing considerable damage to U.S. overseas shipping.[55] Lansky and U.S. intelligence authorities also worked out a deal to have Luciano released from a New York state prison, where he was serving a thirty- to fifty-year sentence for running prostitutes, so that he could recruit U.S. mafia deportees willing to return to Sicily and gather intelligence for the coming Allied invasion.[56]

After the war, our recurring player, James J. Angleton, an OSS official in Italy who later became chief of counterintelligence for the CIA, used the Mafia deportees to counter the growing power of the Communists in Sicily.[57] In much the same way, Angleton, along with French intelligence, recruited Corsican gangsters to work against the Communists who threatened to take control of the key Mediterranean port of Marseille.[58] Angleton's close relationships with key figures in organized crime included Jay Lovestone of the AFL's Free Trade Union Committee, who passed on funds from the CIA to the French gangs in Marseille. The Marseille gangs, in turn, worked with the Corsican heroin labs and distributors that Lansky had integrated into the drug-trafficking network known as The Marseille Connection – the mainline of heroin to the United States.[59]

As Alfred McCoy explains in *The Politics of Heroin*, intelligence agencies and criminal syndicates have a natural affinity. Both are versed in the clandestine arts – "the basic skill of operating outside the normal channels of civil society."[60] On a more practical level, they both need each other – intelligence agencies rely on the street-smarts and confidentiality of syndicates to muscle the enemy while keeping their own hands clean; syndicates rely on the protection of intelligence agencies to keep law enforcement officials off their backs.[61]

To see through all the possible lenses in the JFK assassination, two more chains of connection must be considered. In the summer of 1963, Oswald was often seen in the New Orleans office of Guy Banister, a former FBI agent and rabid anti-Communist and racist who performed regular duties for the CIA.[62] One of Banister's employees was David Ferrie, who also worked as a private investigator for Louisiana syndicate boss Carlos Marcello. Ferrie, a pilot who had instructed Oswald as a teenager in the Civil Air Patrol, was famous for having flown dangerous missions to Cuba to supply anti-Castro forces.[63]

During his five months in New Orleans prior to the assassination, Oswald was seen on several occasions in the company of both Ferrie and Shaw.[64] In the 1962 edition of *Who's Who in the South and Southwest*, Shaw included in his biographical information that he was on the board of directors of CMC-Permindex. Interestingly, the connection was eliminated from the 1963-64 edition of *Who's Who*.[65] The top stockholder in Permindex, and at one point president of its board, was Bloomfield, who had connections both to the FBI, as a working partner with division chief William Sullivan, and to Lansky, with whom he had smuggled arms to the Jewish underground in Palestine prior to the formation of Israel.[66] Several investigators, including those at *Life* magazine, discovered that Permindex had banking connections with Lansky and his Bahamas gambling operations in the early 1960s.[67] But none pointed out the broader links through Permindex among Shaw, Bloomfield, the CIA, the OAS, and Israel.

The CMC-Permindex connection to the OAS and the assassination attempts on de Gaulle hardly seem relevant to the JFK assassination until another piece of evidence is added to the puzzle. Two days after JFK was killed, Jean Rene Souetre, an assassin for the OAS, was secretly deported by U.S. officials from Texas after he had spent the morning of the assassination in Fort Worth, where Kennedy had given a speech in front of the Hotel Texas, and the afternoon of that day in Dallas, where Kennedy was assassinated.[68] JFK researcher Mary Ferrell stumbled upon the document among the thousands that were released by the CIA prior to 1977. The photocopied document was heavily redacted with a magic marker, but by using strong backlighting and a powerful magnifying glass, Ferrell was able to make out its contents.[69] Neither Souetre's deportation from Texas nor the existence of the CIA document was ever reported to the Warren Commission. The CIA generated the memo after the French secret service contacted U.S. diplomats with concerns that Souetre was in Mexico, where de Gaulle was planning a visit.[70]

The U.S. media and most independent JFK researchers have ignored the presence of Souetre in Houston and Dallas on November 22, 1963, an oversight that has baffled Brad O'Leary and L.E. Seymour, authors of *Triangle of Death*.[71] Souetre, who somehow had managed to get a U.S. passport, had been implicated in the assassination attempts on de Gaulle and was considered a suspect by the FBI in the Kennedy murder before his deportation.[72] O'Leary and Seymour weave Souetre, who also used the aliases of Michel Roux and Michel Mertz, into an assassination plot involving the U.S. Mafia, the Marseille or Corsican Mob, and the highest echelons of the South Vietnamese government. The South Vietnamese, the authors argue, were avenging Kennedy's assassination of South Vietnamese President Ngo Dinh Diem and the Mafia and Corsican Mob were protecting their French Connection in the global heroin syndicate.[73]

Ignoring Souetre – or any other French assassin, such as Michel Mertz, who some researchers argue was using Souetre's name as an alias – is even harder to understand in light of detailed warnings about the assassination from U.S. Army private Eugene B. Dinkin, a codebreaker with a top security clearance stationed in Metz, France in 1963. FBI and CIA documents show that Dinkin had predicted the JFK assassination with uncanny accuracy several weeks before it took place, including a potential date (in November 1963, most likely Nov. 28), the location (Texas), the perpetrators ("the 'military' of the United States, perhaps combined with an 'ultra right wing economic group'") and possible patsies (a communist or "Negro").[74]

Richard Russell, author of *The Man Who Knew Too Much* who has perhaps delved the deepest into the Dinkin's story, argues that the Army codebreaker was decrypting cable traffic from the French OAS.[75] Dinkin's first warning was in an Oct. 22, 1963 letter to Attorney General Robert Kennedy. Realizing his letter might never reach its destination, Dinkins traveled to Luxembourg and attempted to alert several foreign embassies there. Only the Israeli ambassador would give him an audience, redirecting him to the proper channels at the U.S. embassy. Dinkin took his message there, where he was told the ambassador was playing tennis. Not surprisingly, he was also told that he should return to his military base and the ambassador would notify him of an appointment, which, of course, never happened.[76]

Learning that he was about to be confined for psychiatric treatment, Dinkin went AWOL and, using phony identification papers, traveled to Geneva, Switzerland, where he got the ear of the editor of the *Geneva Diplomat*. Before returning to his base, Dinkin also went to Frankfurt, Germany and, on November 6, 1963, gave his final warning to the now-defunct *Overseas Weekly*, an English-language newspaper whose primary audience was U.S. military personnel in Europe. Upon his return to base, Dinkin was indeed locked up in a psychiatric unit on November 13, 1963, nine days before the assassination. Dinkin refused to talk as long as he was confined.

After the assassination, on December 5, 1963, Dinkin was transferred for "therapy" to the Army's Walter Reed Hospital in Washington, D.C. Dinkin later told the FBI that his psychiatric evaluation was "an attempt on [the Army's part] to cover up the military plot which he had attempted to expose."[77] According to Russell, Dinkin faked cooperation with his "therapists" that he was indeed mentally ill in order to avoid electro-shock treatments. Even so, Russell argues, they managed to brainwash him as subsequent developments show. Dinkin was released from both the hospital and the Army on a medical discharge. Years later, in filing a 1975 lawsuit against the U.S. government, Dinkin professed that he had somehow managed to predict details of the Kennedy assassination by analyzing information from military newspapers.[78]

Within a week of JFK's murder, John Scelso, the high-ranking spy who was initially in charge of the counterintelligence investigation of the JFK assassination for the CIA, revealed to his superiors and to The White House that Dinkin had predicted details of the assassination, including that it would take place in Texas.[79] Scelso also told those above him that there was no evidence that Oswald was part of a communist conspiracy in Mexico City. A week later, however, Scelso was replaced as head of the CIA's counterintelligence investigation by Angleton, the CIA's chief of counterintelligence.[80]

Years before the assassination, Angleton had an intense but secret interest in Oswald. Angleton's counterintelligence department in the CIA was keen enough on Oswald to intercept and read his mail under a top-secret, illegal program called HT/LINGUAL. Yet, despite Oswald's attempt in 1959 to defect to the Soviet Union and to provide the Soviets with sensitive radar information on the U2 spy program, the CIA did not open a counterintelligence file on Oswald until fourteen months after his attempted defection.[81] Nor did Angleton's department alert the Secret Service that, in October of 1963, Oswald (or an Oswald impersonator) had visited the Soviet Embassy in Mexico City and talked with Valery Kostikov, the Soviets' top assassin and terrorist in the Western Hemisphere.[82] Still missing or sealed is a good deal of CIA evidence related to Oswald's visit to Mexico City in the month before the assassination, including surveillance photos of Oswald (or an impersonator) entering the Cuban Embassy as well as tape recordings of intercepted calls that Oswald (or an impersonator) made to the Soviet Embassy.[83] In 1971, when Winston Scott, head of the CIA's Mexico City bureau, died of a heart attack, Angleton flew to Mexico City and personally collected the contents of Scott's safe. [84]

Angleton, who was the CIA's liaison to the Warren Commission, is at the center of much of the mystery and muddle that surrounds JFK's assassination. A fervent anti-Communist with a deep streak of paranoia and a love of poetry and orchids, Angleton was a spook's spook with a genius for deception, but a drinking problem that worsened with age. Years after the Warren Report was released, JFK researchers discovered that it was Angleton's staff that raised the false flag that Oswald had been working for the Soviets.[85] It was no secret in Washington that Angleton loathed Kennedy for his peace overtures to the Soviet Union and perhaps for personal reasons as well – Kennedy's "soul mate" and mistress, Mary Pinchot Meyer, had been married to Cord Meyer, one of Angleton's top agents and his close friend, enough so that Angleton was the godfather of his children. Meyer's affair with the president was secretly recorded and closely watched by Angleton, who bragged about the intrusion several times to CIA associates.[86]

According to Peter Janney, author of *Mary's Mosaic*, Meyer may, in fact, have had some influence on JFK in his desire to end the Cold War with the Soviet Union after the Cuban Missile Crisis nearly brought both countries to nuclear annihilation. In the last year of his presidency, Janney says, Kennedy had been quietly mulling the idea of disarmament while seeking to avoid the scrutiny of military and intelligence oversight. During this period, he was also experimenting with LSD at the suggestion of Meyer and her circle of psychedelic-pioneering friends, including LSD guru Timothy Leary. Janney argues that Kennedy's months of personal transformation are what led to his famous, and surprising, commencement speech at American University on June 10, 1963 in which he called for a nuclear test ban treaty and, more importantly, a long-term world peace based on mutual trust rather than mutual destruction.[87]

> Not a Pax Americana enforced on the world by American weapons of war. Not the peace of the grave or the security of the slave. I am talking about genuine peace – the kind of peace that makes life on earth worth living – the kind that enables man and nations to grow and to hope and to build a better life for their children – not merely peace for Americans but peace for all men and women – not merely peace in our time but peace for all time.[88]

As head of CIA counterintelligence from the mid-1950s to the mid-1970s, Angleton was legendary for his furtiveness and alcohol-fueled, anti-Communist paranoia, including his suspicions that W. Averell Harriman and Henry Kissinger were both Soviet spies.[89] Angleton had his own secret channels of communication to which other departments in the CIA were not privy.[90] He was known for one more thing – his long and close ties to Israel's secret intelligence services, prior even to the formation of Israel and Mossad.

Angleton's connections went back to his OSS post in Italy during World War II when he worked with Italian Jews as part of the resistance to German and Italian fascists.[91] Toward the end of the war, the Jewish Agency, against the wishes of the British government, began moving Jewish refugees and arms through Italy to Palestine for the Jewish colonization effort. Angleton was certainly aware of, and perhaps assisted, the effort. What is known for certain is that, during this period, he formed close relationships with the founders of Mossad, including Teddy Kollack and Meir Deshalit.[92] Angleton felt it was important to build up and to form an alliance with Israeli intelligence to provide the U.S. greater access in the Middle East and to act as a bulwark against Soviet and Communist influence there.[93]

In the mid-1950s, when Angleton was moved from collection of foreign intelligence to the head of counterintelligence, he was also given the highly unusual and independent position as head of the Israeli desk of the CIA, in which the two countries shared their intelligence.[94] Angleton's relationship with Mossad was so intimate that he was known to assign Mossad agents to CIA operations, including, as he told the Church Committee in 1973, placing a Mossad agent in Havana to spy on Castro.[95]

Today, there are not one but two monuments to Angleton in Israel – large stones with bronze plaques, one in Jerusalem and one on a hill outside the city – which leads to an obvious question: What did Israel owe to Angleton? As Michael Holzman points out in his biography, *James Jesus Angleton: The CIA, and the Craft of Counterintelligence*, the answer may never be known until the secret files of both Mossad and the CIA are revealed.[96]

Beginning in the late 1950s, Angleton knew from his personal contacts in Israel of its secret plans to build a nuclear weapon "but never learned – or, at least, never reported – the extent to which Israel was deceiving Washington about its nuclear weapons progress," wrote former *New York Times* investigative reporter Seymour Hersh in his book about the secret history of Israel's nuclear weapons program, *The Samson Option*.[97] There is at least one report that Angleton actively aided Israel in its development of a nuclear bomb, despite the fervent opposition of the Kennedy administration to nuclear proliferation. *New York Times* foreign correspondent Tad Szulc testified to that effect before the Church Committee in 1975:

> I was told by one of my news sources that a situation had occurred in the 1960s in which the CIA delivered to the Israeli government classified information, technical knowledge, know-how, the services of distinguished physicists and fissionable material in the form of plutonium to assist in the development of an Israeli nuclear weapon at the Dimona Israeli Nuclear Testing grounds.... I have raised the subject in a private conversation with Mr. James Angleton in the spring of this year [April 1975]. Mr. Angleton told me that essentially this information was correct.[98]

Angleton later denied that Israel had been supplied with any nuclear material and that the technical assistance to Israel was provided in the late 1950s, not the early 1960s, when JFK was in office.[99] Hersh, however, claims that Angleton's technical assistance continued into the 1960s.[100]

During this same period, Angleton was deeply connected to the National Crime Syndicate and organized crime on both sides of the Atlantic. After his forced retirement in 1976, he told an investigator that he knew which mobsters had killed Sam Giancana. He blamed the Church Committee for the deaths of both Giancana and Roselli for having subpoenaed them to testify in clear violation of the Mafia code of silence.[101] As part of the Army's Operation X after World War II, Angleton had been in charge of recruiting Mafia deportees to work against the communists in Sicily and continued to use them in the years that followed. Through his connections with Jay Lovestone and Irving Brown of the AFL Free Trade Union Committee, Angleton was able to pass on CIA funds to the Marseille Mob, which was part of The French Connection organized by Lansky to distribute heroin in the U.S.[102]

Trying to stretch one's arms around the intertwining connections and motives for assassinating JFK is akin to Hercule Poirot trying to solve the case in *Murder on the Orient Express*. Agatha Christie's famous fictional detective needed a good deal of imagination to explore the possibility that all twelve suspects took part in the murder. As in Christie's novel, it is possible that all, or some groups, of the suspects in the JFK assassination could have worked together; although, in this case, only a very few people at the top would have needed to know the full spectrum of the conspiracy to coordinate the actions of those below them.

Compartmentalizing top-secret projects was a strategy developed and refined by the U.S. military during World War II, with the Manhattan Project as perhaps its best example.[103] Thousands of people in scores of locations across America worked on different parts of the Manhattan Project to develop the nation's first atomic bomb, but only a few top scientists and military leaders were privy to its larger design and purpose. Vice President Harry Truman would not learn of the bomb until after FDR's death, just months before his decision to use the awful device against Japan. The top-secret project, launched in 1942, did not become public until after the first two bombs were dropped on Japan in the late summer of 1945.

Another example comes from a lesser-known secret enterprise during World War II – the U.S. Navy's successful attempt to design and build a computer-like codebreaking machine that would help the Allies crack the Nazi's advanced U-boat Enigma codes. More than a thousand people, including some six hundred U.S. Navy WAVES, worked on the project between 1942 and 1945 inside NCR's Building 26 in Dayton, Ohio. Not a single participant broke the silence for nearly fifty years until documents related to the project were declassified in the mid-1990s. Evelyn Hodges Vogel, a plucky Missouri native who had lied about her age to enlist in the WAVES at age eighteen, said a combination of fear and pride kept the women from speaking to anyone about the project, including their own families, for half a century. Their commanding officers "told us they would shoot us at sunrise if we talked about what we were doing," Vogel said in an interview with the author in 2002. "And we did keep our mouths shut. Men always think women have big mouths, but we didn't. We were so proud to be serving in the armed forces and doing something women had never done before."[104]

There are hints of a broad conspiracy in the JFK murder in sightings of several suspicious persons who appeared to trail the president during his visit to Texas. Souetre, the OAS assassin, was in Fort Worth the morning JFK appeared there and then traveled that afternoon to Dallas.[105] Eugene Hale Brading (aka Jim Braden), an ex-convict with ties to Lansky and organized crime, was stopped by Dallas police for "suspicious behavior" in a Dealey Plaza office building minutes after the assassination. He was taken in for questioning and let go. (Brading, who used numerous aliases, also happened to be visiting in Los Angeles on the night that Robert F. Kennedy was killed, a mile from the hotel where RFK was gunned down. Again, he was questioned by police and released.)[106] According to a Secret Service report, Ruby was seen by five witnesses hanging around the

400 block of Milam Street in Houston for several hours on November 21, 1963, a block from JFK's entrance route to his hotel.[107]

Piper was one of the first JFK researchers to argue in his 1994 book *Final Judgment* that a small cabal at the top of the intelligence and organized crime communities could have coordinated the extensive but secretive collaboration needed to murder a president of the United States:

> The number of those involved in the conspiracy who actually knew that JFK was going to be assassinated was probably very limited indeed – yet those who were "in the know" had vast resources at their command to influence substantially larger numbers of people who would never necessarily know that they were indeed participating in an assassination conspiracy aimed at President Kennedy.[108]

Piper's theory would appear to explain a remarkable *non sequitur* that slipped from Angleton's tongue during a 1974 interview with then-*New York Times* reporter Seymour Hersh. Angleton, who observers at the time say was increasingly at the mercy of his alcoholism, was asked by Hersh about the CIA's illegal covert operations against U.S. antiwar protesters that eventually led to his forced retirement. "I've got problems," Angleton said. He then explained his domestic counterintelligence activities by saying, "A mansion has many rooms, and there were many things going on during the period of the [anti-war] bombings." With no prodding, Angleton added out of nowhere, "I'm not privy to who struck John."[109] Angleton later denied in court that he was referring to John F. Kennedy but offered no explanation for his cryptic comment. Years later, JFK researcher and *Salon.com* founder David Talbot asked Hersh if he knew what Angleton had meant. "I would be absolutely misleading you if I told you I had any fucking idea," Hersh said in his usual colorful language. "But my instinct about it is he was basically laying off [blame] on somebody else inside the CIA, and the whole purpose of the conversation was to convince me to go after somebody else and not him. And also that he was a completely crazy fucking old fart."[110]

Over the last fifty years, JFK researchers have employed diverse and sometimes conflicting lenses for investigating a conspiracy that, in more recent years, have coalesced into a smaller number of composite views. In the early decades after the assassination, there were two main camps of researchers who often exchanged harsh words in print; those who believed the CIA and military intelligence were primarily responsible for the assassination[111] and those who pinned the blame exclusively on organized crime.[112] As new documents came to light, however, especially after the JFK Records Act in 1992, most researchers adopted the view that elements of both the CIA and organized crime may have been working together. Two of the most recent books on the JFK assassination, one by journalist David Talbot (*Brothers*) and one by historian Larry J. Sabato (*The Kennedy Half Century*), blend together the two lenses without distortion.

Outliers among investigative lenses include those that implicate LBJ along with big oil interests and/or the Secret Service.[113] Other more credible lenses, however, have been given short shrift by the community of conspiracy researchers and have been ignored, even attacked, by the mainstream media. The Marseille or French connection to the assassination has been taken up by only a handful of JFK researchers, even though evidence for the link surfaced in the late 1970s with the discovery of the CIA memo revealing Souetre's deportation from Texas.[114]

In *Triangle of Death*, one of the few assassination books to look closely at the French connection, TV and print journalist Brad O'Leary wrote that he was mystified that so many high-profile JFK researchers, including former BBC producer Anthony Summers, former U.S. special operations chief L. Fletcher Prouty, and investigative reporters Henry Hurt and Jim Marrs, have all but ignored the presence of so deadly and mysterious a figure on the heels of Kennedy's final appearances in Texas.[115] Even Scott, who chides other researchers for the narrowness of their lenses, fails to acknowledge Souetre's presence in Dallas (or possibly another French assassin who may have taken Souetre's name as a cover, Michael Mertz[116]) on the day of the assassination. None of the books incorporating the French connection, including O'Leary's, has been reviewed or even acknowledged by the elite media.

Piper argues that to acknowledge a French connection in the JFK assassination is to acknowledge the possibility of an Israeli connection – a lens that both the mainstream media and the JFK research community have been careful to avoid. Allied in the 1950s against France's withdrawal from Algeria and the formation of a new Arab state in the Middle East, French and Israeli intelligence officials often worked together in the years before and after the JFK assassination. Israeli investigative journalist Barry Chamish, author of *Who Killed Yitzhak Rabin?*, concluded that "French intelligence provided the operational guidance behind Rabin's murder" by a lone gunman and alleged Zionist.[117]

The more immediate nexus between the French and Israeli lenses is CMC and its subsidiary Permindex, the front corporations that were ex-

pelled from Switzerland and Italy after being accused of financing the assassination attempts on de Gaulle as well as anti-Communist subversion
in Europe. Europe in the early 1960s, and especially France, was a hotbed
of political violence from both Left and Right. As a reporter in Paris in
1962, British spy novelist Frederick Forsyth described the tense atmo-
sphere in his autobiography *The Outsider: My Life in Intrigue*:

> The Paris into which I landed that May 1962 was in turmoil. The
> biggest Communist Party in Europe, west of the Iron Curtain, was
> French, completely loyal to Moscow, which had been arming and
> funding the Algerians. Far-left students marched and clashed vio-
> lently on the streets of Paris with those supporting the right. Plastic
> bombs exploded in cafes and restaurants.[118]

CMC-Permindex may have had ties to the CIA as well. As we have
seen, both its board member Clay Shaw and top stockholder Louis
Bloomfield had worked with U.S. intelligence. Bloomfield also may have
had ties to Lansky and Israel's Mossad. Like Lansky, Bloomfield was part
of the gun-running operation to the Jewish terrorist underground prior to
the formation of Israel in 1948.[119] Later, he became director of the Israe-
li-Canadian Maritime League and chairman in Canada of the Histadrut
Campaign, Israel's national labor federation.[120] As an attorney, Bloomfield
represented the Bronfman distillery family, which built its fortune in Canada working with Lansky in the bootleg trade.[121] The French OAS-Israeli
link is further strengthened by another top investor, Banque de Credit
International (BCI), whose founder Tibor Rosenbaum was the longtime
chief financial officer for Israel's Mossad.[122]

In the *Paesa Sera* articles in March 1967, CMC-Permindex was publicly called "a creature of the CIA ... set up as a cover for the transfer
of CIA ... funds in Italy for illegal political-espionage activities."[123] But
it was decades later in 2001 that Max Holland, a pro-Warren historian,
came to the CIA's defense in an article for the agency's website (later re-
published in *The Wilson Quarterly*) in which he cited KGB documents,
obtained through the CIA, that claim the *Paesa Sera* article was part of a
KGB disinformation campaign to smear the CIA.[124] However, Holland's
defense does not explain the involvement of Shaw and Bloomfield in the
organization, nor does it counter allegations that CMC-Permindex had
links to the OAS and Mossad. Agreeing at least partly with Piper's theory,
Chamish accepts that "Permindex ... was a Mossad front for covert operations" and that "the real killers [of JFK] were OAS-employed Corsican

hit men, or at least one was for certain, and they were recruited by the Mossad's European chief assassin, Yitzhak Shamir."[125]

So far, only one published JFK researcher, Piper, has tried to view the conspiracy through all the lenses of Scott's deep politics, including links to the CIA, Israel/Mossad, the French OAS, and Lansky's National Crime Syndicate, and he paid a price for it. After turning to the ultraconservative newspaper *American Free Press* as the only media outlet willing to publish his book, Piper was accused of anti-Semitism, an *ad hominem* form of flak, by the Anti-Defamation League of B'Nai Brith.[126] Piper's one mainstream public speaking engagement, as part of a community college non-credit course on the JFK assassination in California in 1997, was canceled after pro-Israel supporters protested to college administrators, who received more than two-hundred angry calls.[127] In media coverage leading up to the seminar, the ADL accused Piper of being a Holocaust denier, a charge he said was false.[128] The ADL also accused another speaker, Chicago court reformer and journalist Sherman Skolnick, of being on the board of *The Spotlight* (now *The American Free Press*), which it called "the most anti-Semitic publication in America." Skolnick denied being on the board and called himself "a traditional Jew."[129]

One pair of national journalists pushed for cancellation of the course with no qualms about academic freedom or First Amendment rights. Arianna Huffington and Stephanie Miller, co-hosts of CNBC's *Equal Time*, said the college had no "free speech" right to conduct a course on JFK conspiracy theories.[130] The co-hosts were given a strong on-air assist from guest panelist Gerald Posner, author of the Warren Report apologia *Case Closed*, who repeated the accusation that Piper was a Holocaust denier.[131] "The people that say the Holocaust didn't happen, they don't even get past [a] screener on a radio talk show," Miller said. "I mean, where do these people get off teaching a course?" After radio talk show host and guest panelist Holly McClure pointed out that courses on Satanism and other bizarre topics have been taught on college campuses without an outcry, Huffington responded, "If Satanism is being taught, it clearly shouldn't be taught because, after all, this is not an issue of free speech; this is a college course."[132]

Piper's *Final Judgment* has many flaws. For one thing, Piper badly needed a good editor. His book is poorly organized and indexed, maddeningly repetitious, often self-congratulatory, and full of less-than-ironclad certitudes. And he did not help the case for his book when he called one of its critics, a Jewish Defense League member, "a bizarre troll,"[133] and members of a young military group in Dallas "five Jewish boys,"[134] or pointed out irrelevancies such as how many members of the Warren Commission were Jewish or married to Jewish women.[135]

Piper also admitted ties to the Liberty Lobby, a right-wing organization that has often been critical of the pro-Israel lobby in the United States.[136] But his book has 746 footnotes, nearly all of them to credible sources, and it cannot be discounted in its entirety for its flaws.

The Israeli/Mossad lens has been marginalized by the media in the JFK assassination debate by a number of means, with the threat of being labeled an anti-Semite the most obvious one. But more subtle means can be discovered by analyzing the other lenses in the debate. Many JFK researchers, for instance, use the misleading label of "Mafia" or "La Cosa Nostra" to describe the network of organized crime in America, as though Italian-Americans are its only, or even its most powerful, members. Scott tackles this misleading characterization in his critique of the HSCA investigation, citing this excerpt from its report as a case of "committee doublethink":

> A major reason for suspecting conspiracy was Oswald's murder by Jack Ruby. Organized crime – specifically the national syndicate known as La Cosa Nostra or the mafia – was a logical choice for the study. A number of leads to organized crime existed, mostly through Ruby:
>
> Ruby had moved from Chicago to Dallas in 1946, at a time when the Mafia was said to be moving into that city. It has been alleged that Ruby was a front man...
>
> Ruby had made several unexplained phone calls to underworld figures in the months preceding the assassination.[137]

Scott goes on to point out that 1) Ruby (who had changed his last name from Rubinstein) was a Jew; 2) of the fifteen Chicago mobsters who had moved to Dallas with Ruby, nine were Jewish, according to the same HSCA memo; and 3) according to another HSCA report, of the seven or eight mob-linked individuals whom Ruby called, only one was Italian. Why, then, does the HSCA tie Ruby to "La Cosa Nostra or the mafia"?[138]

In his unauthorized biography of Meyer Lansky published in 1971, Hank Messick wrote in an author's note that "I try to show [in this book] that organized crime isn't the province of any one ethnic group or secret society. Just as no such group has a monopoly on virtue, neither does one have a monopoly on evil."[139]

And by detailing in his book how Lansky had risen to the top of the National Crime Syndicate in America, "I've been smeared as anti-Semitic from coast to coast by gangsters who used religion as a cloak."[140] Messick, an investigative journalist and one-time reporter for the *Louisville Courier-Journal*, wrote extensively about organized crime and conducted much of his research where the action was taking place – interviewing the key players in the back rooms and streets of America's most corrupt cities.[141]

While the HSCA report suggests that Carlos Marcello of Louisiana and Santos Trafficante of Florida were at the center of the intrigue surrounding JFK's assassination, Messick makes a strong case that both were front men for Lansky. Messick points out that Marcello was an obscure immigrant struggling in the Algerian section of New Orleans when Lansky cut him in on the syndicate's lucrative slot machine operations in Louisiana.[142] By 1959, according to Messick, Lansky was "the Chairman of the Board of the National Crime Syndicate with no one left to contest that fact."[143] And while the public heat was on the "Mafia" from 1960 to 1965, Lansky "succeeded in keeping his name completely out of the newspapers" during a period that for Lansky "was one of the most active, and profitable, eras he had known."[144]

When Messick once asked a "high-ranking Justice [Department] official" why investigators emphasized the Mafia rather than the National Crime Syndicate, the official answered:

> The Mafia was small and handy. The feeling was the American people would buy it with its family relations and blood oaths a lot quicker than they could understand the complex syndicate. You must remember, we wanted to get public support behind the drive on crime.[145]

JFK researchers who cite the involvement of organized crime in JFK's murder seldom go up the chain of command to name Lansky as the head of the National Crime Syndicate or to bring up Lansky's ties to those involved in the assassination. Only Piper and the authors of *Coup d'Etat in America*, Alan J. Weberman and Michael Canfield, draw Lansky into their investigative lenses.[146] Piper argues that Lansky worked with both Mossad and the CIA's Angleton to pull off the assassination.[147] Weberman and Canfield do not mention Mossad or Israel, but list a number of links between Lansky and key suspects in the assassination, including Ruby, who had worked under Lansky running guns to Cuba.[148] When the national syndicate needed another man to direct affairs in Dallas, it sent Ruby.[149] Weberman and Canfield also point out that Ruby's close friend, Lewis McWillie, was a henchman for Lansky.[150]

Other researchers who argue that organized crime was part of the JFK assassination plot are careful to avoid any connection to Lansky. In *Mafia Kingfish: Carlos Marcello and the Assassination of John F. Kennedy*, author John H. Davis notes that Lansky was key in elevating Marcello to the head of syndicate operations in Louisiana, but leaves Lansky entirely out of his discussion of the events leading up to the assassination.[151]

Numerous JFK researchers point the blame at mobsters Trafficante, Giancana, Roselli, and, to varying degrees, Jimmy Hoffa, but drop syndicate chairman Lansky out of the equation. The list includes authors David Kaiser (*The Road to Dallas*), Jim Marrs (*Crossfire*), David Scheim (*Contract on America*), Dale Peter Scott (*Deep Politics and the Death of JFK*), and Lamar Waldron (*Ultimate Sacrifice*). And even though Marrs details the ties among Lansky, McWillie, and Ruby, he distances Lansky from the anti-Castro groups involved in the assassination by quoting HSCA investigator Robert Blakey that Trafficante, not Lansky, was "the undisputed Mafia gambling boss in Havana."[152]

Historian Larry J. Sabato mentions Ruby's ties to numerous organized crime figures, including Sam Giancana and Lewis McWillie, but does not mention the close connection of both men to Lansky.[153] O'Leary is one of the few JFK researchers to delve into the possible Marseille connection to the assassination and, although he notes that Lansky set up the longstanding deal to supply America's underworld with heroin via the French connection, he fails to include Lansky among "the U.S. Mafia, the Marseille Mafia, and the highest echelons of the South Vietnamese government," whom he accuses of murdering JFK.[154] In an authorized 1991 biography of Meyer Lansky, *Little Man*, author Robert Lacey defends Lansky against accusations of involvement in the JFK assassination[155] but also avoids any reference in his book to Marcello, whom Lansky sponsored as head of the Louisiana syndicate. Even so, Lacey acknowledges that Lansky ran guns to Israel in 1948 and that he tried to use his contribution to the formation of the Israeli state as political leverage when he sought Israeli citizenship in 1977. Lansky was denied because of his criminal history.[156]

Likewise, many JFK researchers have been careful to distance the curious maneuverings of mobster Eugene Hale Brading (aka Jim Braden) from Lansky, even though Brading was a "personal courier" for Lansky, according to CBS producer Peter Noyes, author of *Legacy of Doubt*.[157] In his book, *Fatal Hour*, Blakey wrote that he and other staff investigators for the HSCA had interviewed Brading extensively but had come to no conclusions.[158] Brading, a charter member of the syndicate-financed La Costa

Country Club in Southern California,[159] visited the same Dallas office of the H.L. Hunt Oil Company on the same afternoon that Ruby did, one day before the assassination.[160] Brading was staying at the Cabana Motel in Dallas at the time, a mob hangout where Ruby had visited a friend around midnight before the assassination. Brading showed up again the next day in the Dal-Tex Building overlooking Dealey Plaza, where not long after the assassination he was arrested for "acting suspiciously" and taken in for questioning. Brading told police he had gone into the building to make a phone call related to his oil business dealings in Dallas. He was released without charge.[161] In the months leading up to the assassination, Brading was seen in New Orleans frequenting an office in the Pere Marquette Building (Room 1701) just down the hall from where Marcello's attorney, G. Wray Gill, employed David Ferrie as an investigator (Room 1707).[162]

In interviews and testimony where a reference to "Jew" or "Jews" has been used in relation to the JFK assassination, many researchers tread lightly, if it all – again, likely because they expect to receive flak. This aversion has kept many journalists and researchers from adhering to one of the primary rules of investigative reporting – follow the money. In *Coup d'Etat in America*, first released in 1975, Weberman and Canfield quote an FBI informant who was in the process of selling weapons to a Cuban exile group just prior to the JFK assassination. The informant, Thomas Mosley, reported that a member of the exile group, Homer Echevarria, told him on November 21, 1963 that "we now have plenty of money – our new backers are the Jews – as soon as they take care of JFK."[163] Yet when David Scheim's book, *Contract on America: The Mafia Murder of President John F. Kennedy*, was released in 1988, Scheim trimmed the reference to Jewish backers and altered Echevarria's quote to read "as soon as we take care of Kennedy."[164]

Echevarria may have been involved in an earlier plot to kill Kennedy in Chicago in early November. After Mosley reported his conversation to the Secret Service, the agency began probing what it called "a group in the Chicago area who may have a connection with the JFK assassination." Echevarria belonged to the 30th November group, an anti-Castro organization with ties to the student-run DRE, whom Oswald had been in contact with the previous summer in New Orleans.

The FBI took over the case from the Secret Service but quickly dropped it. The Warren Commission, which was also aware of Mosley's report, ignored it. Interestingly, in 1995, the Secret Service destroyed its protection reports from some of Kennedy's trips during the fall of 1963, including the canceled Chicago trip for November 2.[165] Abraham Bolden, an African-American Secret Service agent in Chicago, claims he tried to inform the Warren Commission about the Chicago plot but was framed for a counterfeiting crime to silence him. JFK had handpicked Bolden in 1961 to break the Secret Service color barrier at the White House but he lasted only three months there after he complained about being assigned to separate quarters on trips to the South and about the laxity and heavy drinking among Secret Service staff. As a result of these complaints, Bolden says he was returned to the Chicago office for routine anti-counterfeiting duties.[166]

It was in October 1963 that Bolden says the Chicago Secret Service office received a teletype from the FBI warning that a four-man hit squad from "a dissident Cuban group" – armed with high-powered rifles – would try to kill the president when he visited the city for the Army-Air Force football game on November 2. When Bolden later discovered this information was being kept from the Warren Commission, he was warned by his superiors "to keep his mouth shut." Bolden traveled to Washington instead and telephoned Warren Commission Counsel J. Lee Rankin. But he was soon arrested and taken back to Chicago on charges of discussing a bribe with known counterfeiters. Eventually found guilty, Bolden was sentenced to six years in prison and was placed in solitary confinement when he tried to draw attention to his case. Sam DeStefano, one of Bolden's two accusers, was close to members of the Chicago mob, including Sam Giancana, Charles Nicoletti, and Richard Cain. DeStefano was murdered in 1973, possibly by Cain, who himself was murdered soon after.[167] One of Bolden's earliest and strongest supporters was Chicago activist Sherman Skolnick,who filed a lawsuit and a legal petition on his behalf. Skolnick died in 2006.[168]

Jeanne de Mohrenschildt, the wife of George de Mohrenschildt – Oswald's closest friend and, some say, CIA handler – told Marrs that her husband, following his nervous breakdown, thought that "the Jewish Mafia and the FBI" were out to get him.[169] George de Mohrenschildt killed himself with a shotgun on the day that the HSCA served him with a subpoena to testify in its investigation. De Mohrenschildt's statements to his wife have been dismissed by researchers and the media as evidence only of his increasing paranoia. In the two months leading up to his suicide, however, de Mohrenschildt had been receiving injections and prescriptions for chronic bronchitis from a mysterious physician, Dr. Charles Mendoza, who appeared in Dallas soon after the HSCA was established.

Mendoza disappeared with a nonexistent forwarding address just a few months after Jeanne de Mohrenschildt insisted her husband stop treatments.[170] Even the most comprehensive accounts of the JFK assassination and its aftermath fail to include references to Echevarria's or de Mohrenschildt's statements. John Simkin's 7,000-page encyclopedia on the JFK assassination,[171] which includes more than a hundred references to the Mafia, forty-one references to Irish or Irishman, and nine references to Sicilians, contains not a single reference to the words Jew or Jewish Mafia or even to Homer Echevarria.

Potential Israeli/Mossad connections to the assassination have long been ignored by both the U.S. media, JFK researchers, and government investigators. While hanging around the Dallas police station where Oswald was in custody after the assassination, Ruby told a number of witnesses at the scene that he was there to translate for "Israeli reporters."[172] Piper asks in *Final Judgment* why Ruby would make such a claim (Israeli newspapers had no competent English-speaking correspondents?) and why federal investigators have never sought the identities of the newspapers and their reporters.[173]

At least one respected U.S. journalist has claimed there were ties between Ruby and Israeli intelligence. In a 1968 *Midlothian (Texas) Mirror* column, publisher W. Penn Jones wrote:

> Jack Ruby was a close intimate of the members of the Dallas Police force and other United States law enforcement agencies, as well as the Israeli counter intelligence organization. His one-time employee, Nancy Zeigman Perrin Rich, was also close to the same forces. Identifying Ruby and Nancy as being involved with the Israeli intelligence opens up a completely overlooked area concerning the assassination of President Kennedy.[174]

Foreign media, including Israeli newspapers, have been less reluctant to report on possible Israeli links to the assassination. On July 25, 2004, Israel's *Jerusalem Post* carried the headline: "Vanunu: Israel was behind JFK assassination." The *Post* based its story on an interview that Israeli nuclear physicist, Mordechai Vanunu, had reportedly given to a London-based Arabic paper in violation of his parole agreement not to talk to foreign media. Vanunu had just been released after eighteen years in an Israeli prison for exposing Israel's covert nuclear weapons program, which today is still part of a "don't ask, don't tell" agreement between the U.S. and Israel. In the interview, Vanunu said that "according to 'near-certain indications,' Kennedy was assassinated due to 'pressure he exerted on then head of government, David Ben-Gurion, to shed light on Dimona's nuclear reactor,'" where Israel had been secretly developing nuclear weapons.[175] Newspapers around the world picked up the report but none did so in the United States, except for the Washington-based weekly, the *American Free Press*, which had also published Piper's book. The *American Free Press* conducted its own interview with Vanunu several weeks later, in which he made the same claims.[176]

Originally called the *Spotlight*, the *American Free Press* was founded by Willis Carto, whom the ADL calls "one of the most influential American anti-Semitic propagandists of the past 50 years."[177] Piper fired back in *Final Judgment* that the ADL is "the primary intelligence and propaganda arm of Israel's Mossad in the United States."[178] His source is the *Executive Intelligence Review* (EIR), a weekly news magazine founded by Lyndon LaRouche, the controversial head of the LaRouche Movement and eight-time presidential candidate for the U.S. Labor Party. LaRouche has been called a racist and an anti-Semite by the mainstream media and the Democratic Party.

In later editions of *Final Judgment*, Piper points out that only thirty of his 746 footnotes are culled from LaRouche publications, including EIR.[179] Piper argues that the notes were not key to his thesis of Israeli and Lansky involvement in the JFK assassination. The thirty notes break down in the following ways: eight tie the ADL to bankers who also had ties to Lansky; three involve Rabbi Tibor Rosenbaum and Banque de Credit International and their ties to CMC-Permindex; three involve gun-running to Israel in the 1940s; four contain background information on people connected to Rosenbaum and CMC-Permindex; one ties the law firm of Louis Bloomfield and its client the Bronfman family to CMC-Permindex, and one refers to reports that the French OAS received money from Guy Banister, an associate of CMC-Permindex board member Clay Shaw.[180]

Obviously, supporters of Piper and supporters of Israel both have agendas in the JFK assassination debate. Researchers and journalists must proceed with caution about claims made by either side, but to dismiss either side's arguments based solely on their alleged reputations is a disservice to public discourse. As Noam Chomsky reminds us, the intellectual's only obligation is to the truth.[181]

A further word of caution is important here. To explore the possibility of Israeli involvement in the JFK assassination should not be equated with "blaming it on the Jews." The covert operations of Israeli government and intelligence officials no more represent all Jews, or even all Israelis, than the covert operations of the CIA and its leaders represent all Americans. By that same logic, if members of an Israeli cabal were found to be complicit in the assassination, it should not give license to those who would try to extend the blame to all Israelis, much less to Jews of other nations.

Whatever his reasons, Ruby also feared a backlash against Jews would follow the Kennedy assassination. On three occasions, Ruby reportedly told his attorney, William Kunstler, that "I did this [killed Oswald] so they wouldn't implicate Jews."[182] On Kunstler's last visit to his jail cell, Ruby handed him a note that stressed again his wish to protect Jews from a pogrom that he feared would follow the nation's outrage over the assassination.[183] Kunstler attributed Ruby's "convoluted thinking" to Oswald's ties to Fair Play for Cuba, whose members included Jews.[184] But even for someone as reportedly paranoid about anti-Semitism as Ruby, this logic seems a stretch when few Americans had even heard of Fair Play for Cuba and Oswald himself was not Jewish.

And yet, as we shall see in the next chapter, exploring Israel's possible involvement in the assassination of JFK is a sensitive, highly complex subject that can, indeed, foster anti-Semitism if not conducted in the right context.

Endnotes

1. John Lewis Gaddis, *The Landscape of History: How Historians Map the Past* (New York: Oxford University Press, 2002), 65.

2. G. Robert Blakey and Richard N. Billings, *Fatal Hour: The Assassination of President Kennedy by Organized Crime* (New York: Berkley Books, 1992), xi.

3. Mark Lane, *Plausible Denial: Was the CIA Involved in the Assassination of JFK?* (New York: Thunder's Mouth Press, 1991), 98.

4. Jim Marrs, *Crossfire: The Plot That Killed Kennedy* (New York: Carroll and Graf Publishers, 1989), 170.

5. Bradley S. O'Leary and L.E. Seymour, *Triangle of Death: The Shocking Truth about the Role of South Vietnam and the French Mafia in the Assassination of JFK* (Nashville, Tenn.: WND Books, 2003), 50.

6. Michael Benson, *Encyclopedia of the JFK Assassination* (New York: Checkmark Books, 2002), 116-117; and Peter Dale Scott, *Deep Politics and the Death of JFK* (Berkeley: University of California Press, 1993), 212-14.

7. Michael Collins Piper, *Final Judgment: The Missing Link in the JFK Assassination Conspiracy* (Washington, D.C.: Wolfe Press, 1993), 31.

8. L. Fletcher Prouty, *JFK: The CIA, Vietnam, and the Plot to Assassinate John F. Kennedy* (New York: Skyhorse Publishing, 2009), 147-52.

9. John Simkin, *The Assassination of John F. Kennedy* (Spartacus Educational, 2010), Kindle locations 108561-108578.

10. See Piper, *Final Judgment*; and Seymour M. Hersh, *The Samson Option: Israel's Nuclear Arsenal and American Foreign Policy* (New York: Random House, 1991), 98, 101.

11. Shavit, *My Promised Land*, 77; "The Algerian Revolution and the Soviet Bloc Countries," *Wilson Center Digital Archive*, http://digitalarchive.wilsoncenter.org/collection/229/

the-algerian-revolution-and-the-communist-bloc

12. Peter Dale Scott, *Deep Politics and the Death of JFK* (Berkeley: University of California Press, 1993), 19.

13. Benson, *Who's Who in the JFK Assassination*, 42.

14. Ibid, 44.

15 Benson, *Who's Who in the JFK Assassination*, 44.

16. Ibid., 43; Paris Flammonde, "A Few Excerpts from *The Kennedy Conspiracy: An Uncommissioned Report on the Jim Garrison Investigation* (New York: Merideth Press, 1969), 214-224," http://www.maebrussell.com/Articles%20and%20Notes/Kennedy%20Conspiracy.html.

17 Ibid.

18. Ibid.

19. Ibid., 214-224.

20 Ibid.

21. John Simkin, "William Torbitt," Spartacus Educational, August 2014, http://spartacus-educational.com/JFKtorbitt.htm

22 Simkin, "William Torbitt," Spartacus Educational.

23. CanWest News Service, "Dispute over releasing archives keeps lid on potential link to JFK's death," Canada.com, January 27, 2007, http://www.canada.com/story.html?id=54a1746c-a136-4fbb-8b40-288d337b8f0c

24. Piper, *Final Judgment*, 248; and Flammonde, *The Kennedy Conspiracy*, 219.

25. Jim Hougan, Spooks: The Haunting of America – The Private Use of Secret Agents (New York: William Morrow & Co., Inc., 1985), 172.

26. Piper, *Final Judgment*, 249.

27. Ibid., 268.

28. Ibid., 255.

29. Ibid., 259.

30. Ibid.

31. Marrs, *Crossfire*, 499.

32. Stephen Schneider, *Iced: The Story of Organized Crime in Canada*, (Ontario: John Wiley & Sons, 2009), 203.

33 Brian Dowling Quig, "The Death in Arizona of the Kemper Marley Machine," *Monetary and Economic Review*, October 1991, http://www.apfn.net/dcia/marley.html.

34. Piper, *Final Judgment*, 253.

35 Piper, *Final Judgment*, 254.

36. Ibid., 266.

37. Michael Kurtz, *The JFK Assassination Debates: Lone Gunman versus Conspiracy* (Lawrence: University Press of Kansas, 2006), 209.

38. Ibid., 210.

39. Ibid., 211.

40. Anthony Summers, *Not in Your Lifetime: The Defining Book on the JFK Assassination* (New York: Open Road Multimedia, 2013), Kindle edition, Kindle location 6432.

41. Ibid.

42. Scott, *Deep Politics,* 111.

43. Simkin, *Assassination of John F. Kennedy,* Kindle location 94195.

44. Alan J. Weberman and Michael Canfield, *Coup d'Etat in America: The CIA and the Assassination of John F. Kennedy* (San Francisco: Quick American Archives, 1992), 155.

45. Hank Messick, *Lansky* (New York: Berkley Publishing, 1971), 219.

46. Scott, *Deep Politics*, 133.

47. Ibid., 184.

48. Ibid., 180.

49. "Jack Ruby," Spartacus Educational website, http://spartacus-educational.com/JFKruby.htm)

50. Kantor, *Jack Ruby*, 24.

51. Piper, *Final Judgment*, x.

52. Kantor, *Jack Ruby*, 15.

53. Scott, *Deep Politics*, 137, 233.

54. Ibid, 133; and *HSCA Final Report, Volume IX: V – Possible Associations between Jack Ruby and Organized Crime*, 125-46, https://www.maryferrell.org/mffweb/archive/viewer/showDoc.do?docId=955&relPageId=133.

55. O'Leary and Seymour, *Triangle of Death*, 72.

56. Scott, *Deep Politics*, 165.

57. Ibid., 195.

58. Alfred W. McCoy, *The Politics of Heroin: CIA Complicity in the Global Drug Trade* (Brooklyn: Lawrence Hill Books, 1991), 18.

59. Ibid., 44-45.

60. Ibid., 15.

61. Ibid.

62. Kurtz, *JFK Assassination Debates*, 158.

63. Benson, *Encyclopedia*, 81-82.

64. Kurtz, *JFK Assassination Debates*, 158-59.

65. Marrs, *Crossfire*, 499.

66. Piper, *Final Judgment,* 187.

67. Marrs, *Crossfire*, 500.

68. O'Leary and Seymour, *Triangle of Death,* 60; and "Document Page Re Jean Souetre," Mary Ferrell Foundation website, accessed July 17, 2014, http://www.maryferrell.org/mffweb/archive/viewer/showDoc.do?docId=64996&relPageId=2.

69. Ibid., 63. Mary Ferrell devoted her life to obtaining records on the JFK assassination and making them available to other researchers and the public, but she never published anything herself. See Benson, *Encyclopedia*, 81.

70. O'Leary and Seymour, *Triangle of Death*, 62.

71. Ibid., 63-65.

72. Ibid., 75-78.

73. Ibid., 156.

74. Richard Russell, *The Man Who Knew Too Much*, p. 533; and NARA Document I.D. no 1993.06.30.08.29.3).

75. Ibid., 557.

76. Ibid., 554.

77. NARA 179-40005-1-10114

78. Russell, *Man Who Knew*, 556-557.

79. HSCA Interview of John Scelso, 16 May 1978

80. Noel Twyman, *Bloody Treason*, 34.

81. John Newman, *Oswald and the CIA: The Documented Truth about the Unknown Relationship between the U.S. Government and the Alleged Killer of JFK (New York*: Skyhorse Publishing, 2008), 421-422.

82. Ibid., 428.

83. Jefferson Morley, *Our Man in Mexico: Winston Scott and the Hidden History of the CIA* (Lawrence: University Press of Kansas, 2008), 189.

84. Ibid., 286.

85. Scott, *Deep Politics*, 195.

86. David Talbot, *Brothers: The Hidden History of the Kennedy Years* (Glencoe, Ill.: Free Press, 2007), 197,202-203, 275; Janney, Mary's Mosaic, 435-436.

87. Peter Janney, *Mary's Mosaic: The CIA Conspiracy to Murder John F. Kennedy, Mary Pinchot Meyer, and Their Vision for World Peace* (New York: Skyhorse Publishing, 2102), 256-257.

88. John F. Kennedy, "1963 Commencement," American University archive, http://www1.american.edu/media/speeches/Kennedy.htm

89. Scott, *Deep Politics*, 304.

90. Michael Holzman, *James Jesus Angleton: The CIA, and the Craft of Counterintelligence* (Amherst: University of Massachusetts Press, 2008), 170.

91. Ibid., 151.

92. Ibid.

93. Ibid., 152.

94. Ibid., 153.

95. Ibid., 192.

96. Ibid., 155.

97. Hersh, *The Samson Option*, 147.

98. Holzman, *James Jesus Angleton*, 167-68.

99. Ibid.

100. Ibid., 164.

101. Scott, *Deep Politics*, 195.

102. Scott, *Deep Politics*, 195.

103. "Security and Secrecy," Atomic Heritage Foundation, http://www.atomicheritage.org/history/security-and-secrecy

104. Jim DeBrosse and Colin Burke, *The Secret in Building 26* (New York: Random House, 2004), 128.

105. O'Leary, *Triangle of Death*, 62.

106. David E. Scheim, *Contract on America* (New York: Zebra Books, 1988), 45-47: Summers, *Not in Your Lifetime*, 452-3, Blakey and Billings, *Fatal Hour*, 306, 396-97; and Kantor, *Jack Ruby*, 32-37.

107. Ibid., 291-93.

108. Piper, *Final Judgment,* 559.

109. Seymour Hersh, "Huge C.I.A. Operation Reported in US against Antiwar Forces, Other Dissidents During Nixon Years," *New York Times*, December 22, 1974, 1.; and Weberman and Canfield, *Coup d'Etat in America*, 194.

110. Talbot, *Brothers*, 275.

111. Lane, *Plausible Denial;* Marrs, *Crossfire*; Prouty, *JFK*; and Weberman and Canfield, *Coup d'Etat.*

112. Blakey, *Fatal Hour*; John H. Davis, *Mafia Kingfish: Carlos Marcello and the Assassination of John F. Kennedy* (New York: Signet, 1989); and Scheim, *Contract on America*.

113. See David S. Lifton, *Best Evidence: Disguise and Deception in the Assassination of John F. Kennedy* (New York: McMillan, 1980); Barr McLellan, *Blood, Money and Power: How LBJ Killed JFK* (New York: Hannover House, 2003); and Fred T. Newcomb, *Murder from Within: Lyndon Johnson's Plot Against President Kennedy* (Bloomington, IN.; Author House, 2011).

114. O'Leary and Seymour, *Triangle of Death*, 60.

115. Ibid., 64.

116. Piper, *Final Judgment*, 143.

117. Barry Chamish, "A Zionist Looks at Final Judgment," Rense.com, December 14, 1999, http://www.rense.com/politics5/zionist.htm.

118. Frederick Forsyth, *The Outsider: My Life in Intrigue* (New York: GP Putnam's Sons, 2015), 100.

119. Piper, *Final Judgment*, 86-87.

120. Piper, *Final Judgment,* 192.

121. Ibid., 191.

122. Ibid., 187.

123. Ibid., 221.

124. Max Holland, "The Power of Disinformation: The Lie that Linked CIA to the Kennedy Assassination," *The Center for the Study of Intelligence*, Vol. 45, no. 5, CIA Library website, last updated August 3, 2011, https://www.cia.gov/library/center-for-the-study-of-intelligence/kent-csi/vol45no5/html/v45i5a02p.htm.

125. Chamish, "A Zionist Looks at *Final Judgment*."

126. Piper, *Final Judgment*, Author's Foreword (pages not numbered).

127. "College Cancels Controversial JFK Course," *St. Louis Post-Dispatch*, August 22, 1997, LexisNexis Academic.

128. Piper, *Final Judgment,* Author's Foreword (pages not numbered).

129. "College Cancels Controversial JFK Course," *St. Louis Post-Dispatch*.

130. "Community College Offers Seminar on JFK Assassination Conspiracy Theory," CNBC *Equal Time*, August 22, 1997, LexisNexis Academic.

131. Ibid.

132. "Community College Offers Seminar on JFK Assassination Conspiracy Theory," CNBC Equal Time, August 22, 1997, LexisNexis Academic.

133. Piper, *Final Judgment*, Author's Foreword (pages not numbered).

134. Ibid., 544.

135. Ibid., 430.

136. Ibid., Author's Foreword (pages not numbered).

137. Scott, *Deep Politics*, 183.

138. Ibid.

139. Hank Messick, *Lansky* (New York: Berkley Publishing, 1971), 11.

140. Ibid., 10.

141. John Harney, "Hank Messick: Journalist and Author on Organized Crime," *New York Times*, November 20, 1999, LexisNexis Academic.

142. Messick, *Lansky*, 86-7.

143. Ibid., 87, 214, 219.

144. Ibid., 241.

145. Ibid., 242.

146. Weberman and Canfield, *Coup d'Etat,* 151, 155, 163, 294.

147. Piper, *Final Judgment,* 2, 85.

148. Weberman and Canfield, *Coup d'Etat,* 155

149. Ibid., 154.

150. Ibid., 294.

151. Davis, *Kingfish*, 50.

152. Marrs, *Crossfire*, 168-69.

153. Sabato, *Kennedy Half Century*, 202.

154. O'Leary, *Triangle of Death*, 151.

155. Robert Lacey, *Little Man: Meyer Lansky and the Gangster Life* (Boston: Little, Brown and Company, 1991), 386.

156. Ibid., 387-388.

157. Piper, *Final Judgment*, 177; and Peter Noyes, *Legacy of Doubt: Did the Mafia Kill JFK?* (Wellington, New Zealand: Pinnacle Books, 1973), 240.

158. Blakey and Billings, *Fatal Hour*, 430.

159. Ibid.

160. Blakey and Billings, *Fatal Hour*, 430.

161. Simkin, *Assassination of John F. Kennedy*, Kindle locations 82319-82322.

162. Piper, *Final Judgment*, 178.

163. Weberman and Canfield, *Coup d'Etat*, 41.

164. Scheim, *Contract on America*, 218.

165. "Homer Echevarria - Taking Care of Kennedy," Mary Ferrell Foundation website, https://www.maryferrell.org/pages/omer_Echevarria_-_Taking_Care_of_Kennedy.html?search=echevarria).

166. John Simkin, "Abraham Bolden," Spartacus Educational website, http://spartacuseducational.com/JFKbolden.htm).

167. Ibid.

168. "Skolnick's Case In Limbo," The Daily Calumet, Chicago. June 24, 1970; and "Suit asks JFK data; Skolnick on new plot trail," *The Southeast Missourian*, Cape Girardeau, Missouri, Associated Press, April 7, 1970, p. 7.)

169. Marrs, *Crossfire*, 285.

170. Ibid., 286.

171. Simkin, *Assassination of John F. Kennedy*.

172. "Warren Commission Documents: Commission Document 355 – DOJ Criminal Division Listing of Witnesses Interviewed," Mary Ferrell Foundation website, 256, accessed July 17, 2014, http://www.maryferrell.org/mffweb/archive/viewer/showDoc.do?mode=searchResult&absPageId=345628.

173. Piper, *Final Judgment*, 232.

174. Penn Jones Jr., *Forgive My Grief III* (Midlothian, Texas: Midlothian Mirror, 1969), 51.

175. Ariah O'Sullivan, "Vanunu – Israel Was Behind JFK Assassination," July 25, 2004, Rense.com, http://www.rense.com/general54/jfk.htm accessed.

176. Christopher Bollyn, "Vanunu Speaks: Israeli Nuclear Whistleblower Risks Jail to Talk Exclusively to AFP," July 31, 2004, *American Free Press*, http://www.americanfreepress.net/html/vanunu.html.

177. "Extremism in America: Willis Carto," The Anti-Defamation League archive website, 2005, http://archive.adl.org/learn/ext_us/carto.html.

178. Piper, *Final Judgment*, 141.

179. Piper, *Final Judgment*, 516-17.

180. Ibid., 517.

181. Noam Chomsky, "The Responsibility of Intellectuals," The New York Review of Books, February 23, 1967, http://www.chomsky.info/articles/19670223.htm.

182. William M. Kunstler, *My Life as a Radical Lawyer* (New York: Birch Lane Press, 1994), 158.

183. Ibid.

184. Ibid.

Chapter 5

The Firewall

Why does an Israeli-Mossad/French-OAS connection to the assassination deserve consideration? First of all, because it has created a simmering underground of speculation and anti-Semitism that ought to be brought into the light of day and analyzed with candor, reason, and empathy. Outright dismissal of this hypothesis without a closer examination only fuels further unreasoned speculation and, quite frankly, feeds the anti-Semitism its opponents deplore. Piper was able to boast that *Final Judgment* was the best-selling banned book of all time, a claim that strengthens the legitimacy of his argument while at the same time casting those who have banned the book as villains hiding the truth. Secondly, one can hardly write about the marginalization of JFK conspiracy theories without examining the theory that has been most marginalized and even reviled without an honest and open debate of its merits.

Indeed, there are good reasons to tread carefully and, as I have said, with empathy in exploring the Israeli-French connection. As John Mearsheimer and Stephen Walt point out in *The Israel Lobby*, the horrors of the Holocaust are still deeply ingrained in the American Jewish consciousness, and so is the fear that anti-Semitism will arise again at any moment, even in the United States, where Jews have been relatively free in recent decades of open discrimination.[1] What a few leaders and/or intelligence agents of Israel may or may not have done more than fifty years ago is neither a reflection on Israel of the present day nor Jews in general – no more than the possible involvement of America's leaders and intelligence officials in the assassination is a reflection on all Americans.

In *Deep Politics*, Peter Dale Scott observed that transnational links are common among intelligence officials who share information when it works to their advantage, "often in intrigues of which heads of government may be, at best, dimly aware."[2] Transnational, Scott reminds us, does not necessarily mean government involvement but rather elements of intelligence and organized crime that transcend national boundaries.[3] Widening and unfiltering the investigative lens to include the possibility of a French/Mossad/CIA connection is logical and yet daunting. The logic stems from an understanding of the secret history at the time, and the fact that Israeli leaders felt that JFK's policies threatened their nation's very existence. The exploration is daunting, however, because of the legal and logistical challenges of investigating transnational covert operations as well as the likelihood of censorship from the pro-Israel lobby in the U.S. The two barriers form a firewall around a complete examination of the assassination of JFK.

To understand the possible motivation of Israel's leaders requires a detailed knowledge of what was happening behind the scenes between the U.S. and Israel in the early 1960s – crucial developments that continue to have major foreign policy repercussions for both countries and yet have been largely ignored by the U.S. media. It was not until 1991, nearly three decades after Israel acquired its own nuclear arsenal, that investigative journalist Seymour Hersh blew the lid off the secret history of Israel's nuclear weapons development, and America's complicity in that secret, in his book *The Samson Option*. In a one-page author's note, Hersh by necessity avoided details about his sources, many of whom were confidential. But it is clear from his research that he talked to dozens of U.S. and Israeli journalists, scientists, diplomats, and intelligence officials. He points out that none of his interviews was conducted in Israel because he refused to submit his research to Israeli military censors. He concludes his note with this observation: "Those Israelis who talked weren't critics of Israel's nuclear capability, nor would they feel secure without the bomb. They spoke because they believe that a full and open discussion of the Israeli nuclear arsenal – and of the consequences of its development – is essential in a democratic society."[4]

Hersh's book was groundbreaking both for its subject matter and its implications for U.S. foreign policy and world peace.[5] The *New York Times* did not review the book, but it ran a front-page story summarizing the news contained in its pages.[6] The *Washington Post*'s review called the book "a good read" and a "welcome" addition to the topic.[7] However, according to Hersh biographer Robert Miraldi, most reviews coalesced around a negative frame that questioned Hersh's use of unnamed sources and cast doubt on his findings. Nuclear physicist Peter D. Zimmerman dismissed Hersh's work as "trust me" journalism that was weak and poorly sourced. Journalist Steve Emerson accused Hersh of "outright inventions."[8] On the other hand, in a capsule review for *Foreign Affairs*, Yale history professor Gaddis Smith called the book a "fascinating work of investigative history [that] sifts hard fact from the decade's rumors and half-confirmed reports about Israel's nuclear weapons program."[9] Twelve years later, Israeli journalist Ari Shavit would confirm much of what Hersh found in his own book, *My Promised Land: The Triumph and Tragedy of Israel.*[10]

According to Miraldi, *The Samson Option* became a bestseller in Europe, but American Jews, whom Miraldi called a big part of the book-buying public, quickly turned against Hersh. The book did not sell well in Manhattan bookstores patronized heavily by Jews, Miraldi said, and synagogues that invited Hersh to speak about the book canceled the invitations once they discovered that he did not favor Israel possessing the atomic bomb.[11]

Hersh's book revealed new information about the close working relationship between the Mossad and the CIA. When the Carter administration "abruptly cut back [its] intelligence liaison with Israel," Hersh wrote, "[it] perhaps didn't fully understand how entwined Israel's primary intelligence agency, Mossad, had become with the CIA during the Cold War."[12] He went on to write that "the complex amalgamation of American financing and Israeli operations remains one of the great secrets of the Cold War."[13] It remains so today.[14] The possibility that this long-held secret could be implicated in the JFK assassination has been ignored by the mainstream media while independent researchers who have tried to explore the connection have been dismissed as cranks or bigots.

Both Hersh and Shavit make abundantly clear in their books how Israel's leadership in the early 1960s believed that the development of nuclear arms was both urgent and vital to the fledgling nation's survival. Hersh also shows how President Kennedy was just as determined to halt the proliferation of nuclear weapons in the wake of the Cuban Missile Crisis when, over a thirteen-day period, the world was brought to its closest point of mutual annihilation.

The depth and animosity of the rift between Kennedy and Israeli Prime Minister David Ben-Gurion is still locked in the classified U.S. records of their private meetings and phone calls and the pages of their personal correspondence.[15] Even so, Hersh was able to uncover through interviews and available documents a struggle between the two men that surely marks a low point in the relations between the two longtime allied nations. Yuval Neeman, an Israeli intelligence officer who drafted Ben-Gurion's responses to JFK, told Hersh "it was not a friendly exchange. Kennedy was writing like a bully. It was brutal."[16]

More recently, a declassified letter from the National Security Archive at George Washington University shows how adamant Kennedy was in demanding inspections of the Israeli nuclear facilities. Just ten days after Levi Eshkol replaced Ben-Gurion as Israeli prime minister, Kennedy wrote what amounted to an ultimatum on July 5, 1963 asking for a series of inspections by U.S. scientists of the Dimona project, including "a visit early this summer, another visit in June 1964, and thereafter at intervals of six months." The letter included this sentence:

> As I wrote to Mr. Ben-Gurion, this Government's commitment to and support of Israel could be seriously jeopardized if it should be thought that we were unable to obtain reliable information on a subject as vital to peace as the question of Israel's effort in the nuclear field.[17]

The letter also makes clear that Ben-Gurion had lied to Kennedy about the true purpose of the Dimona facility:

> We welcomed the former Prime Minister's strong affirmation that Dimona will be devoted exclusively to peaceful purposes…[18]

JFK was at an immediate disadvantage in his relations with Israel because of his father's perceived anti-Semitism among many Jewish leaders at the time. As ambassador to England just before World War II, Joseph P. Kennedy had opposed going to war against Germany, as did many people in Catholic Ireland, where the Kennedys had their roots.[19] JFK was also seen as being ungrateful for both the financial support he received from the Jewish community during his presidential campaign and the overwhelming support of Jewish voters who helped elect him (81 percent, or 8 percentage points higher than even those voters who shared Kennedy's Catholic faith).[20]

In his drive to head off what he felt would be a disaster for world and Middle Eastern peace, Kennedy pressed hard and often for thorough inspections of the Dimona nuclear facility in the Negev desert, where Israel was secretly engaged in a massive and intensive effort to develop nuclear weapons.[21] Kennedy not only demanded inspections of the plant but also the right to convey the results to Israel's arch-nemesis at the time, Gamal Abdul Nasser, the Egyptian dictator and charismatic leader whose vision of a unified Arab world seemed predicated on the destruction of Israel.[22]

Israel's leaders, and perhaps especially Ben-Gurion, were convinced that Israel must have nuclear weapons to assure the survival of its nation – and, ultimately, its race – against an increasingly hostile Arab world and the growing menace of the Soviet Union. What cannot be forgotten is that the horrors of the Nazi concentration camps, and Hitler's "ultimate solution" of eradicating the Jewish people, was then less than two decades old – still painfully acute in the minds of Israel's leadership. Then, in late April 1963, a short-lived alliance among Egypt, Syria, and Iraq seemed an Israeli nightmare come true.[23] Ben-Gurion appealed to Kennedy to declare jointly with the Soviet Union a guarantee of the territorial integrity and security of every nation in the Middle East. Kennedy declined, as well as rejecting Ben-Gurion's offer of a White House visit. The Israeli leader's fears, and frustrations, can be gauged in the letter that he sent to Kennedy five days later: "Mr. President, my people have the right to exist ... and this existence is in danger."[24] He asked that the United States sign a security agreement with Israel. Again, Kennedy declined.[25]

Under pressure from his own party in Israel, and in part for his inability to work with Washington, Ben-Gurion resigned a few weeks later after fifteen years as Israel's prime minister and defense minister. But under Israel's new leader, Golda Meir, Israel's nuclear weapons program at Dimona continued unimpeded and Ben-Gurion, in an unofficial capacity, only enhanced his role as one of its chief supporters.[26]

At the same time JFK was trying to prevent Israel from acquiring nuclear weapons, he was reaching out to Nasser, offering a combination of economic aid and promises that he would oppose nuclear proliferation in the Middle East.[27] Kennedy's aim was to put the United States on a better footing with Arab extremists, both to assure Western access to Middle Eastern oil and to thwart the growing reliance of Arab nations on the Soviet Union.[28] He also tried to bring stability and peace to the troubled region with a failed plan to resolve the Arab-Israeli conflict over the issue of Palestinian refugees, including the right to return to their homeland.[29]

To put it mildly, Kennedy's policy goals in the Middle East were not popular with Israeli leaders or the growing number of Jewish supporters of Israel in America.[30] To see Egypt receiving U.S. economic aid while also being supplied with advanced Soviet weapons must have been one of Ben-Gurion's deepest fears come true.[31] As a result of pressure from Israel and its supporters at home, Kennedy was forced to balance his overtures toward Egypt by supplying Israel with HAWK defensive missiles and greater U.S. assurances of Israel's security.[32]

In a 2009 article published in *Israel Affairs*, University of Haifa professor Abraham Ben-Zvi, who has long written about U.S.-Israeli relations, viewed Kennedy's compromise with Israel as the "unintentional" beginning of the U.S.-Israeli military alliance and "the Rubicon" that was crossed prior to LBJ's supplying of offensive weapons to Israel. Ben-Zvi wrote that Kennedy "emerges – in terms of his basic attitudes and policies toward Israel – as neither a villain nor a hero but, essentially, as a cold, calculating, and unsentimental statesman."[33] Ben-Zvi argues that Kennedy had realized in his final months that he could not force Israel to drop its plans for developing nuclear weapons and, therefore, offered Israel "upgraded security guarantees without insisting any longer on a reciprocal Israeli concession concerning Dimona."[34] What Ben-Zvi does not mention is that Israel went to extreme lengths to deceive Kennedy and his administration that Dimona was aimed solely at generating nuclear power rather than nuclear weapons.

After Kennedy agreed to supply Israel with HAWK missiles in 1962, Ben-Gurion agreed to allow a team of U.S. inspectors into the facilities at Dimona. But what they would find was an elaborate "Potemkin Village and never know it," according to Hersh.[35] With the help of its French allies, Israel went so far as to construct a false control room, replete with computerized measuring devices, that appeared to operate a working nuclear power reactor. The U.S. team, none of whom could speak Hebrew, spent two days inspecting Israel's elaborate ruse and, of course, found nothing suspicious.[36]

In a visit with JFK later in April 1963, then-Israeli Deputy Defense Minister Shimon Peres lied to the president by saying Israel had no interest in developing nuclear weapons and added that "our interest is in de-escalating" the arms race in the Middle East.[37] Hersh writes in *The Samson Option* that JFK was passionately opposed to an Israeli bomb up until the moment of his death and clearly believed that Israel had not yet developed a nuclear capability.[38] A month after the assassination, the reactor at Dimona went critical.[39]

The fear and panic of Israel's early leaders, whose memories of the Holocaust were far from faded, were a major factor in the development of its nuclear arsenal – and one of its biggest strategic blunders, according to Shavit. By the mid-1950s, Britain had withdrawn its protection from Israel and the Arab world surrounding it was uniting and mustering its forces, eventually with the help of the Soviet Union. "Israel's leaders discovered that the protective umbrella of the West was slowly furling," Shavit writes. "The colonial era was coming to an end, Europe was in retreat, and Israel was left on its own in a hostile desert. At the same time, Arab nationalism was coalescing, being transformed by rapid modernization and swift military build-up."[40] Ben-Gurion, with an able assist from Shimon Peres, manipulated French scientists and intelligence officials into aiding Israel in its nuclear quest – despite the opposition of French President Charles de Gaulle – while he lied to and deceived U.S. officials opposed to nuclear proliferation, especially Kennedy.[41]

Israel's nuclear shield may have worked for forty-six years, but has become more a strategic curse than a blessing, Shavit argues. As JFK and many of Israel's more cautious leaders feared at the time, Israel's nuclear quest has triggered an arms race in the Middle East that has become its biggest threat.[42] Shavit has chosen not to cast those early Jewish leaders as either villains or heroes, but as fearful, loyal men caught up in the race to keep Israel one step ahead of its enemies. For them, he wrote, thinking was paralysis and paralysis was doom.[43]

After Kennedy's assassination, the administration of President Lyndon Johnson would mark a sea-change in U.S.-Israeli military relations. Johnson and his team continued to request inspections of the Dimona reactor, but certainly not with the rigor or insistence of JFK.[44] Like Kennedy before him, LBJ had no inkling of how far Israel had advanced toward a nuclear capability, even though there is evidence that his own national security adviser, McGeorge Bundy, had been aware of the progress.[45] In fact, as early as 1960, CIA officials knew that Israel had broken ground at Dimona for a chemical reprocessing plant – a crucial step in developing a nuclear bomb – but withheld the information from the U.S. inspection team at Dimona and from Kennedy himself.[46]

Regardless of whether Kennedy was aware of what was truly happening at Dimona, Israel's leaders knew that LBJ was far more sympathetic to the Israeli cause than Kennedy had been. As a young congressman from Texas prior to World War II, LBJ had pushed hard to cut the red tape for European Jews seeking asylum from Nazi Germany and to prevent the deportation of those refugees already in the U.S., including the eminent conductor Erich Leinsdorf.[47] Johnson visited Dachau just days after its liberation at the end of World War II, and had returned to the U.S., according to his wife Lady Bird, "just shaken, bursting with overpowering revulsion and incredulous horror at what he had seen. Hearing about it is one thing, being there is another."[48]

As Senate Majority Leader, Johnson was perhaps the strongest voice in Congress to oppose Eisenhower's sanctions against Israel for refusing to withdraw from the Gaza Strip after the 1956 Suez Crisis. LBJ detailed his objections in a much-publicized letter to Secretary of State John Foster Dulles, and privately told an Israeli diplomat that the Eisenhower administration was "not going to get a goddamn thing here (Congress) until they [treat you fairly]."[49] Unlike Kennedy's staff, two of LBJ's closest advisers, Abe Fortas (whom he named to the Supreme Court) and Edwin L. Weisl Sr., had been strong supporters of Israel's security.[50] By the mid-1960s, LBJ and his advisers had adopted an unofficial policy of pretending that America's cursory inspections proved that Israel was not going nuclear while appearing to continue JFK's policy of nonproliferation.[51] By 1967, Israel had the capability to build its own bomb – the ultimate answer, its leaders felt, to its existential anxieties.

LBJ proved a staunch supporter of Israel's security in other ways as well. Under his administration, the United States supplanted France as Israel's top arms supplier in 1968.[52] As David Schwam found while researching his master's thesis, "The Forgotten Legacy of Lyndon Johnson: US-Israel Arms Policy Development, 1963-1968," few historians, and by extension even fewer journalists, have noted this dramatic turning point in the relations between the United States and Israel – a move that would entrench the United States in the quagmire of the Middle East conflict up to the present day.[53] The pivotal year was 1964, when LBJ agreed to supply Israel with offensive weapons but did so secretly through a third party, West Germany, which sold Israel its best tanks.[54]

Prior to the LBJ administration, the U.S. held mostly to a policy of not selling military weapons of any kind to Israel, and only twice granted exceptions for defensive armaments under Eisenhower and Kennedy. Between 1949 and 1963, total U.S. military aid to Israel was $27.4 million. In four years of the Johnson administration, however, total outlays rose to $134.9 million for both defensive and offensive weaponry, including tanks and advanced aircraft.[55] Today U.S. military aid to Israel is about $3 billion annually.[56] As Schwam pointed out, LBJ was not only sympathetic to the Israeli cause but savvy about the growing political strength of the American Jewish community and the pro-Israel lobby, both of which had been vital to the election of JFK in 1960.[57]

Once again, it is imperative to point out that the American Jewish community is not synonymous with the pro-Israel lobby and even less so with Mossad. That said, Mossad has shown its willingness to subvert and manipulate U.S. policy for its own aims. In the last years of the George W. Bush administration, CIA memos reveal, Mossad officers posed as CIA agents – equipped with U.S. passports and U.S. dollars – to recruit operatives from the terrorist group Jundallah for a covert war against Iran. The aim was to raise a "false flag" that the U.S. was conspiring with terrorists against the Iranian regime even though U.S. agents had been told to avoid all contact with the terrorist group, whose members had assassinated Iranian government officials and killed Iranian women and children.[58] The story did not find its way into the *New York Times* or the *Washington Post*.

JFK researchers, even those with a more balanced outlook than *Final Judgment* author Michael Collins Piper, would certainly face accusations of anti-Semitism if they dared to investigate, or speculate upon, the possibility of Mossad's having a role in the JFK assassination. There is much anecdotal evidence to show that those in the U.S. media who criticize Israeli policies are often accused of being "anti-Semitic" or "not a friend of Israel," as detailed by two prominent American scholars, John J. Mearsheimer of The University of Chicago and Stephen M. Walt of Harvard University, in their book *The Israel Lobby and U.S. Foreign Policy*.[59] The evidence includes the personal attacks on former President Jimmy Carter after the 2006 publication of his book, *Palestine: Peace Not Apartheid*, in which he urged Israel to return to its pre-1967 borders and to end Jewish settlements in the occupied territories as the basis for negotiating peace between Israel and the Arab world.[60] In 2002, media coverage showing the destruction of homes and the loss of life in the West Bank following the Israeli military's response to Palestinian suicide bombings led supporters of Israel to boycott the *New York Times*, the *Los Angeles Times,* and the *Washington Post*.[61]

The U.S. media have long been chided by foreign journalists and media watchdogs for a reluctance to criticize Israeli policies in the Middle East or to question U.S. support for Israel and its policies. Mearsheimer and Walt have argued that media coverage of U.S.-Israeli relations has been dominated by the influence of pro-Israel lobbies, in particular the American Israel Public Affairs Committee, or AIPAC. "Channeling public discourse in a pro-Israel direction is critically important, because an open and candid discussion of Israeli policy in the Occupied Territories, Israeli history, and the lobby's role in shaping America's Middle East policy might easily lead more Americans to question existing policy toward Israel and to call for a relationship with Israel that more effectively serves the U.S. national interest," Mearsheimer and Walt wrote.[62]

AIPAC is broadly viewed as one of the most influential lobbying organization in America. Along with more than sixty allied Political Action Committees and individual contributors, it is collectively the nation's biggest single-issue donor to political campaigns.[63] Beyond its monetary influence, its sixty-thousand active members, as well as several hundred thousand of its supporters in Jewish communities, can generate flak through intimidating letters, emails, and phone calls on a scale that editors and reporters seldom see on other issues. A *Time* magazine cover story on September 13, 2010, with the headline "Why Israel Doesn't Care about Peace" – based on a poll that showed just 8 percent of Israelis rated the conflict with Palestine as the nation's top concern – drew more than a thousand letters, most of them protests from Israeli supporters, according to an editor's note in the September 27, 2010, issue of the magazine. In a press release issued September 18 of that year, The Anti-Defamation League of B'nai Brith charged *Time* with "calling up age-old anti-Semitic stereotypes about Jews and money" and demanded an apology from the magazine's editors.[64] Prior even to the release of *Time*'s story, a *Haaretz* headline and kicker read: "ADL: *Time* Magazine Israel Cover Story Rehashes anti-Semitic Lies. Israelis are depicted as caring more about cafés, booming economy than striking a peace deal with the Palestinians."[65]

Accusations of "anti-Semitism" in varying forms have become one of the most powerful tools in the pro-Israel lobby's arsenal of flak for silencing those in the media who question Israel's treatment of Palestinians or America's unconditional support for Israel.[66] "In fact, anyone who says there is an Israel lobby runs the risk of being charged with anti-Semitism, even though [the lobbyists themselves] are hardly bashful about describing their influence," Mearsheimer and Walt wrote.[67]

The silencing campaign against U.S. critics of America's pro-Israeli foreign policy also extends to American universities, where the media often turn to find experts who can provide analysis and commentary on news events in the Middle East. Campus Watch, sponsored by the pro-Israel organization Middle East Forum, posts articles attacking the work of academics it calls "enemies of the Israeli state."[68] The site encourages donors to withhold their contributions from the academics' institutions and to urge university officials to dismiss or block the promotion of offending academicians. Rachid Khalidi, a professor of Arab studies at Columbia University, told the *New York Times* that he believes the aim of Campus Watch is to have "a chilling effect" on free speech.[69] "There is a dearth of proper debate in the media and politics about the Middle East. The only place where these views can be found is in academia. They want to shut down this last window."[70]

Seth Ackerman, a staff member of the media watchdog Fairness and Accuracy in Reporting, has pointed out that "American journalists probably feel more pressure about their coverage of Israel than any other subject."[71] That was true even at FAIR, he said, where "despite having a readership that is overwhelmingly sympathetic to our progressive critique of the media, our Middle East coverage invariably elicits angry letters and complaints, sometimes resulting in canceled subscriptions."[72]

U.S. support for Israel was a primary reason that the architects of the 9/11 attack targeted the United States and killed nearly three thousand innocent civilians in September 2001, according to the 9/11 Commission Report. Khalid Sheik Muhammad, cited by the report as "the mastermind of the 9/11 attack" and a top al-Qaeda leader, was driven "by his violent disagreement with U.S. foreign policy favoring Israel.... KSM himself was to land [a hijacked plane] at a U.S. airport and, after killing all adult male passengers on board and alerting the media, deliver a speech excoriating U.S. support for Israel, the Philippines and repressive governments in the Arab world."[73] The report also states that Osama Bin Laden, then leader of al-Qaeda and KSM's superior, had twice urged KSM to advance the date of the attack to coincide with media events tied to Israel's occupation of Jerusalem – the first time after then-Israeli opposition party leader Ariel Sharon's visit to the Temple Mount and the second "supposedly after Bin Laden learned from the media that Sharon would be visiting the White House."[74]

Media critics and foreign journalists alike have taken the U.S. media to task since 9/11 for, one, failing to make the connection in its coverage between the al-Qaeda attack and U.S. foreign policy and, two, obscuring the issues in the Palestinian-Israeli conflict that might have made clearer the animus that al-Qaeda and other Arab extremists have toward the United States.[75] That animus has led to two wars in the Middle East initiated by the U.S. – those in Iraq and Afghanistan – at a considerable cost in lives, taxpayers' dollars, and investment at home. By at least one estimate that includes disease, injuries, and mental health issues, U.S. casualties in Afghanistan and Iraq exceed 500,000.[76] According to a Harvard researcher, the cost to U.S. taxpayers for those wars, including the treatment of veterans, will run from $4 trillion to $6 trillion, or more than a third of the U.S. total debt of $17 trillion.[77]

More recently, the pro-Israel lobby pressured Congress and President Obama to end negotiations with Iran and take military action instead to stop Iran's quest to join Israel in the region's nuclear club. In the case of Arkansas Senator Tom Cotton, "pressure" came in the form of a nearly $1 million campaign donation from The Kristol Emergency Committee for Israel. Cotton, in turn, spurred 46 of his Senate Republican colleagues to write letters to Iranian officials, warning them not to trust the United States during sensitive negotiations.[78]

A nuclear arms race in the tinder box of the Middle East was exactly what President Kennedy was trying to prevent when he insisted on meaningful inspections of Israel's Dimona facility. With the assassination of JFK and the change in leadership to LBJ, the balance of power in the Middle East took a dramatic and destabilizing turn – not only by introducing nuclear weapons into a deeply divided region but by allying America's interests with that of Israel as its chief arms supplier. This, indeed, is LBJ's forgotten legacy.

As a leading leftist intellectual and a hero of the progressive media, Noam Chomsky has disappointed many critics of the Warren Commission by chastising JFK researchers for wasting their time chasing after the conspirators in the JFK assassination. Why bother, he argues in *Rethinking Camelot*, when Kennedy would not have changed the course of history. Despite the hopes for peace infused in him by an adoring generation of baby boomers, Chomsky says, Kennedy would have continued and escalated the war in Vietnam and continued to serve the needs of the military-industrial complex and the nation's business elite.[79]

But could JFK have prevented a nuclear-armed Israel? Perhaps not, not when Israel had a decisive start at Dimona by 1963 and an iron-willed determination to see it through. But there can be little doubt that Kennedy, up to the moment of his death, intended to try.[80] Nor can there be any doubt that he favored a more even-handed policy in the Arab-Israeli conflict than the president who succeeded him. The question then becomes whether Kennedy's policies toward Israel, and their dramatic reversals after this assassination, might have been a motive in his murder.

No one in the mainstream media or in the nation's academic circles has dared to explore or even to suggest that connection. As we have seen, more than self-censorship is involved. There is a well-based fear that one's reputation and livelihood will be harmed by such a venture.

Many respected JFK researchers now believe that James J. Angleton, the chief of counterintelligence for the CIA and the agency's liaison to Mossad during much of the Cold War, was at the very center of a broad conspiracy to assassinate President Kennedy. Only Angleton had the authority and the access to pull off what Scott calls a two-phase "dialectical cover-up," the first of which led U.S. leaders, including LBJ and Federal Bureau of Investigation Chief J. Edgar Hoover, to believe that Oswald had been an agent for the Kremlin.[81] Their fear was that, if the American public learned the truth, it would lead to a nuclear confrontation with the Soviet Union and the instant obliteration of tens of millions of Americans.[82] But by the time the nation's leaders realized there was no truth to the Oswald-Soviet connection, they were trapped by their own hastiness inside Phase II of the cover-up – the lone nut gunman theory devised by the Warren Commission in 1964 and patched and jerry-rigged over the past fifty years like the wheezing engine of an old jalopy.[83]

In the epilogue of the 2008 edition of his book, *Oswald and the CIA*, author and former military intelligence analyst John Newman argues that only Angleton could have coordinated the cover-up for the Crime of the Century. He details how Angleton played a shell game with the records in Oswald's CIA files so that, on the day of the assassination, "a World War III virus" implicating Oswald as a Soviet agent would suddenly emerge within the agency. The resulting national security crisis could be stemmed only by a massive cover-up reaching all the way to the White House and into the Warren Commission:

> It is now apparent that the World War III pretext for a national security cover-up was built into the fabric of the plot to assassinate President Kennedy. The plot required that Oswald be maneuvered into place in Mexico City and his activities there carefully monitored, controlled, and, if necessary, embellished and choreographed. The plot required that, prior to 22 November, Oswald's profile at CIA HQS and the Mexico station be lowered; his 201 file had to be manipulated and restricted from incoming traffic on his Cuban activities. The plot required that, when the story from Mexico City arrived at HQS, its significance would not be understood by those responsible for reacting to it. Finally, the plot required that, on 22 November, Oswald's CIA files would establish his connection to Castro and the Kremlin.
>
> The person who designed this plot had to have access to all of the information on Oswald at CIA HQS. The person who designed this plot had to have the authority to alter how information on Oswald was kept at CIA HQS. The person who designed this plot had to have access to project TUMBLEWEED, the sensitive joint agency operation against the KGB assassin, Valery Kostikov [whom Oswald had made contact with in Mexico City]. The person who designed this plot had the authority to instigate a counterintelligence operation in the Cuban affairs staff (SAS) at CIA HQS. In my view, there is only one person whose hands fit into these gloves: James Jesus Angleton, Chief of CIA's Counterintelligence Staff.[84]

Newman points out that, from the time of Oswald's attempted defection to the Soviet Union in 1959 to his dual dalliances with both pro-Castro and anti-Castro organizations in New Orleans and on to his alleged visits to the Soviet and Cuban embassies in Mexico City, Angleton and his closest staff members kept the files on Oswald, and kept them very close to the vest, until after the assassination. Newman continued:

> In my view, whoever Oswald's direct handler or handlers were, we must now seriously consider the possibility that Angleton was probably their general manager. No one else in the Agency had the access, the authority, and the diabolically ingenious mind to manage this sophisticated plot. No one else had the means necessary to plant the WWIII virus in Oswald's files and keep it dormant for six weeks until the president's assassination. Whoever those who were ultimately responsible for the decision to kill Kennedy were, their reach extended into the national intelligence apparatus to such a degree that they could call upon a person who knew its inner secrets and workings so well that he could design a failsafe mechanism into the fabric of the plot. The only person who could ensure a national security cover-up of an apparent counterintelligence nightmare was the head of counterintelligence.[85]

Yet Newman fails to mention Angleton's role as liaison to Mossad and his close ties to Israeli intelligence officials, whom Angleton often lunched with at his favorite Washington, D.C., restaurant.[86] Likewise, in his best-selling biography of Angleton, *Cold Warrior,* author Tom Mangold gives short-shrift to Angleton's partnership with Mossad, writing in a footnote that it was irrelevant to the narrative of his book.[87] A more telling point, however, may have been made in another of Mangold's footnotes, in which he points out that the CIA's officially designated historian for the counterintelligence staff, Richard Klise, was told flatly by Angleton in 1968 that the records on the Israeli desk were all "off limits."[88]

In fact, according to Angleton biographer Michael Holzman, Angleton's connection to Israeli intelligence officers made much of his work "off limits" to the rest of the CIA. "Through his control of the Israeli account, Angleton had virtually a second career in the Agency, supporting operational activities quite distinct from his main counterintelligence responsibilities. It is difficult to exaggerate the importance of this second power base within the CIA. It made him virtually unassailable.[89]

The elite media also have glossed over Angleton's close ties to Israel. The *New York Times'* obituary on Angleton, who died in 1987, mentions in just a sentence that Angleton handled "the Israeli account" at the CIA for more than a decade.[90] The *Washington Post* obituary includes two sentences on Angleton's ties to Israel, including that he helped "establish what came to be the CIA's 'special relationship' with Israel's secret service, the Mossad, that resulted in the United States obtaining vast quantities of data on Soviet military hardware and on conditions in the Soviet Union."[91]

Angleton's long and close relationship with Mossad is given the same circumspect treatment in Israel, where eight months after his death, the top leaders of Israel's intelligence community gathered in a secret ceremony outside Jerusalem and planted a tree on a barren hillside to honor a "friend" for services that were never specified. In the only story in either elite U.S. newspaper to provide more than a passing reference to Angleton's ties to Israel, *Washington Post* foreign correspondent Glenn Frankel wrote from Jerusalem about the secret tribute to Angleton following his death in 1987:

> The head of the pathologically secretive spy agency, the Mossad, was there, as was his counterpart with Shin Bet, the Israeli internal security service. Five former heads of those agencies and three former military intelligence chiefs were also present. Their mission: to pay final tribute to a beloved member of their covert fraternity – the late CIA chief of counterintelligence, James Jesus Angleton.
>
> The tree planting, a traditional ceremony of reverence here, took place at noon at a site about ten miles west of here. Eventually there will be hundreds of trees at the spot, just across the road from a similar forest dedicated to the late Israeli war hero Moshe Dayan.
>
> Following the planting, the group gathered again in Jerusalem behind the King David Hotel at a scenic spot not far from the walls of the Old City that Angleton often visited on his trips here. There they dedicated a memorial stone that read, in English, Hebrew and Arabic: "In memory of a dear friend, James (Jim) Angleton" but that gave no indication of who Angleton was or what he did.[92]

Angleton more than any other JFK assassination suspect was in a key position of power and secrecy to coordinate the actions among all those with a motive to kill the president, including elements of the CIA, organized crime, the French OAS, and Israel's Mossad. Angleton, more than any other suspect, likewise emerges at pivotal moments in the gathering of evidence in the JFK case – as the CIA liaison to the Warren Commission and as the "friend" who, soon after their deaths, visited the home of CIA Mexico City bureau chief Winston Scott to confiscate cartons of sensitive files, photos and tapes,[93] and likewise broke into the Georgetown home of JFK's closest mistress, Mary Pinchot Meyer, to confiscate her sensitive diary.[94]

Could Angleton, who was at least complicit in hiding Israel's nuclear development program from JFK and who may have actively aided in its secret development, have partnered with Israel and the Mossad in Kennedy's assassination? Is this the "partnership" that the CIA fears is at risk if they release all of the documents in the JFK files? Is this the "identifiable harm" to foreign relations that the JFK Records Act allows as an exemption for withholding key documents from Americans? These questions need to be asked and explored without demonizing journalists and historians who venture there.

The firewall must come down.

Endnotes

1. John J. Mearsheimer and Stephen M. Walt, *The Israel Lobby and U.S. Foreign Policy* (New York: Farrar, Straus and Giroux, 2007), 192.

2. Peter Dale Scott, *Deep Politics and the Death of JFK* (Berkeley: University of California Press, 1993), 301.

3. Ibid., 300.

4. Seymour M. Hersh, *The Samson Option: Israel's Nuclear Arsenal and American Foreign Policy* (New York: Random House, 1991), author's note.

5. Dan Charles, "Review: Israel Has Its Nuclear Demons," *New Scientist* magazine 1796, November 1991, 58.

6. Joel Brinkley, "Israeli Nuclear Arsenal Exceeds Earlier Estimates, Book Reports," *New York Times*, October 20, 1991. See also, Seymour M. Hersh, "U.S. Said to Have Allowed Israel to Sell Arms to Iran," *New York Times*, December 8, 1991.

7. William B. Quandt, "How Far Will Israel Go?" *Washington Post*, November 24, 1991.

8. Robert Miraldi, *Seymour Hersh: Scoop Artist* (Lincoln, NE: Potomac Books, 2013), 280.

9 Gaddis Smith, "The Samson Option: Israel's Nuclear Arsenal and American Foreign Policy," *Foreign Affairs*, Spring 1992, http://www.foreignaffairs.com/articles/47574/gaddis-smith/the-samson-option-israels-nuclear-arsenal-and-american-foreign-p.

10 Ari Shavit, *My Promised Land: The Triumph and Tragedy of Israel* (New York: Spiegel & Grau, 2013), 185-187.

11. Miraldi, *Seymour Hersh*, 280.

12. Hersh, *The Samson Option*, 5.

13. Ibid.

14. Alcibiades Bilzerian, "How Much does Israel Cost the Average American?" Veterans Today, July 17, 2013, ://www.veteranstoday.com/2013/07/17/how-much-does-israel-cost-the-average-american/; and "The CIA and Mossad: A Murderous Alliance," WL Central, December 3, 20011, http://wlcentral.org/node/2370.

15. Hersh, *The Samson Option*, 101-2.

16. Ibid, 121.

17. "Letter from John F. Kennedy to Levi Eshkol, July 5, 1963," National Security Ar-

chive, George Washington University, http://nsarchive.gwu.edu/israel/documents/exchange/01-01.htm, accessed January 20, 2016.

18. Ibid.

19. Hersh, *The Samson Option,* 95.

20. Ibid., 96-97.

21. Ibid., 119-28.

22. Ibid., 101-2.

23. Ibid., 121.

24. Ibid.

25. Ibid.

26. Ibid., 129.

27. Abraham Ben-Zvi, "Stumbling into an Alliance," *Israel Affairs* 15, no. 3 (2002): 226; and Jeffrey Michael Nadaner, "Shifting Sands: John F. Kennedy and the Middle East" (PhD diss., Yale University, 2002), ix.

28. Ben-Zvi, "Stumbling into an Alliance," 233; and Nadaner, "Shifting Sands," 2.

29. Nadaner, "Shifting Sands," x.

30. Ibid.

31. Ben-Zvi, "Stumbling into an Alliance," 240.

32. Ibid., 226-27.

33. Ibid., 226.

34. Ibid., 240.

35. Hersh, *The Samson Option,* 111.

36. Ibid., 112.

37. Ibid., 119.

38. Ibid., 125.

39. Shavit, *My Promised Land,* 186.

40. Ibid., 77.

41. Ibid., 179, 185-86.

42. Ibid., 194.

43. Ibid., 197.

44. Hersh, *The Samson Option*, 135-136.

45. Ibid., 133.

46. Hersh, *The Samson Option,* 112; and Michael Holzman, *James Jesus Angleton: The CIA, and the Craft of Counterintelligence* (Amherst: University of Massachusetts Press, 2008),166.

47. Hersh, *The Samson Option,* 127.

48. Ibid.

49. "Letter From Senator Lyndon B. Johnson to the Secretary of State," Washington, February 11, 1957, U.S. Department of State, Office of the Historian, *Foreign Relations of The Unit-*

ed States, 1955–1957, Volume XVII, Arab-Israeli Dispute, 1957, Document 83, https://history.
state.gov/historicaldocuments/frus1955-57v17/d83; and Edward Tivnan, *The Lobby: Jewish Political Power and American Foreign Policy* (New York: Simon and Schuster, 1987), 51.

50. Hersh, *The Samson Option*, 126.

51. Ibid., 143.

52. David S. Schwam, "The Forgotten Legacy of Lyndon Johnson: U.S.-Israeli Arms Policy Development, 1963-1968" (master's thesis, University of Houston, 1994), 125-26; and Hersh, *The Samson Option*, 160.

53. Schwam, "The Forgotten Legacy," viii, 1.

54. Hersh, *The Samson Option*, 133; and John W. Finney, "U.S. Secretly Let Germans Transfer Tanks to Israelis," *New York Times*, January 31, 1965.

55. Schwam, "The Forgotten Legacy," 2; and Clyde R. Mark, "Israel: U.S. Foreign Assistance," *Congressional Research Service*, April 26, 2005, 13, http://fas.org/sgp/crs/mideast/IB85066.pdf.

56. Jeremy M. Sharp, "U.S. Foreign Aid to Israel," *Congressional Research Service*, April 11, 2014, Summary, http://fas.org/sgp/crs/mideast/RL33222.pdf.

57. Schwam, "The Forgotten Legacy," 19.

58. Mark Perry, "False Flag," *Foreign Policy*, http://www.foreignpolicy.com/articles/2012/01/13/false_flag, January 13, 2012.

59. Mearsheimer and Walt, *The Israel Lobby*, v, 9, 171, 188.

60. Ibid., ix.

61. Felicity Barringer, "Mideast Turmoil: The News Outlets; Some U.S. Backers of Israel Boycott Dailies Over Mideast Coverage They Deplore," *New York Times*, May 23, 2002.

62. Mearsheimer and Walt, *The Israel Lobby*, 168.

63. E.S. Herman, "The Pro-Israel Lobby," *Canadian Dimension* 36, no. 3 (2002): 27; and Mearsheimer and Walt, *The Israel Lobby*, 120.

64. Natasha Mosgavaya, "ADL: *Time* Magazine Cover Story Rehashes Anti-Semitic Lies," *Haaretz*, September 10, 2010; and "CAMERA Alert: *Time* Magazine Cover Story Update," *JewishIndy*, http://www.jewishindy.com/modules.php?name=News&file=article&sid=13377, September 22, 2010.

65. Mosgavaya, "ADL," *Haaretz*.

66. Mearsheimer and Walt, *The Israel Lobby*, 188-96.

67. Ibid., 188.

68. Michael North, "We Have Our Eye On You … So Watch Out," *Times Higher Education Supplement*, January 25, 2005.

69. Ibid.

70. Ibid.

71. Seth Ackerman, "Al-Aqsa Intifada and the U.S. Media," *Journal of Palestine Studies* (Winter 2001): 73.

72. Ibid., 74.

73. The 9/11 Commission Report, http://govinfo.library.unt.edu/911/report/911Report.pdf, 154.

74. Ibid., 250.

75. Shahira Fahmy, "How Could So Much Produce So Little? Foreign Affairs Reporting in the Wake Of 9/11" (conference paper, International Communication Association, 2007); Herman, "The Pro-Israel Lobby"; and Mearsheimer and Walt, *The Israel Lobby*, 64-70, 169-75.

76. "Iraq, Afghanistan: American Casualties Total 500,000, Counting Injury and Disease, Writer Claims," *Los Angeles Times*, June 24, 2010, http://latimesblogs.latimes.com/babylonbeyond/2010/06/iraqafghanistan-.html#sthash.lXCadj1Q.dpuf.

77. Ernesto Londono, "Iraq, Afghan Wars Will Cost $4 Trillion to $6 Trillion, Harvard Study Says," *Washington Post,* March 28, 2013, http://www.washingtonpost.com/world/national-security/study-iraq-afghan-war-costs-to-top-4-trillion/2013/03/28/b82a5dce-97ed-11e2-814b-063623d80a60_story.html.

78. John Hudson, "Despite AIPAC Lobby, Obama Calms Congress on Iran Talks," *Foreign Policy*, October 23, 2013, http://thecable.foreignpolicy.com/posts/2013/10/23/despite_aipac_lobbying_obama_admin_pacifies_congress_on_iran; and Keith Foote, "Israel Paid Senator Tom Cotton $1 Million To Block The Iran Nuclear Deal," Liberal America website, September 1, 2015, http://www.liberalamerica.org/2015/09/01/israel-paid-senator-tom-cotton-1-million-block-iran-nuclear-deal/.

79. Noam Chomsky, "Vain Hopes, False Dreams," *Z Magazine*, September 1992, http://www.chomsky.info/articles/199209--.htm.

80. Hersh, *The Samson Option*, 125.

81. Scott, *Deep Politics*, 38-44.

82. John Newman, *Oswald and the CIA: The Documented Truth about the Unknown Relationship between the U.S. Government and the Alleged Killer of JFK* (New York: Skyhorse Publishing, 2008), 618.

83. Scott, *Deep Politics*, 44-57.

84. Newman, *Oswald and the CIA*, 636-37.

85. Ibid.

86. Pamela Kessler, "Cloak-and-Swagger," *Washington Post,* March 3, 1989.

87. Charles R. Babcock, "Obsessions of a Spymaster," *Washington Post*, July 7, 1991; and Tom Mangold, *Cold Warrior* (New York: Simon Schuster, 1991), 362.

88. Mangold, *Cold Warrior*, 433.

89. Michael Holzman, *James Jesus Angleton, the CIA, and the Craft of Counterintelligence* (Amherst: University of Massachusetts Press, 2008), 169.

90. Stephen Engelberg, "James Angleton, Counterintelligence Figure, Dies" *New York Times*, May 12, 1987.

91. Richard Pearson, "James Angleton, Ex-Chief Of Counterintelligence, Dies," *Washington Post*, May 12, 1987.

92. Glenn Frankel, "The Secret Ceremony: Israel's Memorial to the CIA's James Angleton," *Washington Post,* December 5, 1987.

93. Jefferson Morley, *Our Man in Mexico: Winston Scott and the Hidden History of the CIA* (Lawrence: University of Kansas Press, 2008), 1-9.

94. Peter Janney, *Mary's Mosaic: The CIA Conspiracy to Murder John F. Kennedy, Mary Pinchot Meyer, and Their Vision for World Peace* (New York: Skyhorse Publishing, 2012), 75-85.

Chapter 6

Lost in the Master's Mansion

*My Father's mansion has many rooms; if that were not so, would I
have told you that I am going there to prepare a place for you?*
                                                            – John 14:2

O n the eve of his firing from the CIA in 1975, chief counterin-
       telligence officer James Jesus Angleton tried to explain to *New
       York Times* reporter Seymour Hersh how his division could have
been involved in illegal covert tactics against Vietnam War protesters.

"A mansion has many rooms, and there were many things going on during
the period of the [anti-war] bombings," Angleton said. He then added with
a now-famous slip of the tongue, "I'm not privy to who struck John."[1]

It is anybody's guess as to which "John" Angleton was referring to in
the last sentence of his quote, although he later testified in court, without
being asked directly, that it was not John F. Kennedy.[2] Nor can we be certain how he was applying the biblical reference in his opening clause ("A
mansion has many rooms...") to his counterintelligence operations. But
many biblical scholars interpret the passage as the Apostle John's promise
that those who have faith in Jesus will be saved no matter what their religious differences.

On many levels, the passage can be seen as an apt metaphor for the
mysteries surrounding the assassination of John F. Kennedy. There are sol-
id clues that suspects with varying loyalties but a shared interest in killing
the president may have worked together in Angleton's labyrinthine mansion, among them elements of the CIA, organized crime, the anti-Castro
community, right-wing political groups, the French OAS, the Dallas police, and perhaps even Israel's Mossad. As the CIA liaison to the Mossad
and a personal friend of Mossad agents, Angleton was in a position to
recruit, or be recruited by, Israel for counter-intelligence operations that
only he was privy to. Most, if not all, of these foregoing players shared a
rabid fear of the Soviet menace and communism in the early 1960s. But,

for more than fifty years, the mainstream media have been lost in the master's mansion without the nerve or the insight to start knocking on doors.

"Master" in this metaphor refers, above all, to Herman-Chomsky's Propaganda Model in which an elite media serve the interests of those in power because news "makers" and news "producers" share a common mindset through ownership, management, overlapping social circles, and mutual self-interests. For-profit media organizations are by economic necessity conservative in their outlook because they are dependent upon the advertising revenue and financial investment provided by powerful business interests.[3]

"Master" refers as well to Angleton, who used his legendary skills in the art of counter-intelligence to fashion mirrors throughout the mansion that continue to confuse and deceive those who try to navigate its halls and rooms. Like most people who work in a top-down culture where the lines of command are clear and straightforward, journalists have a hard time thinking beyond the centralized, hierarchical structure of non-covert operations. But counterintelligence operations are alien to everyday working life. They are more often free-floating, decentralized, and oblique in achieving their aims. Agents, or those working for agents, are often asked to do things that appear to be in their own self-interest (or the interest of some larger entity to which they are loyal) when, in truth, they may be serving an entirely different or even antagonistic purpose of which the actor is unaware.

For instance, based on what we now know about Lee Harvey Oswald's activities and associates, we might well ask if he was pro-Castro or anti-Castro? His carefully crafted public persona showed him to be pro-Castro, but in his personal life, he associated primarily with those who were anti-Castro and anti-communist, including his closest friend George de Mohrenschildt and his family's primary benefactors, Ruth and Michael Paine. Or was Oswald simply a psychotic sociopath with no allegiances at all? Certainly, supporters of the Warren Report would like us to think so. But others who knew him well believed him to have been intelligent, confident to the point of cockiness, and entirely sane.

Many JFK researchers believe that Oswald was working as a double agent – that is, he appeared to be a Castro supporter while, in truth, he was gathering information for the CIA on the activities of Castro supporters in New Orleans. The same JFK researchers will tell you that the deception probably did not stop there. They argue that Oswald did not realize that his ultimate purpose for the CIA, or more likely for rogue elements within the CIA, was to be set up as a pro-communist patsy who would be blamed for the assassination of JFK.

For those who have not seriously studied the record of Oswald's conflicting associations and contorted maneuverings in the months leading up to the assassination, or the details of what happened in Dealey Plaza on November 22, 1963 – and that includes the vast majority of journalists, past and present – Oswald's public claim that he was "a patsy" seems like so much guilty denial.

Journalists especially are skeptical of conspiracy theories because they don't know what they don't know and what they do know is often served up by those in positions of power and authority that give them instant credibility with journalists. This bit of circular logic has its origins in the Propaganda Model. Unconsciously more often than not, journalists do the bidding of the rich and powerful because that is who controls and finances them – from their corporate owners and their major advertisers to the army of "experts," spin doctors, and public relations people who serve up irresistibly easy-to-use information from the points of view of those who can afford to pay them. Coercion is seldom needed, Herman and Chomsky tell us, because "right-thinking" journalists will be hired in a corporate environment to begin with.[4]

Reporters and editors at the *New York Times* and the *Washington Post* are perhaps the most susceptible to being co-opted because of their proximity to the centers of power and their ambition to be a part of the inner circle where they can "scoop" whatever the power structure is willing to provide as "news." Those inner circles are more than happy to invite journalists in where they can be more easily manipulated and perhaps even recruited as "patriots" for spying and propaganda purposes, as the CIA's Operation Mockingbird did with more than four hundred top journalists and publishers during the Cold War. It's little wonder then that *Washington Post* editor Ben Bradlee felt he could not direct his news staff to investigate the Kennedy assassination. Bradlee was not only close to JFK and his family, but he was the brother-in-law of JFK's most intimate mistress, Mary Pinchot Meyer, whose ex-husband Cord Meyer ran the CIA program that recruited high-powered journalists – including Bradlee – to work for the CIA. For Bradlee, probing the Crime of the Century would have been like tattling on one circle of friends for what they did to another circle of friends.

It's no wonder that, when then-*Washington Post* reporter Jefferson Morley landed the first interview in 1994 with a CIA agent acknowledging that Oswald had been under the agency's surveillance for years prior to the assassination, his editors at the *Post* were "simply not comfortable with the story," Morley said. "No CIA agent had ever talked about the pre-assassination surveillance of Oswald. I thought this was a cool A1 story that lots of people would be interested in." But he was wrong about his editors. After a five-month vetting process that lasted from November 1994 to April 1995, the story didn't run on page one, but in the Outlook features section where Morley was an editor. "I could sense the lack of comfort with this whole topic," he said. "And this was summarized for me when a friend of mine took me aside and said, 'Jeff, this isn't good for your career.'"[5]

Journalists are at a distinct disadvantage in reporting on events that occur at the level of what JFK researcher Peter Dale Scott calls "deep politics" – the underworld of fluid connections among government leaders, intelligence officials, and organized criminals that respects neither law nor international boundaries. The players in deep politics are not likely to leave behind records of their illegal activities, especially details of how those operations were financed. And when they do leave a money trail, it is often through complex international money-laundering operations such as CMC-Permindex, the murky world trade promotion group whose board member Clay Shaw of New Orleans may have acted as paymaster for the JFK assassination. Obviously, too, sources operating at the level of deep politics are not likely to talk to the media and, when they do, they are not likely to tell the truth. For those engaged in counterintelligence activities, the media are just one more tool to be used and, if necessary, lied to and misled.

Indeed, in the first hours after the assassination, the media became a tool to spread the disinformation that Oswald, whom the FBI and Dallas police were already identifying as the president's assassin, had ties to the Soviet Union and Cuba. Angleton's counterintelligence division was directly responsible for generating this lie, which effectively shut down both media and government inquiries into the details of the assassination for fear of provoking a nuclear confrontation with the Soviet Union.

When it became clear that Oswald had no such ties, the media switched horses and galloped off in a different direction at the behest of government and intelligence officials who insisted that Oswald acted alone. The official theory was backed by a pantheon of authority figures on the Warren Commission, from respected members of the Senate and House to the heads of the CIA and the World Bank, with esteemed Chief Justice

Earl Warren as its chairman. How could members of the media possibly think that such a distinguished body would conduct anything less than a complete and impartial investigation into the murder of the nation's highest elected official?

From the beginning, the elite media were careful not to question or criticize the work of the commission. Just hours after the assassination, Time-Life purchased the Zapruder film and then suppressed evidence in the footage for more than a decade that appears to show Kennedy being shot in the head from the front of his motorcade, indicating there were at least two assassins in Dealey Plaza that day. The *New York Times* dropped its investigation into the Kennedy assassination in 1966 and, of course, the *Washington Post* never launched one. In 1967, CBS secretly altered and misrepresented a broadcast so that it would show that its panel of marksmen had reproduced Oswald's apparent feat of firing off three rifle shots in 5.6 seconds and hitting a moving target at the distance of the president's limousine.

By choosing the appearance of stability over truth, however, the media established their passive role in the JFK mystery for the next half century, allowing government and intelligence officials to control and manipulate the information that has so far reached the American public. The media have failed in their duty as government watchdogs by failing to conduct their own investigations into the case and by endorsing the patchwork of inconsistencies, improbabilities, and outright deceptions that have sustained the Warren Report for fifty-plus years.

Despite the mainstream media's unquestioning support, the lone gunman theory is, indeed, just a theory, and a weak one at that. It takes into account only a narrow range of eyewitness testimony, physical evidence, possible motivations, and known linkages among suspects in the case. To reach its conclusions, the Warren Commission ignored both Oswald's and Jack Ruby's ties to the CIA and organized crime as well as the testimony of scores of eyewitnesses to the shooting in Dealey Plaza and to the arrival of the president's body at Parkland Hospital. Doctors, nurses, technicians, and law enforcement officials at the hospital that afternoon swore they saw a small entry wound in JFK's throat and a large blow-out in the back of his head, indicating a second shooter from the front. The commission also ignored the testimony of numerous eyewitnesses, including Dallas Deputy Sheriff Roger Craig, who said their advance on the grassy knoll immediately after the assassination was blocked by several men who identified themselves as Secret Service agents. In truth, there were no Secret Service agents in Dealey Plaza at the time; all of them had gone on to Parkland with the president's speeding motorcade.

The cornerstone of the Warren Commission's lone gunman theory, the so-called Magic Bullet, continues to hold sway with the mainstream media, despite the high improbability that a single bullet could have caused seven wounds in two men (including the shattered bones in Connally's rib cage and wrist) and remain essentially intact, and despite the belief of the two closest eyewitnesses to the shooting, Texas Governor John Connally and his wife, Nellie, that Connally had been wounded by a separate bullet, again indicating a second shooter. Further suspicion is cast upon the Warren Report by 1) eyewitnesses who say the president's head was surgically altered prior to its autopsy at Bethesda Naval Hospital, 2) the burning of the original autopsy report, 3) missing and/altered photos and X-rays from the autopsy and 4) the disappearance of the president's brain and original casket.

As we've learned from historian John Lewis Gaddis, pivotal historical events often have multiple and interdependent causes, none of which can be ignored if we are to gain a satisfactory understanding of how and why the transition occurred. Yet JFK researchers who have dared to knock on other rooms in Angleton's mansion in search of conspirators have been marginalized as "kooks" and "buffs" by a mainstream media that have never ventured out of the foyer. In truth, researchers who pursue broader and more inclusive theories than the lone gunman narrative of the Warren Report are guided by a more compelling logic than their timid counterparts.

The inner-most rooms in the master's mansion, those that may hold Angleton himself, his CIA counter-intelligence operatives and possibly the Mossad along with their allies in organized crime and the French OAS, continue to be locked and barred by social ostracism and outright censorship. Those who go knocking on all the doors face accusations of anti-Semitism and "blaming it on the Jews" when the covert actions of errant leaders and intelligence officials are no more representative of a people than such actions are amenable to their control. So far, only one JFK researcher – one with an extremist agenda, Michael Collins Piper – has publicly tried to fit all the pieces together in the assassination puzzle, including potential links to past Israeli leaders, Mossad, the French OAS, and Meyer Lansky's National Crime Syndicate. For his failure to share what Loury calls the "dearest communal values," Piper was labeled anti-Semitic and his work has been shunned by the JFK research community, even by those who most passionately disagree with the findings of the Warren Report.

Whether the full story of the JFK assassination is ever revealed depends not only on what evidence has been destroyed or withheld in our own country but in other countries as well, including Israel, France, Cuba, Russia, and Mexico, where Oswald and/or an Oswald impostor contacted the Soviet and Cuban embassies in Mexico City in the weeks prior to the assassination. Unfortunately, while we Americans can try to pressure our own government to reveal the last of the documents still sealed in the Kennedy case, we have no such leverage with foreign governments. Even so, an aggressive pursuit of the truth in this country could encourage investigators and government officials in other countries to release new information in the case.

By no means has this book argued that Mossad's involvement in the JFK assassination is a certainty. With so much evidence in the case now missing, destroyed, altered, or still classified, few things in the assassination are known for certain, and that includes the Warren Commission's lone gunman theory. As Gaddis informs us, we will never have full knowledge of all the circumstances surrounding any historical event – a fact that should not deter historians and journalists from seeking a narrative "fit" that is as close as possible to the knowable truth.

More than half-a-century after the Kennedy assassination, the quest for the truth is no longer about finding and punishing those responsible for his death; most, if not all, of the key players are dead. The quest now is about the defense of our democracy against those who may have subverted and taken control of it.

If, as many JFK researchers now believe, rogue elements of the CIA and U.S. military intelligence were involved in the killing of our nation's top elected leader, we are long overdue in placing oversight and constraints on those agencies. And if foreign elements were also involved, no matter how marginally, we as a nation have an even bigger task ahead of us in protecting our democratic processes. Exposing the transnational, covert connections among intelligence officials and organized crime – Scott's "deep politics" – will require international cooperation among journalists and researchers at a level never seen before.

We must keep in mind that seeking truth has a value beyond finding definitive answers. Even when our knowledge of a national tragedy is incomplete, the pursuit of truth keeps us alert to similar dangers and to the emergence of clues that may ultimately point to its causes. The mysteries surrounding the murder of one of our nation's most beloved and perhaps most pivotal presidents may never be entirely vanquished. Yet we as a nation cannot afford to abandon, now or in the future, the search into every dark corner of its circumstances – an investigation that ought to be led by the nation's ultimate guardians of honest government, its media.

As Justice Hugo Black said in his concurring opinion in the Supreme Court decision that turned over the Pentagon Papers to the *New York Times*: "Only a free and unrestrained press can effectively expose deception in government. And paramount among the responsibilities of a free press is the duty to prevent any part of the Government from deceiving the people..."

In her last published piece about the JFK assassination on September 5, 1965, two months before her death from an overdose under suspicious circumstances, Dorothy Kilgallen wrote in the column's final sentence, "This story isn't going to die as long as there's a real reporter alive – and there are a lot of them."[6]

The American people can only hope so.

Endnotes

1. Seymour Hersh, "Huge C.I.A. Operation Reported in US against Antiwar Forces, Other Dissidents During Nixon Years," *New York Times*, December 22, 1974, 1.

2. David Talbot, *Brothers: The Hidden History of the Kennedy Years* (Glencoe, Ill.: Free Press, 2007), 275.

3. Edward S. Herman and Noam Chomsky, *Manufacturing Consent: The Political Economy of the Mass Media* (New York: Pantheon Books, 2002), xi.

4. Herman and Chomsky, *Manufacturing Consent,* xi.

5. "The JFK Assassination and the Media," Passing the Torch conference, Senator John Heinz History Center, Pittsburg, Pennsylvania, October 17, 2013. Video download.

6. Lee Israel, *Kilgallen: A Biography of Dorothy Kilgallen* (New York Delacorte Press: 1979), 403-404.

Bibliography

ARTICLES

Abramson, J. "The Elusive President." *The New York Times*, October 27, 2013. LexisNexis Academic.

Achenbach, Joel. "JFK Conspiracy: Myth vs. the Facts." *The Washington Post*, February 28, 1992. LexisNexis Academic.

Ackerman, Seth. "Al-Aqsa Intifada and the U.S. Media." *Journal of Palestine Studies* 30, no. 2 (2001): 61-74.

Auchincloss, Kenneth. "Twisted History," a review of the film *JFK* directed by Oliver Stone. December 23, 1991. Academic Search Complete.

Babcock, Charles R. "Israel Uses Special Relationship to Get Secrets." *The Washington Post*, June 15, 1986. LexisNexis Academic.

_____. "Obsessions of a Spymaster," reviews of *Cold Warrior* by Tom Mangold and *Dangerous Liaisons* by Andrew and Leslie Cockburn. *The Washington Post* July 7, 1991. LexisNexis Academic.

Barringer, Felicity. "Some U.S. Backers of Israel Boycott Dailies over Mideast Coverage that They Deplore." *The New York Times*, May 23, 2002. LexisNexis Academic.

Ben-Zvi, Abraham. "Stumbling into an Alliance: John F. Kennedy and Israel." *Israel Affairs* 15, no. 3 (2009): 224-245.

Bollyn, Christopher. "Vanunu Speaks: Israeli Nuclear Whistleblower Risks Jail to Talk Exclusively to AFP." *The American Free Press*, July 31, 2004. http://www.americanfreepress.net/html/vanunu.html.

Bryan Burrough. "Conspiracy . . . Or Not?" *The New York Times*, May 20, 2007. LexisNexis Academic.

Buchwald, Art. "Bugged: The Flu Conspiracy." *The Washington Post*, January 14, 1992. LexisNexis Academic.

"CAMERA Alert: Time Magazine Cover Story Update." *JewishIndy*, September 22, 2010. http://www.jewishindy.com/modules.php?name=News&file=article&sid=13377.

Chomsky, Noam. "The Responsibility of Intellectuals." *The New York Review of Books*, February 23, 1967. http://www.chomsky.info/articles/19670223.htm.

Clark, William. "Rome's Trade Center – How It Came to Be." *Chicago Daily Tribune*, September 17, 1960. ProQuest Historical Newspapers.

Cowles, Gregory. "Inside the List." *The New York Times*, October 27, 2013. LexisNexis Academic.

Dickey, Jack. "The Debunker among the Buffs." *Time*, November 25, 2013. Academic Search Complete.

Engelberg, Stephen. "James Angleton, Counterintelligence Figure, Dies: Obituary." *The New York Times*, May 12, 1987. LexisNexis Academic.

Fahmy, Shahira. "How Could So Much Produce So Little? Foreign Affairs Reporting in the Wake of 9/11." Paper presented at the annual meeting of the International Communication Association, San Francisco, CA, May 23, 2007. http://citation.allacademic.com/meta/p170176_index.html.

Fein, Esther B. "Book Notes." *New York Times*, January 8, 1992.

Fetherling, Douglas. "Dallas: Myth and Memory." *The Toronto Star*, November 20, 1993. ProQuest Historical Newspapers.

Finney, John W. "U.S. Secretly Let Germans Transfer Tanks to Israelis." *The New York Times*, January 31, 1965. LexisNexis Academic.

Fletcher, Suzanne W. and Robert H. Fletcher. "Medical Editors, Journal Owners, and the Sacking of George Lundberg." *Journal of General Internal Medicine* 14, no. 3 (1999): 200-202. Academic Search Complete.

Frank, Jeffrey. "Who Shot JFK? The 30-Year Mystery," review of *Case Closed* by Gerald Posner. *The Washington Post*, October 31, 1993. LexisNexis Academic.

Frankel, Glenn. "The Secret Ceremony; Israel's Memorial to the CIA's James Angleton." *The Washington Post*, December 5, 1987. LexisNexis Academic.

Freund, Charles. "All the President's Triggermen." *The Washington Post*, November 22, 1992. LexisNexis Academic.

Gates, David, Frank Gibney Jr, and Robert Parry. "The Kennedy Conundrum." *Newsweek*, November 28, 1988. LexisNexis Academic.

Goodman, Walter. "Assassination Theories." *The New York Times*, November 1, 1988. LexisNexis Academic.

Greenberg, David. "Every President Wants that JFK Magic," review of *The Kennedy Half Century* by Larry J. Sabato. *The Washington Post*, October 27, 2013. LexisNexis Academic.

Harney, John. "Hank Messick, Journalist and Author on Organized Crime: Obituary (Obit)." *The New York Times*, November 20, 1999. LexisNexis Academic.

Hayes, Andrew F. "Exploring the Forms of Self-Censorship: On the Spiral of Silence and the Use of Opinion Expression Avoidance Strategies." *Journal of Communication* 57, no. 4 (2007): 785-802. Academic Search Complete.

Hennelly, Robert and Jerry Policoff. "JFK: How the Media Assassinated the Real Story." *The Village Voice* 37, no. 13 (1992): 33. Academic Search Complete.

Herman, Edward S. "The Pro-Israel Lobby." *Canadian Dimension* 36, no. 3 (2002): 27.

Holland, Max. "The Demon in Jim Garrison." *The Wilson Quarterly* 25, no. 2 (2001): 10-17. Academic Search Complete.

Horrock, Nicholas M. "Tracing Any Kennedy Conspirator Is Given Little Chance by Officials." *The New York Times,* January 1, 1979. ProQuest Historical Newspapers.

Hudson, John. "Despite AIPAC Lobby, Obama Calms Congress on Iran Talks." *Foreign Policy*, October 23, 2013. http://thecable.foreignpolicy.com/posts/2013/10/23/despite_aipac_lobbying_obama_admin_pacifies_congress_on_iran.

Husting, Ginna and Martin Orr. "Dangerous Machinery: "Conspiracy Theorist" as a Transpersonal Strategy of Exclusion." *Symbolic Interaction* 30, no. 2 (2007): 127-150. Academic Search Complete.

Isikoff, Michael. "H-e-e-e-e-r-e's Conspiracy: Why did Oliver Stone Omit (Or Suppress!) the Role of Johnny Carson?" *The New York Times*, December 29, 1991. LexisNexis Academic.

Jackson, David. "Most Still Believe in JFK Assassination Conspiracy." *USA Today*, November 20, 2013. http://www.usatoday.com/story/theoval/2013/11/17/john-kennedy-assassination-conspiracy-theories-gallup/3618431/.

Kakutani, Michiko. "Oswald and Mailer: The Eternal Basic Questions: Speculation under the Protection of 'He had to Feel' Or 'It is Possible.'" *The New York Times* April 25, 1995. LexisNexis Academic.

Kessler, Pamela. "Cloak-and-Swagger." *The Washington Post*, March 3, 1989. LexisNexis Academic.

Korte, Gregory. "Conspiracy Theories over JFK's Assassination Thrive." *USA Today*, September 26, 2010. http://usatoday30.usatoday.com/news/washington/2010-09-26-jfk-assassination-conspiracy-theories_N.htm?csp=34.

Krauss, Clifford. "28 Years after Kennedy's Assassination, Conspiracy Theories Refuse to Die." *The New York Times*, January 5, 1992. LexisNexis Academic.

Lardner, George Jr. "Archive Photos Not of JFK's Brain, Concludes Aide to Review Board; Staff Member Contends 2 Different Specimens Were Examined." *The Washington Post*, November 10, 1998. LexisNexis Academic.

_____. "Assassinations Committee Turns to Tantalizing Leads." *The Washington Post*, September 27, 1978. ProQuest Historical Newspapers.

_____. "On the Set: Dallas in Wonderland: How Oliver Stone's Version of the Kennedy Assassination Exploits the Edge of Paranoia." *The Washington Post*, May 19, 1991. LexisNexis Academic.

Lehmann-Haupt, Christopher. "Books of the Times; Kennedy Assassination Answers," review of *Case Closed* by Gerald Posner. *The New York Times*, September 9, 1993. LexisNexis Academic.

Leyden, John G. "Historians, Buffs and Crackpots." *The Washington Post,* January 26, 1992. LexisNexis Academic.

Londono, Ernesto. "Study: Iraq, Afghan Wars Will Cost $4 Trillion to $6 Trillion." *The Washington Post*, March 28, 2013. http://www.washingtonpost.com/world/national-security/study-iraq-afghan-war-costs-to-top-4-trillion/2013/03/28/b82a5dce-97ed-11e2-814b-063623d80a60_story.html.

Loury, Glenn C. "Self-Censorship in Public Discourse: A Theory of 'Political Correctness' and Related Phenomena." *Rationality and Society* 6, no. 4 (1994): 428-461.

Lyall, Sarah. "Book Notes." *The New York Times*, December 1, 1993. LexisNexis Academic.

Magnuson, Ed. "Now, a "Two-Casket Argument," *Time*, January 19, 1981. Academic Search Complete.

Morley, Jefferson. "Jefferson Morley: What We Still Don't Know about JFK's Assassination," *Dallas Morning News*, October, 25, 2013. LexisNexis Academic.

———. "Revelation 19.63." *Miami New Times*, April 12, 2010. http://www.miaminewtimes.com/2001-04-12/news/revelation-19-63/7/.

Mosgovaya, Natasha. "ADL: *Time* Magazine Cover Story Rehashes Anti-Semitic Lies." *Haaretz*, September 10, 2010. http://www.haaretz.com/jewish-world/adl-time-magazine-israel-cover-story-rehashes-anti-semitic-lies-1.313096.

Naftali, Tim. "A Complex Journey to the Grassy Knoll," a review of *The Road to Dallas* by David Kaiser. *The Washington Post*, January 15, 2009. LexisNexis Academic.

Noelle-Neumann, Elisabeth. "Turbulences in the Climate of Opinion: Methodological Applications of the Spiral of Silence Theory." *The Public Opinion Quarterly* 41, no. 2 (1977): 143-158.

North, Michael. "We Have Our Eye On You . . . So Watch Out." *Times Higher Education Supplement*, January 25, 2005. http://www.timeshighereducation.co.uk/features/we-have-our-eye-on-youso-watch-out/193711.article.

O'Harrow, Robert Jr. "Conspiracy Theory Wins Converts: Moviegoers Say 'JFK' Nourishes Doubts that Oswald Acted Alone." *The Washington Post*, January 2, 1992. LexisNexis Academic.

Paraeklae, Anssi and Johanna Ruusuvuori. "Analyzing Talk and Text." In *The SAGE Handbook of Qualitative Research*, by Norman K. Denzin and Yvanno S. Lincoln, 529. Thousand Oaks, Calif.: Sage, 2011.

Parshall, Gerald. "The Man with the Deadly Smirk." *U.S. News & World Report* , August 30, 1993. Academic Search Complete.

Pearson, Richard. "James Angleton, Ex-Chief of Counterintelligence, Dies." *The Washington Post*, May 12, 1987. LexisNexis Academic.

Perry, Mark. "False Flag." *Foreign Policy*, January 13, 2012. http://www.foreignpolicy.com/articles/2012/01/13/false_flag.

Powers, Thomas. "The Mind of the Assassin: Norman Mailer Pursues the Secrets of Lee Harvey Oswald," review of *Oswald's Tale* by Norman Mailer. *The New York Times*. April 30, 1995. LexisNexis Academic.

Powers, William F. "The Kennedy Assassination: Last Word?" *The Washington Post*, August 24, 1993. LexisNexis Academic.

Price, Deborah. "A Complete Catalogue of Kennedy Conspiracies," review of *Crossfire* by Jim Marrs. *The Washington Post*, December 24, 1989. LexisNexis Academic.

Riechmann, Deb. "Newly Released JFK Documents Raise Questions about Medical Evidence." *Associated Press*, November 9, 1998. LexisNexis Academic.

Sandbrook, Dominick. "Dallas '63: The Sad, Chilling Truth." *The Daily Telegraph*, June 21, 2008. ProQuest Historical Newspapers.

Sandels, Alexandra. "Iraq, Afghanistan: American Casualties Total 500,000, Counting Injury and Disease, Writer Claims." *Los Angeles Times*, June 24, 2010. http://latimes-blogs.latimes.com/babylonbeyond/2010/06/iraqafghanistan-.html#sthash.lXCadj1Q.dpuf.

Shannon, Ulrich. "Case Closed?" *The Gazette*, September 11, 1993. ProQuest Historical Newspapers.

Sharp, Jeremy M. "U.S. Foreign Aid to Israel." *Congressional Research Service*, April 11. 2013. https://www.fas.org/sgp/crs/mideast/RL33222.pdf.

Sharrett, C. "Debunking the Official History." *Cineaste* 19 [serial online], no. 1 (1992):11-14. Academic Search Complete.

Stone, Oliver. "Who is Rewriting History?: Behind the Media Establishment's Anger Over 'JFK.'" *The New York Times*, December 20, 1991. LexisNexis Academic.

Sturken, Marita. "Personal Stories and National Meanings." In *The Seductions of Biography*, eds. Mary Rhiel and David Bruce Suchoff. New York: Routledge, 1996.

Talbot, David and Vincent Bugliosi. "The Assassination: Was it a Conspiracy?: Yes. No." *Time*, July 2, 2007. Academic Search Complete.

Thompson, Elizabeth. "Do Lawyer's Files Hide JFK Secrets?: Bloomfield Papers. Montreal Lawyer's Widow Asks Federal Archives to Seal Husband's Documents for at Least 25 More Years." *The Gazette (Montreal)*, January 27, 2007. ProQuest Historical Newspapers.

Tuchman, Gaye. "Objectivity as Strategic Ritual: An Examination of Newsmen's Notions of Objectivity." *American Journal of Sociology* 77, no. 2 (1972).

Von Drehle, David. "Broken Trust." *Time*, November 25, 2013. Academic Search Complete.

Ward, Geoffrey C. "The most Durable Assassination Theory: Oswald did it Alone." *The New York Times*, November 21, 1993. LexisNexis Academic.

Weinraub, Bernard. "Substance and Style Criticized in 'J.F.K.' " *The New York Times*, November 7, 1991. LexisNexis Academic.

———. "Valenti Calls 'J.F.K.' 'Hoax' and 'Smear.' " *The New York Times*, April 2, 1992. LexisNexis Academic.

Wolfe, Alan. "Goodbye, Grassy Knoll." *The Washington Post*, May 27, 2007. LexisNexis Academic.

Wrone, David R. "Book Reviews—Case Closed: Lee Harvey Oswald and the Assassination of JFK by Gerald Posner." *The Journal of Southern History* 6 (1995): 186-88. Academic Search Complete.

BOOKS, DISSERTATIONS, AND PUBLIC DOCUMENTS

Baker, Judyth Vary, Edward T. Haslam and Jim Marrs. *Me & Lee: How I Came to Know, Love and Lose Lee Harvey Oswald*. Walterville, OR: Trine Day, 2010.

Barrett, Roby Carol. "'Come Quickly Sweet'" Muslims: American Foreign Policy in the Middle East 1958-1963." PhD Diss., University of Texas at Austin, 2005. ProQuest 3215304.

Becker, Don. *The JFK Assassination: A Researchers Guide*. Bloomington, IN: Author-House, 2011.

Beinart, Peter. *The Crisis of Zionism*. New York: Times Books/Henry Holt and Co., 2012.

Belzer, Richard, and David Wayne. *Hit List: An in-Depth Investigation into the Mysterious Deaths of Witnesses to the JFK Assassination*. New York: Skyhorse Publishing, 2013.

Benson, Michael. *Encyclopedia of the JFK Assassination*. New York: Checkmark Books, 2002.

———. *Who's Who in the JFK Assassination: An A-to-Z Encyclopedia*. Secaucus, NJ: Carol Publishing Group, 1993.

Berlin, Isaiah, Henry Hardy and Roger Hausheer. *The Proper Study of Mankind: An Anthology of Essays*. New York: Farrar, Straus and Giroux, 1998.

Blakey, G. Robert, and Richard N. Billings. *Fatal Hour: The Assassination of President Kennedy by Organized Crime*. New York: Berkley Books, 1992.

Bocco, Michael. "Unintended Alliances: Kennedy, Israel, and Arab Nationalism." Master's thesis, Florida Atlantic University, 2008. ProQuest 1460509.

Bratich, Jack Zeljko. "Grassy Knoll-Edges: Conspiracy Theories and Political Rationality in the 1990s." PhD Diss., University of Illinois at Urbana-Champaign, 2001. ProQuest 3023024.

Broderick, James F and Darren W. Miller. *Web of Conspiracy; a Guide to Conspiracy Theory Sites on the Internet*. Medford, NJ: Information Today, 2008.

Bugliosi, Vincent. *Parkland*. New York: W.W. Norton & Company, 2013.

Bugliosi, Vincent. *Four Days in November: The Assassination of President John F. Kennedy*. New York: W.W. Norton & Co., 2007.

Chomsky, Noam, David Barsamian, and Arthur Naiman. *The Common Good*. Monroe, ME: Odonian Press, 1998.

"Commission Document 355—DOJ Criminal Division Listing of Witnesses Interviewed." Warren Commission Documents, 256. *Mary Ferrell Foundation* website, accessed March 17, 2014, http://www.maryferrell.org/mffweb/archive/viewer/showDoc.do?mode=searchResult&absPageId=345628.

Cornwell, Gary. *Real Answers: The True Story*. Spicewood, TX: Paleface Press, 1998.

Davis, John H. *Mafia Kingfish: Carlos Marcello and the Assassination of John F. Kennedy*. New York: Signet, 1989.

———. *The Kennedy Contract: The Mafia Plot to Assassinate the President*. New York: HarperPaperbacks, 1993.

DeBrosse, Jim, and Colin B. Burke. *The Secret in Building 26: The Untold Story of America's Ultra War against the U-Boat Enigma Codes*. New York: Random House, 2004.

DiEugenio, James, and Lisa Pease, eds. *The Assassinations: Probe Magazine on JFK, RFK, MLK and Malcolm X*. Los Angeles: Feral House, 2002.

Epstein, Edward Jay. *Legend: The Secret World of Lee Harvey Oswald*. New York: Reader's Digest Press, 1978.

Ernest, Barry. *The Girl on the Stairs: The Search for a Missing Witness to the JFK Assassination*. Gretna, LA: Pelican Publishing, 2013.

Fetzer, James H. *Assassination Science: Experts Speak Out on the Death of JFK*. Chicago: Catfeet Press, 1998.

Fishman, Mark. *Manufacturing the News*. Austin: University of Texas Press, 1980.

Flammonde, Paris. *The Kennedy Conspiracy: An Uncommissioned Report on the Jim Garrison Investigation*. New York: Meredith Press, 1969.

Forsyth, Frederick. *The Outsider: My Life in Intrigue*. New York: GP Putnam's Sons, 2015.

Gaddis, John Lewis. *The Landscape of History: How Historians Map the Past*. New York: Oxford University Press, 2004.

Garrison, Jim. *On the Trail of the Assassins*. New York: Sheridan Square Press, 1988.

Hepburn, James. *Farewell America*. Vaduz: Frontiers, 1968.

Herman, Edward S., and Noam Chomsky. *Manufacturing Consent: The Political Economy of the Mass Media*. New York: Pantheon Books, 2002.

Hersh, Seymour M. *The Samson Option: Israel's Nuclear Arsenal and American Foreign Policy*. New York: Random House, 1991.

Heymann, C. David. *The Georgetown Ladies' Social Club*. New York: Atria Books, 2003.

Hinckle, Warren, and William W. Turner. *Deadly Secrets: The CIA-Mafia War against Castro and the Assassination of J.F.K.* New York: Thunder's Mouth Press, 1993.

———. *The Fish is Red: The Story of the Secret War against Castro*. New York: Harper & Row, 1981.

Hogan, Jacob Peter. "Democracy, Duplicity and Dimona: The United States of America, Israel and the Globe since 1949." ProQuest, UMI Dissertations Publishing, 2010.

Holzman, Michael Howard. *James Jesus Angleton, the CIA, and the Craft of Counterintelligence*. Amherst: University of Massachusetts Press, 2008.

Horne, Douglas P. *Inside the Assassination Records Review Board: The U.S. Government's Final Attempt to Reconcile the Conflicting Medical Evidence in the Assassination of JFK*. Falls Church, VA: D.P. Horne: 2009.

Hougan, Jim. *Spooks: The Haunting of America—The Private Use of Secret Agents.* New York: William Morrow & Co., 1985.

House Select Committee on Assassinations. *Findings of the Select Committee on Assassinations in the Assassination of President John F. Kennedy in Dallas, Tex., on November 22, 1963, HSCA Final Assassinations Report.* H.R. REP NO. 95-1828. 1979. http://www.history-matters.com/archive/jfk/hsca/report/html/HSCA_Report_0005a.htm.

Hurt, Henry. *Reasonable Doubt: An Investigation into the Assassination of John F. Kennedy.* New York: H. Holt and Co., 1987.

Israel, Lee. *Kilgallen: A Biography of Dorothy Kilgallen.* New York: Delacorte Press, 1979.

Janney, Peter. *Mary's Mosaic: The CIA Conspiracy to Murder John F. Kennedy, Mary Pinchot Meyer, and their Vision for World Peace.* New York: Skyhorse Publishing, 2012.

Jones Jr. Penn. *Forgive My Grief III.* Midlothian, Texas: Midlothian Mirror, 1969.

Kaiser, David E. *The Road to Dallas: The Assassination of John F. Kennedy.* Cambridge, MA: Belknap Press of Harvard University Press, 2008.

Kantor, Seth. *Who was Jack Ruby?* New York: Everest House, 1978.

Kennedy, John F. "1963 Commencement." *American University* website. http://www1.american.edu/media/speeches/Kennedy.htm

Knight, Peter D. "Plotting the Sixties: The Culture of Conspiracy in the United States of America." PhD diss., The University of York (United Kingdom), 1996. ProQuest C824307.

Kostrzewa-Zorbas, Grzegorz. "American Responses to the Proliferation of Actual, Virtual, and Potential Nuclear Weapons: France, Israel, Japan, and Related Cases, 1939-1997. Lessons for the Multipolar Future." PhD Diss., The Johns Hopkins University, 1998. ProQuest 9832918.

Kross, Peter. *JFK: The French Connection.* Kempton, IL: Adventures Unlimited Press, 2012.

Kunstler, William M. *My Life as a Radical Lawyer.* New York: Birch Lane Press, 1994.

Kurtz, Michael L. *The JFK Assassination Debates: Lone Gunman versus Conspiracy.* Lawrence: University Press of Kansas, 2006.

Lacey, Robert. *Little Man: Meyer Lansky and the Gangster Life.* Boston: Little, Brown, 1991.

Lane, Mark. *Plausible Denial: Was the CIA Involved in the Assassination of JFK?* New York: Thunder's Mouth Press, 1991. Kindle edition.

———. *Last Word: My Indictment of the CIA in the Murder of JFK.* New York: Skyhorse Publishing, 2012.

"Letter from John F. Kennedy to Levi Eshkol, July 5, 1963." National Security Archive, George Washington University. http://nsarchive.gwu.edu/israel/documents/exchange/01-01.htm, accessed January 20, 2016.

Lifton, David S. *Best Evidence: Disguise and Deception in the Assassination of John F. Kennedy.* New York: Macmillan, 1980.

Livingstone, Harrison Edward, and Robert J. Groden. *High Treason: The Assassination of JFK & the Case for Conspiracy.* New York: Carroll & Graf Publishers, 1998.

Mangold, Tom. *Cold Warrior: James Jesus Angleton: The CIA's Master Spy Hunter.* New York: Touchstone, 1992.

Marrs, Jim. *Crossfire: The Plot that Killed Kennedy.* New York: Carroll & Graf, 2001.

Martin, David C. *Wilderness of Mirrors.* Guilford, CT: Lyons Press, 2003.

McAdams, John. *JFK Assassination Logic: How to Think about Claims of Conspiracy.* Washington, D.C.: Potomac Books, 2011.

McClellan, Barr. *Blood, Money & Power: How LBJ Killed JFK.* New York: Hannover House, 2003.

McCoy, Alfred W. *The Politics of Heroin: CIA Complicity in the Global Drug Trade.* Brooklyn, NY: Lawrence Hill Books, 1991.

McKee, Alan. *Textual Analysis: A Beginner's Guide.* London: Sage Publications, 2006.

McKnight, Gerald. *Breach of Trust: How the Warren Commission Failed the Nation and Why.* Lawrence: University Press of Kansas, 2013.

Mellen, Joan. *Jim Garrison: His Life and Times, the Early Years.* Southlake, TX: JFK Lancer Productions and Publications, 2005.

Meagher, Sylvia. *Accessories After the Fact: The Warren Commission, the Authorities, and the Report.* New York: Vintage Books, 1976.

Mearsheimer, John J., and Stephen M. Walt. *The Israel Lobby and U.S. Foreign Policy.* New York: Farrar, Straus and Giroux, 2007.

Messick, Hank. *Lansky.* New York: Berkeley Publishing Corporation, 1971.

Miraldi, Robert. *Seymour Hersh: Scoop Artist.* Lincoln, NE: Potomac Books, 2013.

Morley, Jefferson. *Our Man in Mexico Winston Scott and the Hidden History of the CIA.* Lawrence: University Press of Kansas, 2008.

Morrow, Robert D. *First Hand Knowledge: How I Participated in the CIA-Mafia Murder of President Kennedy.* New York: S.P.I. Books, 1992.

Nadaner, Jeffrey Michael. "Shifting Sands: John F. Kennedy and the Middle East." ProQuest, UMI Dissertations Publishing, 2002.

Nelson, Phillip F. *LBJ: The Mastermind of the JFK Assassination.* New York: Skyhorse Publishing, 2011.

_____, *LBJ: From Mastermind to "The Colossus."* New York: Skyhorse Publishing, 2015.

Newcomb, Fred T. *Murder from Within: Lyndon Johnson's Plot Against President Kennedy.* Bloomington, Indiana: Author House, 2011.

Newman, John M. *Oswald and the CIA the Documented Truth about the Unknown Relationship between the U.S. Government and the Alleged Killer of JFK.* New York: Skyhorse Publishing, 2008.

The 9/11 Commission Report. http://govinfo.library.unt.edu/911/report/911Report.pdf.

Noyes, Peter. *Legacy of Doubt.* Lexington, KY: P&G Publications, 2010.

O'Leary, Bradley S., and L.E. Seymour. *Triangle of Death: The Shocking Truth about the Role of South Vietnam and the French Mafia in the Assassination of JFK.* Nashville, TN: WND Books, 2003.

Piper, Michael Collins. *Final Judgment: The Missing Link in the JFK Assassination Conspiracy.* Washington, D.C.: American Free Press, 2005.

Popkin, Richard Henry. *The Second Oswald.* Raleigh, NC: Boson Books, 2006.

Posner, Gerald L. *Case Closed: Lee Harvey Oswald and the Assassination of JFK.* New York: Random House, 1993.

Prouty, L. Fletcher, Jesse Ventura and Oliver Stone. *JFK: The CIA, Vietnam, and the Plot to Assassinate John F. Kennedy.* New York: Skyhorse Publishing, 2011.

Ragano, Frank, and Selwyn Raab. *Mob Lawyer.* New York: Maxwell Macmillan International, 1994.

Ralston, Ross Frank. "The Media and the Kennedy Assassination: The Social Construction of Reality." ProQuest, UMI Dissertations Publishing, 1999.

Rather, Dan and Mickey Herskowitz. *The Camera Never Blinks: Adventures of a TV Journalist.* New York: William Morrow and Company, 1977.

Rhiel, Mary and David Bruce, eds. *The Seductions of Biography.* New York: Routledge, 1996.

Russell, Dick. *The Man Who Knew Too Much.* New York: Carroll & Graf Publishers, 1992.

Sabato, Larry J. *The Kennedy Half Century: The Presidency, Assassination, and Lasting Legacy of John F. Kennedy.* New York: Bloomsbury, 2013.

_____. *Feeding Frenzy: How Attack Journalism Has Transformed American Politics.* New York: Free Press, 1991.

Scheim, David E. *Contract on America: The Mafia Murder of President John F. Kennedy.* New York: Kensington, 1988.

Schneider, Stephen. *Iced: The Story of Organized Crime in Canada.* Ontario: John Wiley & Sons, 2009.

Schotz, E. Martin. *History Will Not Absolve Us: Orwellian Control, Public Denial, and the Murder of President Kennedy.* Brookline, MA: Kurtz, Ulmer, & DeLucia Book Publishers, 1996.

Schwam, David Samuel. "The Forgotten Legacy of Lyndon Johnson: United States-Israeli Arms Policy Development, 1963-1968." ProQuest, UMI Dissertations Publishing, 1994.

Scott, Peter Dale. *Deep Politics and the Death of JFK.* Berkeley: University of California Press, 1993.

Shavit, Ari. *My Promised Land: The Triumph and Tragedy of Israel*. New York: Spiegel & Grau, 2013.

Summers, Anthony. *Conspiracy*. New York: Paragon House, 1989.

Talbot, David. *Brothers: The Hidden History of the Kennedy Years*. New York: Free Press, 2008.

Tivnan, Edward. *The Lobby: Jewish Political Power and American Foreign Policy*. New York: Simon and Schuster, 1987.

Waldron, Lamar. *The Hidden History of the JFK Assassination*. Carlton North, Australia: Scribe Publications, 2013.

Weberman, Alan J., and Michael Canfield. *Coup d'Etat in America: The CIA and the Assassination of John F. Kennedy*. San Francisco: Quick American Archives, 1992.

Wecht, Cyril H., Mark Curriden, and Benjamin Wecht. *Cause of Death*. New York: E. P. Dutton, 1993.

Weisberg, Harold. *Case Open: The Unanswered JFK Assassination Questions*. New York: Carroll & Graf, 1994.

———. *Never again!: The Government Conspiracy in the JFK Assassination*. New York: Carroll & Graf Publishers, 1995.

Weissman, Steve. *Big Brother and the Holding Company: The World behind Watergate*. Palo Alto, CA: Ramparts Press, 1974.

Wrone, David R. *The Zapruder Film: Reframing JFK's Assassination*. Lawrence: University Press of Kansas, 2003.

Zelizer, Barbie. *Covering the Body: The Kennedy Assassination, the Media and the Shaping of Collective Memory*. Chicago: The University of Chicago Press, 1992.

ELECTRONIC MEDIA

"The Algerian Revolution and the Soviet Bloc Countries." *Wilson Center Digital Archive*. http://digitalarchive.wilsoncenter.org/collection/229/the-algerian-revolution-and-the-communist-bloc.

"Anti-Semites Attempt to Exploit Anti-Government Conspiracy Theories." *ADL.org* archive, April 5, 2010. http://archive.adl.org/nr/exeres/c2bcb515-c582-49d0-b936-9ead0eccdda0,0b1623ca-d5a4-465d-a369-df6e8679cd9e,frameless.html.

"The Assassination of John Kennedy." CNN Live Event/Special, November 23, 2013. LexisNexis Academic.

Associated Press. "Poll: Belief in JFK Conspiracy Slipping Slightly." *USA Today* website, May 11, 2013. http://www.usatoday.com/story/news/nation/2013/05/11/poll-jfk-conspiracy/2152665/.

Chamish, Barry. "A Zionist Looks at *Final Judgment*." *Rense.com*, December 14, 1999. http://www.rense.com/politics5/zionist.htm.

Casey, Sheila. "Confessions of a Conspiracy Theorist." *Dissident Voice*, October 24, 2008. http://dissidentvoice.org/2008/10/confessions-of-a-conspiracy-theorist.

Chomsky, Noam. "American Amnesia: We Forget Our Atrocities Almost as Soon as We Commit Them." *AlterNet*, May 19, 2009. http://www.alternet.org/story/140137/american_amnesia%3A_we_forget_our_atrocities_almost_as_soon_as_we_commit_them.

"College Cancels Controversial JFK Course." *St. Louis Post-Dispatch*, August 22, 1997. LexisNexis Academic.

"Community College Offers Seminar on JFK Assassination Conspiracy Theory." CNBC *Equal Time*, August 22, 1997. LexisNexis Academic.

"Conspiracy Theory; Speaking Out." World News Saturday, ABC, January 12, 2013.

Dankbar, Wim. *JFK Murder Solved* website, accessed November 7, 20114. ttp:jfkmurder-solved.com/film/ferrie.wmv.

"David Lifton, Author, *Best Evidence*, Discusses the Importance of the Newly Released Documents Related to the Assassination of President Kennedy." CBS *This Morning*, June 1, 1999. LexisNexis Academic.

Dickey, Jack. "Interview: Oliver Stone Keeps Rolling." *Time.com*, November 15, 2013. Academic Search Complete.

DiEugenio, Jim. "How Gerald Posner Got Rich and Famous: Or, Bob Loomis and the Anti-Conspiracy Posse." *Citizens for Truth about the Kennedy Assassination* website, accessed March 17, 2014. http://www.ctka.net/posner_jd4.html.

_____. "Noam Chomsky's Sickness unto Death," *Citizens for Truth about the Kennedy Assassination* website, accessed July 17, 2013. http://www.ctka.net/reviews/Chomsky_Sickness_DiEugenio.html.

"Documents Release Show What Happened to JFK's Original Bronze Casket." CBS *Evening News*, June 1, 1999. LexisNexis Academic.

"Examining the Assassination of President Kennedy, 50 Years Later." 48 Hours, CBS, November 16, 2013. LexisNexis Academic.

"Extremism in America: Willis Carto." *The Anti-Defamation League* archive website, 2005. http://archive.adl.org/learn/ext_us/carto.html.

"For November 11, 2013." CBS *This Morning*, November 11, 2013. LexisNexis Academic.

"Government Releases New Information about Events Surrounding the Assassination of President John F. Kennedy." CBS *Morning News*, June 1, 1999. LexisNexis Academic.

"G. Robert Blakey." *Frontline*, PBS, November 19, 2019. http://www.pbs.org/wgbh/pages/frontline/biographies/oswald/interview-g-robert-blakey/#addendum.

Herman, Douglas. "Does Noam Chomsky Matter Any More?" *Rense.com*, May 28, 2008. http://www.rense.com/general82/chom.htm.

"How Geraldo Rivera Changed America (And Why That Is So Hard to Admit)." *JFK-Facts.org*, accessed February 14, 2014. http://jfkfacts.org/assassination/review/how-geraldo-rivera-changed-america-and-why-that-is-so-hard-to-admit/Ibid.

Kelly, Bill. "Journalists and JFK: Real Dizinfo Agent at Dealey Plaza." *JFKcountercoup*, May 24, 2011. http://jfkcountercoup.blogspot.com/2011/05/journalists-and-jfk-re-al-dizinfo-agents.html

"Kennedy Assassination: New Techniques for Analyzing Evidence." *Good Morning America*, ABC, November 20, 2003. LexisNexis Academic.

King, Gary. "Journalists and JFK: How to Succeed in the News Media." *Citizens for the Truth in the Kennedy Assassination*, May 2011. http://www.ctka.net/2011/journal-ist_&_JFK_King.html

"The Kennedy Assassination—Thirty Years Later." *Larry King Live*, CNN, November 22, 1994. LexisNexis Academic.

"Larry Sabato Talks about His Book on the Kennedy Assassination." CBS *This Morning*, October 14, 2013. LexisNexis Academic.

"Lyndon Johnson Expresses Alarm and Disgruntlement Following Kennedy Assassination." CBS Evening News, April 15, 1994. LexisNexis Academic.

McQuigge, Michelle. "Did Canadian-Born Robert MacNeil Meet Lee Harvey Oswald After JFK Shooting?" *Global News.com*, November 21, 2013. http://globalnews.ca/news/981131/did-canadian-born-robert-macneil-meet-lee-harvey-oswald-after-jfk-shooting/

Morley, Jefferson. "Jefferson Morley: What We Still Don't Know about the JFK Assassination." *dallasnews.com*, October 26, 2013. http://www.dallasnews.com/opinion/sunday-commentary/20131025-what-we-still-dont-know-about-jfks-assassination.ece.

_____. "The Kennedy Assassination: 47 Years Later, What Do We Really Know?" *The Atlantic Monthly*, November 22, 2010. http://www.theatlantic.com/national/archive/2010/11/the-kennedy-assassination-47-years-later-what-do-we-really-know/66722/.

_____. "Morley v. CIA: Why I Sued for JFK Assassination Records." *JFKFacts.org*, February 21, 2013. http://jfkfacts.org/assassination/news/morley-v-cia-why-i-sued-for-jfk-assassination-records/.

"Newspaper Quality Rankings." *Journawiki*. Last modified October 25, 2011. http://journalism.wikia.com/wiki/Newspaper_quality_rankings.

"1994 Winners and Finalists." *The Pulitzer Prizes* website, accessed March 17, 2013. http://www.pulitzer.org/awards/1994.

Ontheeearthproduction. "Noam Chomsky Talks about the CIA and Other Topics." *YouTube* video, 12:32, uploaded April 13, 2009. http://www.youtube.com/watch?v=IX-cL5o55q8s.

O'Sullivan, Ariah. "Vanunu—Israel Was Behind JFK Assassination." *Rense.com*, July 25, 2004. http://www.rense.com/general54/jfk.htm.

"Re-Enactment of Shooting of President Kennedy." *NBC Nightly News*, NBC, November 13, 2008. LexisNexis Academic.

"Remembering the Kennedy Assassination." *Today Show*, NBC, November 22, 2013. LexisNexis Academic.

"Secretary John Kerry Doubts Kennedy's Assassination Is Solved." *Anderson Cooper 360 Degrees*, CNN· November 8, 2013. LexisNexis Academic.

Shenon, Philip. "Yes, the CIA Director Was Part of the JFK Assassination Cover-Up." *Politico*, October 6, 2015.

"A Special on the Assassination of John F. Kennedy." CBS *Face the Nation*, November 17, 2013. LexisNexis Academic.

"Special Report." ABC *News*, November 20, 2003. LexisNexis Academic.

"Talking About a New Book on the Kennedy Assassination." CBS *This Morning*, October 25, 2013. LexisNexis Academic.

Shea, Danny. "Gerald Posner RESIGNS From *Daily Beast* over Plagiarism Scandal." *The Huffington Post*, April 13, 2010. http://www.huffingtonpost.com/2010/02/11/gerald-posner-resigns-fro_n_458169.html.

Sickles, Jason. "James Teague, Key JFK Assassination Witness, Dies." *Yahoo News*, March 1, 2014. http://news.yahoo.com/james-tague-key-jfk-assassination-witness-dies-175758762.html.

"Who Shot President Kennedy?" *Nova*, PBS, November 15, 1988. http://dvp-potpourri.blogspot.com/2010/02/who-shot-president-kennedy.html.

Oral Histories

Fetzer, James H. Interview by author. April 2, 2014.

Horne, Douglas P. Interview by author. April 6, 2014.

Janney, Peter. Interview by author. April 4, 2014.

Morley, Jefferson. Interview by author. April 1, 2014.

Millegan, Kris. Interview by author. May 23, 2014.

Scott, Peter Dale. Interview by author. April 19, 2014.

Steele, David. Interview by author. April 8, 2014.

Appendix A

Library of Congress Book Selection

The selection of books began with a simple search on the main page of the Library of Congress website (www.loc.govhttp://catalog.loc.gov/) using the following delimiters:

Search keywords "John F. Kennedy Assassination"

Check "All Items"

Format: Books. Site: Catalog. Language: English.

Years 1988 to 2013

The selection of books was further refined by the use of the following rules to assure quality and comparability:

No ebooks

No self-published books

No contract books

No reference books or guides

Must be aimed at a national market for non-juveniles

Must be non-fiction and non-humorous

Must be primarily about the JFK assassination or someone key to the JFK assassination

Must be published in U.S.

Must be earliest edition of printed book

The lists below include all relevant books found in the Library of Congress catalogue from 1988 to 2013, per the selection rules cited above.

The books were categorized as **pro-Warren**, **anti-Warren** or **Mixed** after either a full reading (those marked with an asterisk) or a reading of some or all of the following: summaries on WorldCat and/or Amazon.com websites, online and/or newspaper reviews, and the introduction and/or selected excerpts from the book.

Finally, each **author's status** was categorized under the following sets of credentials:

1=Witness or Official Investigator

2=Academic Historian (with Ph.D.)

3=Academic Other (with Ph.D., M.D. and/or J.D.)

4=Journalist*

5=Lawyer

6=Independent Researcher

*Must be employed by a media organization at time of publication.

ANTI-WARREN BOOKS: Authors criticize the methods and findings of the Warren Commission and argue against a lone gunman theory.

Adams, Don. *From an Office Building with a High-Powered Rifle: A Report to the Public from an FBI Agent Involved in the Official JFK Assassination Investigation.* Walterville, OR: TrineDay, 2012. Author Status: 1

Albarelli, H. P. *A Secret Order: Investigating the High Strangeness and Synchronicity in the JFK Assassination.* Walterville, OR: Trine Day, 2013. Author Status: 6

Baker, Judyth Vary, Edward T. Haslam, and Jim Marrs. *Me & Lee: How I Came to Know, Love and Lose Lee Harvey Oswald.* Walterville, OR: Trine Day, 2010. Author Status: 1

Belzer, Richard and David Wayne. *Hit List: An In-Depth Investigation into the Mysterious Deaths of Witnesses to the JFK Assassination.* New York: Skyhorse Publishing, 2013.* Author Status: 6

Canal, John A. *Silencing the Lone Assassin.* St. Paul, MN: Paragon House, 2000. Author Status: 6

Chambers, G. Paul. *Head Shot: The Science behind the JFK Assassination.* Amherst, NY: Prometheus Books, 2010. Author Status: 2

Craig, John R., and Philip A. Rogers. *The Man on the Grassy Knoll: Did the CIA Hire a Psychopath to Assassinate JFK?* New York: Avon Books, 1992. Author Status: 1

Crenshaw, Charles A. *JFK: Conspiracy of Silence.* New York: Signet, 1992. Author Status: 1

Crenshaw, Charles A. *Trauma Room One: The JFK Medical Cover-Up Exposed.* New York: Paraview Press, 2001.* Author Status: 1

Cornwell, Gary. *Real Answers: The True Story.* Spicewood, TX: Paleface Press, 1998.* Author Status: 1

Davis, John H. *The Kennedy Contract: The Mafia Plot to Assassinate the President.* New York, N.Y.: HarperPaperbacks, 1993. Author Status: 6

Davis, John H. *Mafia Kingfish: Carlos Marcello and the Assassination of John F. Kennedy.* New York: McGraw-Hill, 1989.* Author Status: 6

DiEugenio, James. *Destiny Betrayed: JFK, Cuba, and the Garrison Case.* New York: Sheridan Square Press, 1992. Author Status: 6

Douglass, James W. *JFK and the Unspeakable: Why He Died and Why It Matters.* New York: Simon & Schuster, 2010. Author Status: 3

Elliott, Todd C. *A Rose by Many Other Names: Rose Cheramie & the JFK Assassination.* Walterville, OR: TrineDay, 2013.* Author Status: 4

Ernest, Barry. *The Girl on the Stairs: The Search for a Missing Witness to the JFK Assassination*. Gretna, LA: Pelican Publishing Company, 2013.* Author Status: 6

Fetzer, James H., ed. *Assassination Science: Experts Speak Out on the Death of JFK*. Chicago: Catfeet Press, 1998.* Author Status: 3

Fetzer, James H. *The Great Zapruder Film Hoax: Deceit and Deception in the Death of JFK*. Chicago: Catfeet Press, 2003. Author Status: 3

Fetzer, James H. *Murder in Dealey Plaza: What We Know Now that We Didn't Know Then about the Death of JFK*. Chicago: Catfeet Press, 2000. Author Status: 3

Fonzi, Gaeton. *The Last Investigation*. New York: Thunder's Mouth Press, 1993. Author Status: 1

Garrison, Jim. *On The Trail of the Assassins: My Investigation and Prosecution of the Murder of President Kennedy*. New York: Sheridan Square Press, 1988. Author Status: 1

Giancana, Antoinette, John R. Hughes and Thomas H. Jobe. *JFK and Sam: The Connection between the Giancana and Kennedy Assassinations*. Nashville, TN: Cumberland House, 2005. Author Status: 1

Groden, Robert J., and Harrison Edward Livingstone. *High Treason: The Assassination of President John F. Kennedy: What Really Happened?* New York: Conservatory Press, 1989.* Author Status: 1

Groden, Robert J. *The Killing of a President: The Complete Photographic Record of the JFK Assassination, the Conspiracy and the Cover-Up*. New York: Viking Studio Books, 1993. Author Status: 1

Hosty, James P. *Assignment: Oswald*. New York: Arcade Publishing, 1996. Author Status: 1

Hepburn, James. *Farewell, America: The Plot to Kill JFK*. Roseville, CA: Penmarin Books, 2002.* Author Status: 6

Heiner, Kent. *Without a Smoking Gun: Was the Death of Lt. Cmdr. William B. Pitzer Part of the JFK Assassination Cover-Up Conspiracy?* Walterville, OR; TrineDay, 2004. Author Status: 6

Janney, Peter. *Mary's Mosaic: The CIA Conspiracy to Murder John F. Kennedy, Mary Pinchot Meyer, and Their Vision for World Peace*. New York: Skyhorse Publishing, 2012.* Author Status: 6

Kaiser, David. *The Road to Dallas: The Assassination of John F. Kennedy*. Cambridge, MA: Belknap Press, 2008.* Author Status: 2

La Fontaine, Ray and Mary. *Oswald Talked: The New Evidence in the JFK Assassination*. Gretna, LA: Pelican Publications, 1996. Author Status: 3

Lane, Mark. *Plausible Denial: Was the CIA Involved in the Assassination of JFK?* New York: Thunder's Mouth Press, 1991.* Author Status: 5

Livingstone, Harrison. *High Treason 2: The Assassination of JFK and the Case for Conspiracy*. New York: Carroll and Graf Publishers, 1992. Author Status: 6

Livingstone, Harrison Edward. *Killing the Truth: Deceit and Deception in the JFK Case*. New York: Carroll & Graf Publishers, 1993. Author Status: 6

183

Livingstone, Harrison E. *Killing Kennedy and the Hoax of the Century*. New York: Carroll & Graf, 1995. Author Status: 6

Marrs, Jim. *Crossfire: The Plot That Killed Kennedy*. New York: Carroll and Graf Publishers, 1989.* Author Status: 6

McClellan, Barr. *Blood, Money and Power: How LBJ Killed JFK*. New York: Hannover House, 2003. Author Status: 6

McKnight, Gerald D. *Breach Of Trust: How the Warren Commission Failed the Nation and Why*. Lawrence: University Press of Kansas, 2005.* Author Status: 2

Melanson, Dr. Phillip. *Spy Saga: Lee Harvey Oswald and U.S. Intelligence*. New York: Praeger, 1990. Author Status: 3

Mellen, Joan. *Jim Garrison: His Life and Times, the Early Years*. Southlake, TX: JFK Lancer Productions and Publications, 2005. Author Status: 3

Menninger, Bonar. *Mortal Error: The Shot That Killed JFK*. New York: St. Martin's Press, 1992. Author Status: 6

Nelson, Phillip F. *LBJ: The Mastermind of the JFK Assassination*. New York: Skyhorse Pub., 2011. Author Status: 6

Newman, John. *Oswald and the CIA: The Documented Truth about the Unknown Relationship between the U.S. Government and the Alleged Killer of JFK*. New York: Skyhorse Publishing, 1995.* Author Status: 6

Nolan, Patrick. *CIA Rogues and the Killing of the Kennedys: How and Why U.S. Agents Conspired to Kill JFK and RFK*. New York: Skyhorse Publishing, 2013. Author Status: 6

North, Mark. *Act of Treason: The Role of J. Edgar Hoover in the Assassination of President Kennedy*. New York: Carroll and Graf Publishers, 1991. Author Status: 6

Oglesby, Carl. *The JFK Assassination: The Facts and the Theories*. New York: Signet Books, 1992. Author Status: 6

Oglesby, Carl. *Who Killed JFK?* Berkeley, CA: Odonian Press, 1992. Author Status: 6

O'Leary, Bradley S. and L. E. Seymour. *Triangle of Death: The Shocking Truth about the Role of South Vietnam and the French Mafia in the Assassination of JFK*. Nashville, TN: WND Books, 2003.* Author Status: 6

Piper, Michael Collins. *Final Judgment: The Missing Link in the JFK Assassination Conspiracy*. Washington, D.C.: Wolfe Press, 1993.* Author Status: 6

Prouty, L. Fletcher. *JFK: The CIA, Vietnam, and the Plot to Assassinate John F. Kennedy*. New York: Skyhorse Publishing, 1996.* Author Status: 6

Russell, Dick. *The Man Who Knew Too Much*. New York: Carroll & Graf Publishers, 1992. Author Status: 6

Russell, Dick. *On The Trail of the JFK Assassins: A Groundbreaking Look at America's Most Infamous Conspiracy*. New York: Skyhorse Publishing, 2008. Author Status: 6

Scheim, David E. *Contract on America: The Mafia Murder of President John F. Kennedy*. New York: Shapolsky Publishers, 1988.* Author Status: 6

Scott, Peter Dale. *Deep Politics and the Death of JFK.* Berkeley: University of California Press, 1993.* Author Status: 3

Shaw, Mark. *The Poison Patriarch: How the Betrayals of Joseph P. Kennedy Caused the Assassination of JFK.* New York: Skyhorse Publishing, 2013. Author Status: 6

Sloan, Bill with Jean Hill. *JFK: The Last Dissenting Witness.* Gretna, LA: Pelican Publications, 1992. Author Status: 1

Stone, Roger J. *The Man Who Killed Kennedy: The Case against LBJ.* New York: Skyhorse Publishing, 2013. Author Status: 6

Talbot, David. *Brothers: The Hidden History of the Kennedy Years.* Glencoe, IL: Free Press, 2007.* Author Status: 4

Ventura, Jesse. *They Killed our President: 63 Reasons to Believe There Was a Conspiracy to Assassinate JFK.* New York: Skyhorse Publishing, 2013. Author Status: 6

Waldron, Lamar. *The Hidden History of the JFK Assassination.* Berkeley, CA: Counterpoint Press, 2013. Author Status: 6

Waldron, Lamar, and Thom Hartmann. *Legacy of Secrecy: The Long Shadow of the JFK Assassination.* Berkeley, CA: Counterpoint Press, 2009. Author Status: 6

Waldron, Lamar with Thom Hartmann. *Ultimate Sacrifice: John and Robert Kennedy, the Plan for a Coup in Cuba, and the Murder of JFK.* New York: Carroll and Graf Publishers, 2005. Author Status: 6

Wecht, Cyril H., Mark Curridan and Wecht, Benjamin. *Cause of Death.* New York: E. P. Dutton, 1993. Author Status: 3

Weisberg, Harold. *Case Open: The Unanswered JFK Assassination Questions.* New York: Carroll & Graf, 1994. Author Status: 6

Weisberg, Harold. *Never Again!: The Government Conspiracy in the JFK Assassination.* New York: Carroll & Graf Publishers, 1993. Author Status: 6

Wrone, David R. *The Zapruder Film: Reframing JFK's Assassination.* Lawrence: University Press of Kansas, 1993. Author Status: 2

PRO-WARREN BOOKS: Authors may criticize aspects of the Warren Report but support its chief finding that Lee Harvey Oswald acted alone in killing JFK.

Belin, David W. *Final Disclosure: The Full Truth about the Assassination of President Kennedy.* New York: Scribner's, 1988. Author Status: 1

Bugliosi, Vincent. *Parkland.* New York: W.W. Norton & Company, 2013.* Author Status: 5

Bugliosi, Vincent. *Reclaiming History: The Assassination of John F. Kennedy.* New York: W.W. Norton & Company, 2007. Author Status: 5

Fuhrman, Mark. *A Simple Act of Murder: November 22, 1963.* New York: William Morrow, 2006. Author Status: 6

Holland, Max. *The Kennedy Assassination Tapes.* New York: Alfred A. Knopf, 2004. Author Status: 2

Lambert, Patricia. *False Witness: The Real Story of Jim Garrison's Investigation and Oliver Stone's Film JFK.* New York: M. Evans, 1998. Author Status: 6

Latell, Brian. *Castro's Secrets: The CIA and Cuba's Intelligence Machine.* New York: Palgrave Macmillan, 2012. Author Status: 6

Mailer, Norman. *Oswald's Tale: An American Mystery.* New York: Random House. 1995. Author Status: 6

Mallon, Thomas. *Mrs. Paine's Garage and the Murder of John F. Kennedy.* New York: Pantheon Books, 2002. Author Status: 6

McAdams, John. *JFK Assassination Logic: How to Think about Claims of Conspiracy.* Washington, D.C.: Potomac Books, 2011.* Author Status: 3

Nechiporenko, Oleg. *Passport to Assassination: The Never-before-Told Story of Lee Harvey Oswald by the KGB Colonel Who Knew Him.* New York: Carol Publishing Group, 1993. Author Status: 6

O'Reilly, Bill. *Kennedy's Last Days: The Assassination that Defined a Generation.* New York: Henry Holt and Company, 2013. Author Status: 4

Posner, Gerald. *Case Closed: Lee Harvey Oswald and the Assassination of JFK.* New York: Anchor Books, 2003.* Author Status: 5

Russo, Gus, and Stephen Molton. *Brothers in Arms: The Kennedys, the Castros, and the Politics of Murder.* New York: Bloomsbury USA, 2008. Author Status: 6

Russo, Gus. *Live by the Sword: The Secret War against Castro and the Death of JFK.* Baltimore: Bancroft Press, 1998. Author Status: 6

Specter, Arlen, and Charles Robbins. *Passion for Truth: From Finding JFK's Single Bullet to Questioning Anita Hill to Impeaching Clinton.* New York: HarperCollinsPub, 2000. Author Status: 1

Swanson, James L. *End of Days: The Assassination of John F. Kennedy.* New York: William Morrow, 2013. Author Status: 5

Willens, Howard P. *History Will Prove Us Right: Inside the Warren Commission Report on the Assassination of John F. Kennedy.* New York: The Overlook Press, 2013. Author Status: 1

MIXED TOWARD WARREN: Authors criticize the methods and findings of the Warren Report but argue there is not enough evidence to develop a conspiracy theory.

Kurtz, Michael L. *The JFK Assassination Debates: Lone Gunman versus Conspiracy.* Lawrence: University Press of Kansas, 2006.* Author Status: 2

Johnson, Scott Patrick. *The Faces of Lee Harvey Oswald: The Evolution of an Alleged Assassin.* Lanham: Lexington Books, 2013. Author Status: 3

Sabato, Larry J. *The Kennedy Half-Century: The Presidency, Assassination, and Lasting Legacy of John F. Kennedy.* New York: Bloomsbury USA, 2013.* Author Status: 2

Shenon, Philip. *A Cruel and Shocking Act: The Secret History of the Kennedy Assassination.* New York: Henry Holt and Company, 2013. Author Status: 4

Author Status

Author Status	Books Published	Books Reviewed	Percent Books Reviewed	Percent of Reviews Positive*
1	16	4	25 %	(1 of 4) 25 %
2	7	3	43 %	(1 of 3) 33 %
3	11	2	18 %	(0 of 2) 0 %
4	4	1	25 %	(0 of 1) 0 %
5	5	3	60 %	(6 of 6) 100 %
6	44	8	18 %	(2 of 10) 20 %

1=Witness or Official Investigator; 2=Academic Historian (with Ph.D.); 3=Academic Other (with Ph.D., M.D. or J.D.); 4=Staff Journalist; 5=Lawyer; 6=Independent Researcher

*Some books received more than one review. See "Coding Results" that follow.

U.S. Book Reviews

CODING SHEET

Book Title: _____
Author: _____
Publisher: _____

Review appeared in: New York Times=1, Washington Post=2 _____
Name(s) of reviewer(s): _____
Date (MM/DD/YEAR): _____
Page and/or Section: _____
Headline: _____
Length (in Words): _____
Type of Review: Single Book=1, Multiple Books=2, Brief=3 _____
<u>How did the reviewer react to the following aspects of the book?</u>

<u>Quality of Research:</u> Positive=1, Negative=2, Mixed=3, Neutral or NA=4 _____
<u>Quality of Reasoning</u>: Positive=1, Negative=2, Mixed=3, Neutral or NA=4 _____
<u>Writing/Organization:</u>   Positive=1, Negative=2, Mixed=3, Neutral or NA=4 _____

<u>Author's Character/Motivations:</u>
Positive=1, Negative=2, Mixed=3, Neutral or NA=4 _____

<u>Based on your previous findings, what was the reviewer's OVERALL reaction to the book?</u>
Choose One. Positive=1, Negative=2 _____

Coders
Coders were three white, college-educated, Midwestern males, author included, in their 50s and 60s.

Coding Results

Author (Status) Reviewer	Headline	Paper	Date	Stance	Research	Reasoning	Writing	Overall
David W. Belin (1) Ronnie Dugger	Final Disclosure	NYT	19890129	PW	2	2	4	2
Vincent Bugliosi (5) Bryan Burrough	Or Not?	NYT	20070520	PW	4	1	3	1
Vincent Bugliosi (5) Alan Wolfe	Goodbye, Grassy Knoll	WP	20070527	PW	1	1	3	1
Max Holland (2) Thomas Mallon	The 11/22 Commission	NYT	20041031	PW	1	1	1	1
Norma Mailer (6) M. Kakutani	Oswald and Mailer	NYT	19950425	PW	2	2	2	2
Norma Mailer (6) Thomas Powers	The Mind of the Assassin	NYT	19950430	PW	1	1	1	1
Thomas Mallon (6) Sara Mosle	Russian Lessons	NYT	20020203	PW	2	2	3	2
Bill O'Reilly (4) Janet Maslin	Unabashed in the Face of Tragedy	NYT	20121011	PW	3	1	2	2
Gerald Posner (5) Jeffrey A. Frank	Who Shot JFK?	WP	19931031	PW	3	3	1	1
Gerald Posner (5) Lehmann-Haupt	Kennedy Assassination Answers	NYT	19930909	PW	1	1	4	1
Gerald Posner (5) Geoffrey Ward	The Most Durable Assassination Theory	NYT	19931121	PW	1	1	1	1
Gus Russo (6) Tim Naftali	A Complex Journey to the Grassy Knoll	WP	20090115	PW	2	2	4	2
Gus Russo (6) Charles Salzberg	Review in Brief	NYT	19990523	PW	1	1	1	1

Author (Status) Reviewer	Headline	Paper	Date	Stance	Research	Reasoning	Writing	Overall
Arlen Specter (1) Allen D. Boyer	Books in Brief: Non-Fiction	NYT	20010114	PW	1	4	2	1
Sums	Total Reviews PW=14							Positive=9 Negative=5
John H. Davis (6) Ronnie Dugger	Reverberations of Dallas	NYT	19890129	AW	2	4	4	2
Gaeton Fonzi (1) Jeffrey A. Frank	Who Shot JFK?	WP	19931031	AW	2	3	2	2
Jim Garrison (1) Ronnie Dugger	Reverberations of Dallas	NYT	19890129	AW	3	4	4	2
David Kaiser (2) Tim Naftali	A Complex Journey to the Grassy Knoll	WP	20090115	AW	2	2	4	2
Mark Lane (5) Rory Quirk	Conspiracies	WP	19911215	AW	3	1	3	1
Jim Marrs (6) Deborah Price	A Complete Catalog	WP	19891024	AW	3	2	1	2
Joan Mellen (3) Jefferson Morley	A Farewell to Justice	WP	20051224	AW	2	3	4	2
Bonar Menninger (6) David Streitfeld	The Accidental Assassination?	WP	19920327	AW	2	4	4	2
Mark North (6) A.G. Theoharis	Conspiracies	WP	19911215	AW	2	2	4	2
Peter Dale Scott (3) Jeffrey A. Frank	Who Shot JFK?	WP	19931031	AW	1	2	1	2
David Talbot (4) Alan Brinkley	Conspiracy	NYT	19930520	AW	3	3	4	2
David Talbot (4) Matthew Dallek	Beyond the Grassy Knoll	WP	19930617	AW	3	3	2	2
Lamar Waldron (6) Jefferson Morley	Conspiracy Theories	WP	19931127	AW	1	2	4	2

Author (Status) Reviewer	Headline	Paper	Date	Stance	Research	Reasoning	Writing	Overall
Sums	Total Reviews AW=13							Positive=1 Negative=12
Larry J. Sabato (2) David Greenberg	Every President Wants that JFK Magic	WP	20131027	Mixed	3	4	2	2
Sums	Total Reviews Mixed=1							Positive=0 Negative=1

Intercoder Results
Positive Overall Review=1; Negative Overall Review=2

Author/Reviewer	Coder J	Coder F	Coder L
Belin/Dugger	2	2	2
Bugliosi/Burrough	1	1	1
Bugliosi/Wolfe	1	1	1
Holland/Mallon	1	1	1
Mailer/Kakutani	2	2	2
Mailer/T. Powers	1	1	1
Mallon/Mosle	2	2	2
O'Reilly/Maslin	2	2	2
Posner/Frank	1	1	2
Posner/LH	1	1	1
Posner/Ward	1	1	1
Russo Brothers/Naftali	2	2	2
Russo Live/Salzberg	1	1	1
Specter/Boyer	1	1	1
Davis/Dugger	2	2	2
Fonzi/Frank	2	1	2
Garrison/Dugger	2	1	2
Kaiser/Naftali	2	2	2
Lane/Quirk	1	1	1
Marrs/Price	2	1	2
Mellen/Morley	2	1	2

Menninger/Streitfeld	2	2	2
North/Theoharis	2	2	2
Scott/Frank	2	2	2
Talbot/Brinkley	2	2	2
Talbot/Dallek	2	2	2
Waldron/Morley	2	2	2
Sabato/Greenberg	2	1	2

Intercoder Reliability Scores

ReCal 0.1 Alpha for 3+ Coders results for file "ReCalc CSV.csv"

File size:	196 bytes
N coders:	3
N cases:	28
N decisions:	84

Average Pairwise Percent Agreement

Average pairwise percent agr.	Pairwise pct. agr. cols 1 & 3	Pairwise pct. agr. cols 1 & 2	Pairwise pct. agr. cols 2 & 3
85.714%	96.429%	82.143%	78.571%

Fleiss' Kappa

Fleiss' Kappa	Observed Agreement	Expected Agreement
0.704	0.857	0.518

Average Pairwise Cohen's Kappa

Average pairwise CK	Pairwise CK cols 1 & 3	Pairwise CK cols 1 & 2	Pairwise CK cols 2 & 3
0.718	0.92	0.65	0.582

Krippendorff's Alpha (nominal)

Krippendorff's Alpha	N Decisions	$\Sigma_c o_{cc}$***	$\Sigma_c n_c (n_c - 1)$***
0.707	84	72	3572

***These figures are drawn from Krippendorff (2007, case C.)

Appendix C

Publisher Analysis

In the charts below, publishers of JFK assassination books have been grouped by the book's Warren Report stance and listed in ascending order of their number of annual titles, unless data was not available. The mean of annual titles was calculated for each category of Anti-Warren, Pro-Warren, and Mixed stance books.

Data for annual titles were drawn from the Literary Market Place catalog for each book's publication year or by direct contact with the publisher.

ANTI-WARREN BOOKS					
Author	Title	Year	City	Publisher	Annual Titles
James DiEugenio	Destiny Betrayed	1992	New York	Sheridan Square Press	1
Carl Oglesby	Who Killed JFK?	1992	Berkeley, CA	Odonian Press	3
James Hepburn	Farewell, America	2002	Roseville, CA	Penmarin Books	6
Don Adams	From an Office Building with a High-Powered Rifle	2012	Waterville, OR	Trine Day	8
H.P. Albarelli	A Secret Order	2013	Waterville, OR	Trine Day	8
Judyth Vary Baker	Me & Lee	2010	Waterville, OR	Trine Day	8
Todd C. Elliott	A Rose by Many Other Names	2013	Waterville, OR	Trine Day	8
Kent Heiner	Without a Smoking Gun	2004	Waterville, OR	Trine Day	8
David Talbot	Brothers	2007	Glencoe, Ill.	Free Press	9
Mark Lane	Plausible Denial	1991	New York	Thunder's Mouth Press	11

David E. Scheim	Contract on America	1988	New York	Shapolsky	20
Gaeton Fonzi	The Last Investigation	1993	New York	Thunder's Mouth Press	24
James H. Fetzer, ed.	Asassination Science	1998	Chicago	Catfeet Press	31
Bill Sloan	JFK: The Last Dissenting Witness	1992	Gretna, LA	Pelican Publishing	51
Gerald D. McKnight	Breach of Trust	2005	Lawrence	Univ. Press of Kansas	55
David Wrone	The Zapruder Film	2003	Lawrence	Univ. Press of Kansas	55
Mark North	Act of Treason	1991	New York	Carroll and Graf	56
Ray and Mary LaFontaine	Oswald Talked	1996	Gretna, LA	Pelican Publishing	65
Barry Ernest	The Girl on the Stairs	2013	Gretna, LA	Pelican Publishing	70
Jim Marrs	Crossfire	1989	New York	Carroll and Graf	85
G. Paul Chambers	Head Shot	2010	New York	Prometheus Books	120
Harrison Livingstone	High Treason 2	1992	New York	Carroll and Graf	120
Dick Russell	The Man Who Knew Too Much	1992	New York	Carroll and Graf	120
Lamar Waldron	Ultimate Sacrifice	2005	New York	Carroll and Graf	120
James Douglass	JFK and the Unspeakable	2010	New York	Simon & Schuster	125
David Kaiser	The Road to Dallas	2008	Cambridge, MA	Belknap Press	130
Harrison Livingstone	Killing Kennedy and the Hoax of the Century	1995	New York	Carroll and Graf	130
Harold Weisberg	Case Open	1994	New York	Carroll and Graf	130
Harold Weisberg	Never Again!	1995	New York	Carroll and Graf	130
Harrison Livingstone	Killing the Truth	1993	New York	Carroll and Graf	150
Carl Oglesby	The JFK Assassination: Facts and Theories	1992	New York	Signet	220

Author	Title	Year	City	Publisher	Pages
Antoinette Giancana	JFK and Sam	2005	Nashville, TN	Cumberland House	240
Peter Dale Scott	Deep Politics and the Death of JFK	1993	Berkeley, CA	Univ. of California Press	260
Robert J. Groden	The Killing of a President	1993	New York	Viking Studio Books	290
James H. Fetzer	Murder in Dealey Plaza	2000	Chicago	Catfeet Press	300
Dr. Phillip Melanson	Spy Saga	1990	New York	Praeger	300
John R. Craig	The Man on the Grassy Knoll	1992	New York	Avon Books	381
John H. Davis	The Kennedy Contract	1993	New York	HarperPaperbacks	388
John A Canal	Silencing the Lone Assassin	2000	St. Paul, MN	Paragon House	400
Phillip F. Nelson	LBJ: The Mastermind of the JFK Assassination	2011	New York	Skyhorse	400
Cyril H. Wecht	Cause of Death	1993	New York	E.P. Dutton	617
Bonar Menninger	Mortal Error	1992	New York	St. Martin's Press	1300
Mean of AW Titles					**166**
Richard Belzer	Hit List	2013	New York	Skyhorse	NA
Charles A. Crenshaw	Trauma Room one	2001	New York	Paraview Press	NA
Gary Cornwell	Real Answers	1998	Spicewood, TX	Paleface Press	NA
John H. Davis	Mafia Kingfish	1989	New York	McGraw-Hill	NA
James H. Fetzer	The Great Zapruder Film Hoax	2003	Chicago	Catfeet Press	NA
Jim Garrison	On the Trail of the Assassins	1988	New York	Sheridan Square Press	NA
Robert J. Groden	High Treason	1989	New York	Conservatory Press	NA
James P. Hosty	Assignment: Oswald	1996	New York	Arcade Publications	NA
Peter Janney	Mary's Mosaic	2012	New York	Skyhorse	NA

Barr McClellan	Blood, Money and Power	2003	New York	Hannover House	NA
Joan Mellen	Jim Garrison	2005	Southlake, TX	JFK Lancer	NA
John Newman	Oswald and the CIA	1995	New York	Skyhorse	NA
Patrick Nolan	CIA Roguesa and the Killing of the Kennedys	2013	New York	Skyhorse	NA
Bradley S. O'Leary	Triangle of Death	2003	Nashville, TN	WND Books	NA
Michael Collins Piper	Final Judgment	1993	Washington, DC	Wolfe Press	NA
L. Fletcher Prouty	JFK: The CIA, Vietnam and the Plot to	1996	New York	Skyhorse	NA
Dick Russell	On the Trail of the Assassins	2008	New York	Skyhorse	NA
Mark Shaw	The Poison Patriarch	2013	New York	Skyhorse	NA
Roger J. Stone	The Man Who Killed Kennedy	2013	New York	Skyhorse	NA
Jesse Ventura	They Killed Our President	2013	New York	Skyhorse	NA

PRO-WARREN BOOKS

Gus Russo	Live by the Sword	1998	Baltimore	Bancroft Press	6
Patricia Lambert	False Witness	1998	New York	M. Evans	25
John McAdams	JFK Assassination Logic	2011	Washington, D.C.	Potomac Books	80
Howard P. Willens	History Will Prove Us Right	2013	New York	The Overlook Press	90
Bill O'Reilly	Kennedy's Last Days	2013	New York	Henry Holt and Co.	100
Gus Russo	Brothers in Arms	2008	New York	Bloomsbury	100

Oleg Nechiporenko	Passport to Assassination	1993	New York	Carol Publishing Group	160
Vincent Bugliosi	Parkland	2013	New York	W.W. Norton and Co.	400
Vincent Bugliosi	Reclaiming History	2007	New York	W.W. Norton and Co.	400
David W. Belin	Final Disclosure	1988	New York	Scribner's (MacMillan)	600
Mark Fuhrman	A Simple Act of Murder	2006	New York	William Morrow (Harper-Collins)	1700
Arlen Specter	Passion for Truth	2000	New York	Harper-Collins	1700
James Swanson	End of Days	2013	New York	William Morrow (Harper-Collins)	1700
Max Holland	The Kennedy Assassination Tapes	2004	New York	Alfred A. Knopf (Random House)	3152
Brian Latell	Castro's Secrets	2012	New York	Palgrave Macmillan	3200
Norman Mailer	Oswald's Tale	1995	New York	Random House	3444
MEAN OF PW TITLES					**1054**
Thomas Mallon	Mrs. Paine's Garage	2002	New York	Pantheon Books (Random House)	NA
Gerald Posner	Case Closed	1993	New York	Random House	NA
MIXED BOOKS					
Michael L. Kurtz	The JFK Assassination Debates	2006	Lawrence	Univ. Press of Kansas	55
Scott Patrick Johnson	The Faces of Lee Harvey Oswald	2013	Lanham	Lexington Books	400
Larry J. Sabato	The Kennedy Half-Century	2013	New York	Blooms-bury	100

Philip Shenon	A Cruel and Shocking Act	2013	New York	Henry Holt and Co.	100
Mean of Mixed					164

Appendix D

News Magazine Analysis

News Magazine	Date	Headline	Author	Slant
Newsweek	19881128	The Kennedy Conundrum	David Gates	PW
Newsweek	19911223	Twisted History	K. Auchincloss	PW
Time	20131125	Broken Trust	David Von Drehle	Neutral
Time	20070702	The Assassination: Was It a Conspiracy? Yes	David Talbot	AW
Time	20131125	Debunker Among the Buffs	Jack Dickey	PW
Time	20070702	The Assassination: Was It a Conspiracy? No	Vincent Bugliosi	PW
Time.com	20131115	Interview: Oliver Stone Keeps Rolling	Jack Dickey	AW
U.S. News	19930830	The Man With the Deadly Smirk	Gerald Parshall	PW
U.S. News	20070611	The Final Verdict	Alex Kingsbury	PW

Appendix E

TV News Analysis

Network	Date	Show Type	PW Sources	AW	Mixed	Neutral	PW Reporters	Mantra
ABC	19920122	Talk	2	5	1			
ABC	19920519	News	2				1	
ABC	19930617	News		2				
ABC	19930823	Book	1					
ABC	19931121	News	1				1	1
ABC	19940503	News	1					
ABC	19981123	News			1			
ABC	20031120	Special	22	1			1	4
ABC	20031120	News	4				2	
ABC	20040803	News	1					
ABC	20130112	News	1	1				
ABC	20130113	News	1	2				
ABC	20131119	Talk	3	2				1
ABC	20131119	News	3	2			2	
ABC	20131122	Talk		2				
CBS	19900806	News		1				
CBS	19911213	News	3	2			1	
CBS	19920205	News	1					
CBS	19920205	Special	1	4				
CBS	19920519	News	1	1				
CBS	19920520	News	2					
CBS	19920521	News	2	1				
CBS	19920521	News	1					
CBS	19930117	News		2				
CBS	19930823	News	1	1				
CBS	19930824	News		2				

CBS	19931118	News	2					
CBS	19960529	News	1					
CBS	19960529	News	1				1	
CBS	19960626	News		1				
CBS	19971008	News	2	2				
CBS	19990601	News		1				
CBS	19990601	News						
CBS	20031121	News	2	1			1	
CBS	20060512	Book			1			
CBS	20120131	News	1			1		1
CBS	20131011	News	1				1	
CBS	20131014	Book		1				
CBS	20131025	Book	1				1	
CBS	20131027	Book	2				1	
CBS	20131028	Book	1					
CBS	20131108	News	1					
CBS	20131111	News	1					1
CBS	20131116	News	1				1	1
CBS	20131116	Special	3				1	1
CBS	20131117	Talk	4				1	1
CBS	20131117	Special	4	1			1	2
CBS	20131122	News	1					1
CNBC	19970822	Talk	3					
CNBC	19990803	Special	3	1	1		1	
CNBC	20010203	Book	1					
CNN	19911120	Talk		1				
CNN	19920116	Talk	1	1				
CNN	19920406	Talk	1	2				
CNN	19920428	News		3				
CNN	19920519	News			1			
CNN	19920519	News	2	1				
CNN	19921126	Talk		1		1		
CNN	19930823	News		3				
CNN	19930830	Book	1	1				
CNN	19931122	Talk	1	1				
CNN	19940415	News	1	2				

Network	Date	Type	C1	C2	C3	C4	C5	C6
CNN	19941118	News	1	1				
CNN	20030919	Book		2				
CNN	20031108	News	1	1		1		
CNN	20031120	News	4	1				1
CNN	20070518	News	1	1				1
CNN	20090108	Book	1	1				
CNN	20120204	News	1					
CNN	20131114	Special	14	5				1
CNN	20131115	Book		1				
CNN	20131120	News	2					
CNN	20131120	News	2					
CNN	20131121	News		1				
CNN	20131122	News		1				
CNN	20131122	Special	1					1
CNN	20131122	News	4	4				
CNN	20131122	News	1	2				
CNN	20131122	News	1	1				
CNN	20131123	Special	4					
CNN	20131123	News	1					
FOX	20060512	News		1	1			
FOX	20131122	News	2					
FOX	20131123	Book		1				
NBC	19971006	Book		1				
NBC	19980929	News	2	1				
NBC	19980930	News	1					
NBC	19981120	News			1			
NBC	19990601	News		1				
NBC	20010809	Special	2			1		
NBC	20040804	News	1			2		
NBC	20070517	News	1	1				
NBC	20081113	News	2					
NBC	20081122	News	1					
NBC	20100309	Book		1				
NBC	20130114	News		1				
NBC	20130912	Book			1			
NBC	20131109	News	2					

NBC	20131110	Special		1				
NBC	20131116	News	2					
NBC	20131122	News	2				2	
Sums			154	84	9	7	20	18

Network	Date	Show Type	PW Sources	AW	Mixed	Neutral	PW Reporters	Mantra
ABC	19920122	Talk	2	5	1			
ABC	19920519	News	2				1	
ABC	19930617	News		2				
ABC	19930823	Book	1					
ABC	19931121	News	1				1	1
ABC	19940503	News	1					
ABC	19981123	News			1			
ABC	20031120	Special	22	1			1	4
ABC	20031120	News	4				2	
ABC	20040803	News	1					
ABC	20130112	News	1	1				
ABC	20130113	News	1	2				
ABC	20131119	Talk	3	2				1
ABC	20131122	Talk		2			2	
Sums			39	15	2		7	6

Network	Date	Show Type	PW Sources	AW	Mixed	Neutral	PW Reporters	Mantra
CBS	19900806	News		1				
CBS	19911213	News	3	2			1	
CBS	19920205	News	1					
CBS	19920205	Special	1	4				
CBS	19920519	News	1	1				
CBS	19920520	News	2					
CBS	19920521	News	2	1				
CBS	19920521	News	1					
CBS	19930117	News		2				
CBS	19930823	News	1	1				
CBS	19930824	News		2				

Network	Date	Show Type	PW Sources	AW	Mixed	Neutral	PW Reporters	Mantra
CBS	19931118	News	2					
CBS	19960529	News	1					
CBS	19960529	News	1				1	
CBS	19960626	News		1				
CBS	19971008	News	2	2				
CBS	19990601	News		1				
CBS	19990601	News						
CBS	20031121	News	2	1			1	
CBS	20060512	Book			1			
CBS	20120131	News	1			1		1
CBS	20131011	News					1	
CBS	20131014	Book		1				
CBS	20131025	Book	1				1	
CBS	20131027	Book	2				1	
CBS	20131028	Book	1					
CBS	20131108	News	1					
CBS	20131111	News	1					1
CBS	20131116	News	1				1	1
CBS	20131116	Special	3				1	1
CBS	20131117	Talk	4				1	1
CBS	20131117	Special	4	1			1	2
CBS	20131122	News	1					1
Sums			40	21	1	1	10	8

Network	Date	Show Type	PW Sources	AW	Mixed	Neutral	PW Reporters	Mantra
CNBC	19970822	Talk	3					
CNBC	19990803	Special	3	1	1		1	
CNBC	20010203	Book	1					
Sums			7	1	1		1	

Network	Date	Show Type	PW Sources	AW	Mixed	Neutral	PW Reporters	Mantra
CNN	19911120	Talk		1				
CNN	19920116	Talk	1	1				
CNN	19920406	Talk	1	2				
CNN	19920428	News		3				
CNN	19920519	News			1			

Network	Date	Show Type	PW Sources	AW	Mixed	Neutral	PW Reporters	Mantra
CNN	19920519	News	2	1				
CNN	19921126	Talk		1		1		
CNN	19930823	News		3				
CNN	19930830	Book	1	1				
CNN	19931122	Talk	1	1				
CNN	19940415	News	1	2				
CNN	19941118	News	1	1				
CNN	20030919	Book		2				
CNN	20031108	News	1	1		1		
CNN	20031120	News	4	1				1
CNN	20070518	News	1	1				1
CNN	20090108	Book	1	1				
CNN	20120204	News	1					
CNN	20131114	Special	14	5				1
CNN	20131115	Book			1			
CNN	20131120	News	3					
CNN	20131120	News	2					
CNN	20131121	News		1				
CNN	20131122	News		1				
CNN	20131122	Special	1					1
CNN	20131122	News	4	4				
CNN	20131122	News	1	2				
CNN	20131122	News	1	1				
CNN	20131123	Special	4					
CNN	20131123	News	1					
Sums			47	37	2	2		4

Network	Date	Show Type	PW Sources	AW	Mixed	Neutral	PW Reporters	Mantra
FOX	20060512	News			1	1		
FOX	20131122	News	2					
FOX	20131123	Book		1				
Sums			2	1	1	1		

Network	Date	Show Type	PW Sources	AW	Mixed	Neutral	PW Reporters	Mantra
NBC	19971006	Book		1				
NBC	19980930	News	1					

NBC	19981120	News			1			
NBC	19990601	News		1				
NBC	20010809	Special	2			1		
NBC	20040804	News	1			2		
NBC	20070517	News	1	1				
NBC	20081113	News	2					
NBC	20081122	News	1					
NBC	20100309	Book		1				
NBC	20130114	News		1				
NBC	20130912	Book			1			
NBC	20131109	News	2					
NBC	20131110	Special		1				
NBC	20131116	News	2					
NBC	20131122	News	2				2	
Sums			14	6	2	3	2	

Foreign Reviews of Oliver Stone's *JFK*

JFK Film Review/Reaction

Content Analysis Template

Case No. _____ Headline _____

_____

Byline: _____

_____

Newspaper: _____

_____

Country: _____

_____

Date of Review: MM_____; DD_____; YEAR _____

SLANT OF ARTICLE/REVIEW TOWARD STONE AND/OR *JFK*_____
1=Positive; 2=Negative; 3=Mixed

Coders

Coders were two, white, Midwestern males, including the author, in their 60s.

Intercoder Results

Headline	Author	Newspaper	Country	Date	Coder A	Coder
JFK: A QUESTION OF PHYSICS	West	Sydney Morning Herald	Australia	2/6/92	1	1
Who Killed JFK	McDonnell	Herald Sun	Australia	12/26/92	1	1
FILM REVIEW JFK	Groen	Globe and Mail	Canada	12/20/91	2	2
Noted critic bestows 1992 Libby Awards	Gelmman	Gazette	Canada	12/21/92	3	3
Gutsy Stone opens JFK assassination wounds	Dunphy	Toronto Star	Canada	12/20/91	1	1
Mini Reviews	None	Financial Post	Canada	4/20/92	1	3
Mini Reviews	None	Financial Post	Canada	1/20/92	1	3
How the movies are faring	Toronto Sun	Financial Post	Canada	1/13/92	1	1
THE PARANOID MYTH OF JFK	Sigal	Guardian	England	1/17/92	2	2
History in the remaking Now Britain	Usher	Daily Mail	England	1/22/92	1	2
Raking the Dallas plot	None	Mail on Sunday	England	1/26/92	2	2
tricky trio's mirth in Venice	Usher	Daily Mail	England	1/24/92	1	1
Camelot Burning	Frank	Daily Yomiuri	Japan	3/28/92	1	1
The tampering and temptations of 'JFK'	Clark	USA Today	US	12/20/91	2	3
NEW IN STORES	Clark	USA Today	US	5/22/92	2	2
No headline	None	Advertiser	US	1/23/92	3	3

POWERFUL BUT NOT PERFECT	Lipper	St. Petersburg Times	US	12/20/91	1	1
WEEKEND; TEENS ON SCREEN	Kelly	St. Petersburg Times	US	12/27/91	2	2
JFK film revives a malicious prosecution	MacKenzie	St. Petersburg Times	US	12/21/91	2	2
Editorial Notebook; Oliver Stone's Patsy	MacKenzie	New York Times	US	12/20/91	2	2

ReCal 0.1 Alpha for 2 Coders
results for file "Film Reliability 2.csv"

File size: 79 bytes
N columns: 2
N variables: 1
N coders per variable: 2

	Percent Agreement	Scott's Pi	Cohen's Kappa	Krippendorff's Alpha (nominal)	N Agreements	N Disagreements	N Cases	N Decisions
Variable 1 (cols 1 & 2)	80%	0.682	0.688	0.69	16	4	20	40

Export Results to CSV (what's this?)

Select another CSV file for reliability calculation below:
Choose File   No file chosen   Calculate Reliability
☐ Save results history (what's this?)

Foreign Reviews of JFK Assassination Books

JFK Assassination Foreign Book Review

Content Analysis Template

Case No. _____ Headline _____

Book Title: _____

Author: _____

Reviewer: _____

Newspaper: _____

Country: _____

Date of Review: MM_____; DD_____; YEAR _____

<u>Was the book reviewed as a package with similar books</u>? Yes/No
Title(s) and Authors(s) of other books reviewed:

HOW DID THE REVIEWER(S) REACT TO THE FOLLOWING ASPECTS OF THE BOOK?

<u>Choose One: 1=Positive; 2=Negative; 3=Not Applicable</u>

<u>Quality of Research</u>: _____

<u>Quality of Reasoning</u>: _____

Writing/Organization: _____

Author's Character/Motivations: _____

REVIEWER'S OVERALL REACTION TO THE BOOK: _____
(Must choose 1 or 2)

Intercoder Results

Case	Date	Headline	Newspaper	Country	Reviewer	Book Title	Author	PW/ AW	Cod-er A	Coder B
1	11/20/93	Dallas: myth and memory	Toronto Star	Canada	Fetherling	Case Closed	Posner	PW	2	2
2	11/21/93	Dallas: myth and memory	Toronto Star	Canada	Fetherling	Deep Politics	Scott	AW	1	1
3	11/22/93	Dallas: myth and memory	Toronto Star	Canada	Fetherling	Kennedy Assassination and the Media	Zelizer	N	1	1
4	07/19/03	AN EXPLOSIVE NEW BOOK	Express	UK	Callan	An Unfinished Life	Dallek	N	1	1
5	09/11/93	CASE CLOSED?; A new book	Gazette	Canada	Shannon	Case Closed	Posner	PW	2	2
8	05/24/03	JFK: monkey business	Globe and Mail	Canada	Ott	An Unfinished Life	Dallek	PW	1	1
9	10/21/13	Robert Kennedy 'stole JFK's missing brain'	Independent	UK	Williams	End of Days	Swanson	PW	1	1
10	03/18/04	Continuing Kennedy	New Strait Times	Malaysia	Mulhall	An Unfinished Life	Dallek	PW	1	1
11	07/18/81	The restless search for answers	Globe and Mail	Canada	Nolan	The Plot to Kill the President	Blakey	AW	1	1
12	07/19/81	The restless search for answers	Globe and Mail	Canada	Nolan	Best Evidence	Lifton	AW	1	1
13	09/18/99	UFOs, JFK and Elvis ... all lies	Straits Times	Singapore	Totten	UFOS, JFK, AND ELVIS	Belzer	AW	1	2
14	03/30/02	More chump than saint	Globe and Mail	Canada	Schuller	Mrs. Paine's Garage	Mallon	PW	2	2
15	09/23/95	Mailer's Lament	Age	Australia	Dowse	Oswald's Tale	Mailer	PW	1	1
16	09/03/95	When Mailer met Oswald	Sunday Age	Australia	Richardson	Oswald's Tale	Mailer	PW	1	1

17	11/01/08	Cracks in the Camelot years	Courier Mail	Australia	Williams	One Minute to Midnight	Dobbs	N	1	1
18	11/02/08	Cracks in the Camelot years	Courier Mail	Australia	Williams	Brothers	Talbot	AW	1	1
20	07/15/95	Not even Mailer can tell us	Sydney Morning Herald	Australia	Sexton	Oswald's Tale	Mailer	PW	1	1
22	05/13/95	Mailer seeks sad ghost	Toronto Star	Canada	Marchand	Oswald's Tale	Mailer	PW	1	1
23	08/31/13	Suspicious minds	Globe and Mail	Canada	Barmak	The United States of Paranoia:	Walker	N	1	1
25	11/19/11	26 seconds we'll never forget	Irish Times	Ireland	Byrne	Zaprudered	Vagnes	N	1	1
26	06/16/12	None	Irish Times	Ireland	Hennigan	Castro s Secrets	Latell	AW	1	1
27	05/23/09	Getting behind the shocking	Irish Times	Ireland	Cunningham	Voodoo Histories	Aaronovich	PW	1	1
28	02/15/13	BOOK OF THE WEEK.	Financial Mail	SA	Steyn	Killing Kennedy	O'Reilly	PW	2	2
29	05/03/09	Book review: Voodoo Histories	Scotland on Sunday	Scotland	Leask	Voodoo Histories	Aaronovich	PW	1	1
30	12/17/94	Yet another confusing episode of Dallas	Herald	Scotland	Black	THE KILLING OF A PRESIDENT	Groden	AW	1	2
32	06/21/08	Dallas '63: the sad, chilling truth	Daily Telegraph	UK	Sandbrook	Four Days in November	Bugliosi	PW	1	1
33	01/08/06	Assassination Saul David Thinks	Sunday Telegraph	UK	David	Ultimate Sacrifice	Waldron	AW	1	1
34	09/01/95	BOOKS: ONCE MORE GRASSY KNOLL	Guardian	UK	Lawson	Oswald's Tale	Mailer	PW	1	1
35	09/02/95	Shadow of a hitman	Independent	Uk	Barnacle	Oswald's Tale	Mailer	PW	1	1
36	11/09/13	JFK's killer is revealed at last	Times	UK	Aaronovitch	The Interloper	Savodnik	PW	1	1
37	12/06/13	Hidden History of JFK Assassination	Independent	UK	Hirst	Hidden History of JFK Assassination	Waldron	AW	2	2

ReCal 0.1 Alpha for 2 Coders
results for file "Intercoder Sheet.csv"

File size: 123 bytes
N columns: 2
N variables: 1
N coders per variable: 2

	Percent Agreement	Scott's Pi	Cohen's Kappa	Krippendorff's Alpha (nominal)	N Agreements	N Disagreements	N Cases	N Decisions
Variable 1 (cols 1 & 2)	93.5%	0.793	0.795	0.797	29	2	31	62

Export Results to CSV   (what's this?)

Select another CSV file for reliability calculation below:
Choose File   No file chosen   Calculate Reliability
☐ Save results history (what's this?)

Index

P

Paesa Sera 107, 108, 123
Paine, Michael 160
Paine, Ruth 29, 160, 186, 197, 211
Palestine: Peace Not Apartheid 147
Paley, William 78, 80
Parrot, James 94
Passport to Assassination: The Never-Before-Told Story of Lee Harvey Oswald by the KGB Colonel Who Knew Him 91, 186, 197
PBS 45, 56, 59, 63, 73, 179-180
Pease, Lisa 44, 75, 85, 90, 101, 173
Peres, Shimon 144
Permindex 12, 33, 34, 84, 97, 107-111, 114, 122-123, 131, 162
Perry, Malcolm 75, 156, 170
Philipps, Maurice 109
Phillips, David Atlee 29, 80, 84
Piper, Michael Collins 48, 96-98, 104, 109-111, 121-126, 130-134, 136-139, 147, 164, 176, 184, 196
Platoon 39
Poirot, Hercule (fictional) 119
Policoff, Jerry 3, 6, 16-17, 75-76, 168
Politico 11-12, 18, 45, 67-68, 73, 180
Politics of Heroin in Southeast Asia, The 81, 101, 113, 134, 175
Porter, Lindsay 41
Posner, Gerald 15, 19, 40, 51, 58-59, 62, 66-67, 73, 87-90, 95, 103, 124, 168-169, 172, 176, 178, 180, 186, 189, 191, 197, 211
Presser, Jackie 95
Prouty, L. Fletcher 122, 132, 136, 176, 184, 196

Q

Quig, Brian Dowling 110, 133

R

Ralston, Ross Frank 47, 95-96, 103, 104, 176
Random House 19, 48, 87, 90, 95, 132, 136, 154, 173, 176, 186, 197

Rankin, Lee 22, 129
Rather, Dan 9, 23, 34, 55-57, 63, 66, 71, 176
Reclaiming History 40, 51, 61, 62, 66, 71, 73, 88, 185, 197
Reed, Ed 37, 46, 116
Rethinking Camelot 150
Reuters 80
Reynolds, Warren 32
Rhodes, James 33
Rivera, Geraldo 34, 45, 179
Road to Dallas, The 62, 73, 127, 170, 174, 183, 194
Robarge, David 34
Robinson, Tom 37, 46
Rolling Stone 3, 8, 80, 100
Roosevelt, Franklin D. (FDR) 120
Roselli, Johnny 29, 30, 112, 119, 127
Rosenbaum, Tibor 110, 123, 131
Rowling, J.K. 59
Ruby, Jack 1, 2, 6, 8, 14, 19, 21, 23-26, 30-32, 43, 62-63, 83, 95, 107, 110, 112-113, 120, 125-128, 130, 132, 134, 136, 163, 174
Rush to Judgment 30, 33, 42, 82
Russell, Richard (Dick) 44, 115, 116, 135, 176, 184, 194, 196

S

Sabato, Larry J. 17, 42, 43, 60, 67-68, 72-74, 86-87, 102-103, 122, 127, 137, 168, 176, 179, 186, 191-192, 197
Salant, Richard 5, 77-79
Salin, Edgar 108
Samson Option, The 48, 118, 132, 135, 140-141, 144, 154-157, 173
Sandbrook, Dominic 89, 102, 171, 212
Saturday Evening Post 80
Scelso, John 116, 135
Schacht, Hjalmar 108
Scheim, David 45, 48, 127-128, 136, 138, 176, 184, 194
Schieffer, Bob 9, 56, 65, 87
Schneider, John 78, 133, 176
Schorr, Daniel 77
Schotz, E. Martin 7, 17, 176

Dr. Mary's Monkey
How the Unsolved Murder of a Doctor, a Secret Laboratory in New Orleans and Cancer-Causing Monkey Viruses are Linked to Lee Harvey Oswald, the JFK Assassination and Emerging Global Epidemics

BY EDWARD T. HASLAM, FOREWORD BY JIM MARRS

Evidence of top-secret medical experiments and cover-ups of clinical blunders The 1964 murder of a nationally known cancer researcher sets the stage for this gripping exposé of medical professionals enmeshed in covert government operations over the course of three decades. Following a trail of police records, FBI files, cancer statistics, and medical journals, this revealing book presents evidence of a web of medical secret-keeping that began with the handling of evidence in the JFK assassination and continued apace, sweeping doctors into cover-ups of cancer outbreaks, contaminated polio vaccine, the genesis of the AIDS virus, and biological weapon research using infected monkeys.

Softcover: **$19.95** (ISBN: 9781634240307) • 432 pages • Size: 5 1/2 x 8 1/2

Hardcover: **$24.95** (ISBN: 9781937584597)

Me & Lee
How I Came to Know, Love and Lose Lee Harvey Oswald

BY JUDYTH VARY BAKER

FOREWORD BY EDWARD T. HASLAM

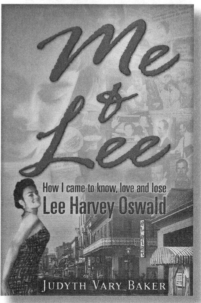

JUDYTH VARY WAS ONCE A PROMISING science student who dreamed of finding a cure for cancer; this exposé is her account of how she strayed from a path of mainstream scholarship at the University of Florida to a life of espionage in New Orleans with Lee Harvey Oswald. In her narrative she offers extensive documentation on how she came to be a cancer expert at such a young age, the personalities who urged her to relocate to New Orleans, and what lead to her involvement in the development of a biological weapon that Oswald was to smuggle into Cuba to eliminate Fidel Castro. Details on what she knew of Kennedy's impending assassination, her conversations with Oswald as late as two days before the killing, and her belief that Oswald was a deep-cover intelligence agent who was framed for an assassination he was actually trying to prevent, are also revealed.

JUDYTH VARY BAKER is a teacher, and artist. Edward T. Haslam is the author of *Dr. Mary's Monkey*.

Hardcover • $24.95 • Softrcover • $21.95 ISBN 9780979988677 / 978-1936296378 • 608 Pages

A Secret Order
Investigating the High Strangeness and Synchronicity in the JFK Assassination
by H. P. Albarelli, Jr.
Provocative new theories that uncover coincidences, connections, and unexplained details of the JFK assassination

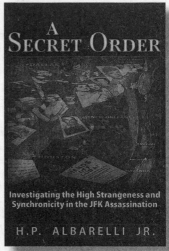

Reporting new and never-before-published information about the assassination of John F. Kennedy, this investigation dives straight into the deep end, and seeks to prove the CIA's involvement in one of the most controversial topics in American history. Featuring intelligence gathered from CIA agents who reported their involvement in the assassination, the case is broken wide open while covering unexplored ground. Gritty details about the assassination are interlaced throughout, while primary and secondary players to the murder are revealed in the in-depth analysis. Although a tremendous amount has been written in the nearly five decades since the assassination, there has never been, until now, a publication to explore the aspects of the case that seemed to defy explanation or logic.

H. P. ALBARELLI JR. is an author and reporter whose previous works can be found in the Huffington Post, Pravda, and Counterpunch. His 10-year investigation into the death of biochemist Dr. Frank Olson was featured on A&E's Investigative Reports, and is the subject of his book, A Terrible Mistake. He lives in Indian Beach, Florida.

Softcover • **$24.95** • ISBN 9781936296552 • 469 Pages

Survivor's Guilt
The Secret Service and the Failure to Protect President Kennedy
by Vincent Michael Palamara
The actions and inactions of the Secret Service before, during, and after the Kennedy assassination

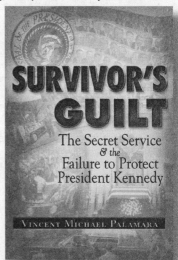

Painstakingly researched by an authority on the history of the Secret Service and based on primary, firsthand accounts from more than 80 former agents, White House aides, and family members, this is the definitive account of what went wrong with John F. Kennedy's security detail on the day he was assassinated.

The work provides a detailed look at how JFK could and should have been protected and debunks numerous fraudulent notions that persist about the day in question, including that JFK ordered agents off the rear of his limousine; demanded the removal of the bubble top that covered the vehicle; and was difficult to protect and somehow, directly or indirectly, made his own tragic death easier for an assassin or assassins. This book also thoroughly investigates the threats on the president's life before traveling to Texas; the presence of unauthorized Secret Service agents in Dealey Plaza, the site of the assassination; the failure of the Secret Service in monitoring and securing the surrounding buildings, overhangs, and rooftops; and the surprising conspiratorial beliefs of several former agents.

An important addition to the canon of works on JFK and his assassination, this study sheds light on the gross negligence and, in some cases, seeming culpability, of those sworn to protect the president.

Vincent Michael Palamara is an expert on the history of the Secret Service. He has appeared on the History Channel, C-SPAN, and numerous newspapers and journals, and his original research materials are stored in the National Archives. He lives in Pittsburgh, Pennsylvania.

Softcover • **$24.95** • ISBN 9781937584603 • 492 Pages

In the Eye of History
Disclosures in the JFK Assassination Medical Evidence
SECOND EDITION
BY WILLIAM MATSON LAW

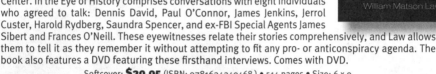

An oral history of the JFK autopsy

Anyone interested in the greatest mystery of the 20th century will benefit from the historic perspective of the attendees of President Kennedy's autopsy. For the first time in their own words these witnesses to history give firsthand accounts of what took place in the autopsy morgue at Bethesda, Maryland, on the night on November 22, 1963. Author William Matson Law set out on a personal quest to reach an understanding of the circumstances underpinning the assassination of John F. Kennedy. His investigation led him to the autopsy on the president's body at the National Naval Medical Center. In the Eye of History comprises conversations with eight individuals who agreed to talk: Dennis David, Paul O'Connor, James Jenkins, Jerrol Custer, Harold Rydberg, Saundra Spencer, and ex-FBI Special Agents James Sibert and Frances O'Neill. These eyewitnesses relate their stories comprehensively, and Law allows them to tell it as they remember it without attempting to fit any pro- or anticonspiracy agenda. The book also features a DVD featuring these firsthand interviews. Comes with DVD.

Softcover: **$29.95** (ISBN: 9781634240468) • 514 pages • Size: 6 x 9

JFK from Parkland to Bethesda
The Ultimate Kennedy Assassination Compendium
BY VINCENT PALAMARA

An all-in-one resource containing more than 15 years of research on the JFK assassination

A map through the jungle of statements, testimony, allegations, and theories relating to the assassination of John F. Kennedy, this compendium gives readers an all-in-one resource for facts from this intriguing slice of history. The book, which took more than 15 years to research and write, includes details on all of the most important aspects of the case, including old and new medical evidence from primary and secondary sources. JFK: From Parkland to Bethesda tackles the hard evidence of conspiracy and cover-up and presents a mass of sources and materials, making it an invaluable reference for anyone with interest in the President Kennedy and his assassination in 1963.

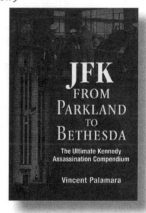

Softcover: **$19.95** (ISBN: 9781634240277) • 242 pages • Size: 6 x 9

The Polka Dot File on the Robert F. Kennedy Killing
Paris Peace Talks connection
BY FERNANDO FAURA

"THE POLKA DOT FILE IS A GEM IN THE FIELD OF RFK ASSASSINATION RESEARCH. READ IT AND LEARN."
—JIM DOUGLASS, AUTHOR, *JFK AND THE UNSPEAKABLE*

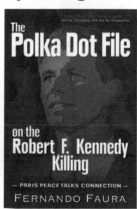

The Polka Dot File on the Robert F. Kennedy Killing describes the day-to-day chase for the mystery woman in the polka-dot dress. The book comments on but does not dwell on the police investigation, and reads like a detective thriller instead of an academic analysis of the investigation. It incorporates actual tapes made by an important witness, and introduces the testimony of witnesses not covered in other books and it is a new take on the assassination and the motives for it introduces a new theory for the reasons behind the assassination. Original and highly personal, it reaches a startling and different conclusion not exposed by other books.

FERNANDO FAURA graduated cum laude with a degree in journalism from the California State University. In 1967 he joined *The Hollywood Citizens News*. Fernando has won awards from the Press Club, the National Newspaper Publishers Association, and was nominated for a Pulitzer Prize.

Softcover: **$24.95** (ISBN: 9781634240598) • 248 pages • Size: 6 x 9

From an Office Building with a High-Powered Rifle
A report to the public from an FBI agent involved in the official JFK assassination investigation
by Don Adams

An insider's look at the mysteries behind the death of President Kennedy

The personal and professional story of a former FBI agent, this is the journey Don Adams has taken over the past 50 years that has connected him to the assassination of the 35th president of the United States. On November 13, 1963, Adams was given a priority assignment to investigate Joseph Milteer, a man who had made threats to assassinate the president. Two weeks later John F. Kennedy was dead, and Agent Adams was instructed to locate and question Milteer. Adams, however, was only allowed to ask the suspect five specific questions before being told to release him. He was puzzled by the bizarre orders but thought nothing more of it until years later when he read a report that stated that not only had Joseph Milteer made threats against the president, but also that he claimed Kennedy would be killed from an office building with a high-powered rifle. Since that time, Adams has compiled evidence and research from every avenue available to him, including his experiences in Georgia and Dallas FBI offices, to produce this compelling investigation that may just raise more questions than answers.

DON ADAMS is a former FBI agent who participated in the investigation of the assassination of John F. Kennedy. He is the author of numerous articles on the subject and is considered a respected authority on the topic. He lives in Akron, Ohio.

Softcover • **$24.95** • ISBN 9781936296866 • 236 Pages

Self-Portrait of a Scoundrel
by Chauncey Holt
A Kennedy insider steps out of the shadows with a riveting account of his life and escapades

Released for the first time 16 years after his death, this startling autobiography by one of the so-called "three tramps" from the John F. Kennedy assassination reveals the details of Chauncey Marvin Holt's many claims. Much mystery and suspicion still swirls around that fateful day in November 1963, and theories abound in nearly every form of media. But one of the major mysteries revolves around the three men spotted and later arrested in Dealey Plaza. Holt's controversial confession to being one of the three tramps has a history of its own, and in his own words he delves into his unique and wild background and life. From his United States Air Force service during Pearl Harbor to his associations with the mob and the CIA, Holt discusses his experiences and encounters in great detail. From a man who truly lived a rare and unique life, the book explains the ins and outs of his associations with Lee Harvey Oswald and the assassination in this unique retrospective of a complex and occasionally dubious life.

CHAUNCEY HOLT came forward claiming to be one of the "three tramps" photographed in Dealey Plaza shortly after the assassination of President John F. Kennedy. At various times in his life, he claimed to be a CIA operative, an accountant for Meyer Lansky, and ostensibly provided false ID documents to Lee Harvey Oswald.

Softcover • **$24.95** • ISBN 9781937584375 • 622 Pages

A Rose by Many Other Names
Rose Cherami & the JFK Assassination

by Todd C. Elliott

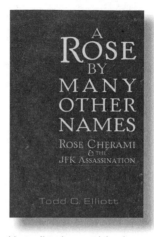

A look into the "birthplace" of the JFK conspiracy

Shifting the focus away from the assassination of John F. Kennedy in Dealey Plaza in Dallas, Texas, to 48 hours prior in Eunice, Louisiana, this book explores the prediction made by Melba Marcades, aka Rose Cherami, that the president would be assassinated on Friday, November 22, 1963 in Dallas. Discounting clairvoyance, the book investigates the possibility that Rose had inside information about the assassination. However, Rose Cherami was not a credible witness: she was a prostitute, a one-time performer in Jack Ruby's Carousel Club, an admitted drug trafficker, a drug addict, and a car thief. But the author's research reveals glaring omissions in her FBI files, questionable admissions regarding her criminal history, and the dubious details of her untimely demise. This book sheds new light on a relatively unknown footnote of the JFK conspiracy theory.

Todd C. Elliott is a former AM talk radio host and a freelance writer and journalist whose work has been featured in the Abbeville Meridian, American Press, the Crowley Post-Signal, the Daily Advertiser, the Eunice News, the Jambalaya News, Lagniappe Magazine, and the Public News. He lives in Lake Charles, Louisiana.

Softcover • **$12.95** • ISBN 9781937584634 • 98 Pages

Betrayal
A JFK Honor Guard Speaks

by Hugh Clark
with William Matson Law

The amazing story that William Law has documented with his historical interviews helps us to understanding our true history. This compelling information shreds the official narrative.In 2015, Law and fellow researcher Phil Singer got together the medical corpsman, who had been present at Bethesda Naval Hospital for President Kennedy's autopsy with some of the official honor guard, who had delivered the president's coffin. What happened next was extraordinary. The medical corpsmen told the honor guards that they had actually received the president's body almost a half-hour before the honor guard got there. The honor guard couldn't believe this. They had met the president's plane at Andrews, taken possession of his casket and shadowed it all the way to Bethesda. The two sides almost broke into fisticuffs, accusing the other of untruths. Once it was sifted out, and both sides came to the understanding that each was telling their own truths of their experience that fateful day, the feelings of betrayal experienced by the honor guards was deep and profound.

Hugh Clark was a member of the honor guard that took President Kennedy's body to Arlington Cemetery for burial. He was an investigator for the United Nations. After Hugh left the service he became a New York City detective and held that position for 22 years.

William Matson Law has been researching the Kennedy assassination for over 25 years. Results of that research have appeared in more than 30 books, including Douglas Horne's magnum opus Inside the Assassination Records Review Board. Law is the producer of the the award-winning documentary RFK, writer, director/producer of the film The Gathering, served as consultant to director Brian McKenna for his theatrical film Killing Kennedy, and worked extensively with bestselling author Matthew Smith's upcoming book about the death of Marilyn Monroe, MARILYN: Murder by Political Entanglement Or How Murder became Suicide in the Three Missing Hours. Law is the author of In the Eye of History and is working on a book about the murder of Robert F. Kennedy with the working title: Shadows and Light. He lives with his family in Central Oregon.

Softcover • **$19.95** • ISBN 9781634240932 • 144 Pages

David Ferrie
Mafia Pilot, Participant in Anti-Castro Bioweapon Plot, Friend of Lee Harvey Oswald and Key to the JFK Assassination

by Judyth Vary Baker

One of the more eccentric characters linked to the JFK assassination

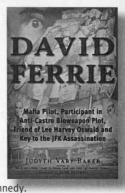

Of the all the people surrounding the assassination of President Kennedy, few are more mysterious and enigmatic than David William Ferrie of New Orleans. Author Judyth Vary Baker knew David Ferrie personally and worked with him in a covert project in New Orleans during the summer of 1963, and this book examines his strange and puzzling behavior both before and after the assassination. At the time of the assassination, Ferrie was a 45-year-old New Orleans resident who was acquainted with some of the most notorious names linked to the assassination: Lee Oswald, Clay Shaw, Guy Banister, Jack Ruby, and Carlos Marcello. He possessed assorted talents and eccentricities: he was at one time a senior pilot with Eastern Airlines until he was fired for homosexual activity on the job; he was also a hypnotist; a serious researcher of the origins of cancer; an amateur psychologist; and a victim of a strange disease, alopecia, which made all of his body void of hair. His odd lifestyle was embellished with an equally bizarre appearance featuring a red toupee and false eyebrows. This is the first book focused solely on David Ferrie and his alleged involvement in the conspiracy to assassinate President John F. Kennedy.

JUDYTH VARY BAKER is an artist, writer, and poet who first became known as a young prodigy in cancer research, then, later, for her assertion that while conducting cancer research in New Orleans in the summer of 1963, she had a love affair with Lee Harvey Oswald. She is the author of *Me & Lee: How I Came to Know, Love and Lose Lee Harvey Oswald*. She lives in Europe.

Softcover • $24.95 • ISBN 9781937584542 • 528 Pages

LBJ and the Kennedy Killing
By Eyewitness

James T. Tague

This is unlike any other book about the assassination of President John F. Kennedy. The author, James Tague, was there and he was wounded by the debris from a missed shot on that fateful day. He stood up to our Government when the Warren Commission was about to ignore what really happened and spoke to the true facts. James Tague's testimony changed history and the "magic bullet" was born in an effort by the Warren Commission to wrongly explain all the wounds to President Kennedy and Governor Connally, and to try and convince the public that Lee Harvey Oswald was the "lone nut assassin." Tague, a long time Dallas area resident, initially believed the Warren Report, but time, diligent research and amazing revelations told to him by prominent Texans has given James Tague an inside look at what really happened. Be prepared to learn new facts, never before published, about one of our nation's darkest moments.

JAMES T. TAGUE spent 5 years in the Air Force, had a career in the automobile business rising to top management and is today recognized as a top researcher on the Kennedy assassination. It was an accident of timing that he was in Dealey Plaza that November day in 1963, receiving a minor injury.

Softcover • $29.95 • ISBN 9781937584740 • 433 Pages

Kennedy & Oswald –The Big Picture–
by Judyth Vary Baker and Edward Schwartz

Unraveling the many strands of hidden history behind the assassination of President Kennedy is not an easy task. Co-authors Baker and Schwartz guide us toward the conclusion that ultimately, the motivation was total governmental control, a coup d'état, changing us from a democratic republic to a oligopoly – a corporatocracy. With help from new witnesses regarding the "Crime of the Century," we are led to the realization that the "War of Terror" and the Patriot Act were predesigned to undermine our US Constitution and our Bill of Rights. The very moment Kennedy died our own government turned against "We the People." Baker and Schwartz provide a compelling narrative showing Oswald's innocence and a condemnation of the conspirators who planned and carried out the assassination of our 35th president and our Republic.

Softcover • $24.95 • ISBN 9781634240963 • 408 Pages

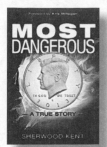

Most Dangerous   *–A True Story–*
by Sherwood Kent

OUT OF THE BOWELS of the sleepy southern town of Tupelo, Mississippi, the birthplace of Elvis Presley, emerges a darkly-humorous true story of staged terror, occult ritual and mind control. The book reads like a Faulkneresque tall tale but is, unfortunately for the main character and those around him, all-too-true. Author S.K. Bain finds himself caught up in the middle of something bigger and uglier than he can at first fathom. Yet, much to his dismay, he catches on rather quickly to what's taking place around him—and near-simultaneously elsewhere across the county in places such as Boston, MA and West, TX—because he's seen this sort of thing before. He wrote the book on it, literally, and he soon realizes just how much danger he and his family are in. The year is 2013, the 50th anniversary of the JFK assassination, and Bain discovers that he is enmeshed in a year-long series of scripted events meticulously planned and brilliantly executed by some of the most ruthless, diabolically-creative, powerful psychopaths on the planet. As the story unfolds, it turns out that Bain has an idea who, specifically, might be behind his woes, and if he's correct, it's even less likely that he's going to get out alive.

Softcover • **$24.95** • ISBN 9781634240406 • 408 Pages

Sinister Forces
A Grimoire of American Political Witchcraft
Book One: The Nine
BY PETER LEVENDA, FOREWORD BY JIM HOUGAN

A shocking alternative to the conventional views of American history.

The roots of coincidence and conspiracy in American politics, crime, and culture are examined in this book, exposing new connections between religion, political conspiracy, and occultism. From ancient American civilization and the mysterious mound builder culture to the Salem witch trials, the birth of Mormonism during a ritual of ceremonial magic by Joseph Smith, Jr., and Operations Paperclip and Bluebird. Fascinating details are revealed, including the bizarre world of "wandering bishops" who appear throughout the Kennedy assassinations; a CIA mind control program run amok in the United States and Canada; a famous American spiritual leader who had ties to Lee Harvey Oswald in the weeks and months leading up to the assassination of President Kennedy; and the "Manson secret.

Softcover: **$24.95** (ISBN 9780984185818) • 432 pages • Size: 6 x 9

Book Two: A Warm Gun

Readers are provided with strange parallels between supernatural forces such as shaminism, ritual magic, and cult practices, and contemporary interrogation techniques such as those used by the CIA under the general rubric of MK-ULTRA. Not a work of speculative history, this exposé is founded on primary source material and historical documents. Fascinating details on Nixon and the "Dark Tower," the Assassin cult and more recent Islamic terrorism, and the bizarre themes that run through American history from its discovery by Columbus to the political assassinations of the 1960s are revealed.

Softcover: **$24.95** (ISBN 9780984185825) • 392 pages • Size: 6 x 9

Book Three: The Manson Secret

The Stanislavski Method as mind control and initiation. Filmmaker Kenneth Anger and Aleister Crowley, Marianne Faithfull, Anita Pallenberg, and the Rolling Stones. Filmmaker Donald Cammell (Performance) and his father, CJ Cammell (the first biographer of Aleister Crowley), and his suicide. Jane Fonda and Bluebird. The assassination of Marilyn Monroe. Fidel Castro's Hollywood career. Jim Morrison and witchcraft. David Lynch and spiritual transformation. The technology of sociopaths. How to create an assassin. The CIA, MK-ULTRA and programmed killers.

Softcover: **$24.95** (ISBN 9780984185832) • 508 pages • Size: 6 x 9